SUNDAY DINNER

SUNDAY DINNER

MEALS FROM FAMILY KITCHENS

Lora Lee Parrott

Illustrated by Crandall Vail

BEACON HILL PRESS OF KANSAS CITY
Kansas City, Missouri

First Printing, 1979

ISBN: 0-8341-0594-2

Printed in the
United States of America

Contents

Reflections on Sunday Dinner

...The Great American Tradition

The great American tradition of Sunday dinner fits the format of Christian family living like it was designed especially for us. Who can fail to recall mental pictures of the entire family gathered around a large table, loaded down with beautiful dishes of mashed potatoes, topped with butter, just waiting for the gravy boat to be passed! Every family has its stories of competition for the chicken legs and the ceremony of the wishbone. Who can forget the variety of fresh vegetables that were standard fare on Sunday, Jello salads that shimmered in the sunlight, and multiple options on the world's most tempting desserts. This was Sunday dinner, the one meal in the week which symbolized family solidarity when married children came home with the highest expectations of food, fun, and fellowship.

Sometimes the honored guests were the pastor and his family. I can still remember some of the prayers our pastor made for grace and the ruffle of napkins and the shuffle of tableware as everyone settled in for the most joyous event of the week, Sunday dinner.

As far as I know, no church sociologist has made a study of Sunday dinner. But if one did, I believe that for millions of Christian families, Sunday school, morning worship, and Sunday dinner are like pearls on a string, each separate but connected. In many homes Sunday dinner has been a weekly family reunion, a celebration of life in the home, a time for thanksgiving, informal supportive counseling with each other, a review of the morning service and its application to life or its lack of it. Mother was loved for her cooking and father was shown respect at the head of the table. As an institution, Sunday dinner has made a significant contribution to Christian families everywhere.

...in the Deep South

One of my good personal friends of long standing is Bertha Shingler who learned to be a good cook in Tennessee and Georgia and refined her craft with the resources of fruits, and vegetables in California where she still knows how to prepare and serve a beautiful Sunday dinner.

In a letter to me, Bertha wrote, "The Sunday dinners my mother used to serve in Tennessee, and the Shingler families served in Georgia, are a far cry from Sunday dinners in households here in California now. For example, a Sunday dinner at my mother-in-law's would consist of a table loaded with such things as a roast beef with mashed potatoes at one end, and at the other end fried chicken (not Colonel Sanders) with rice whose every grain was separated from the other, chicken gravy, beef gravy, ice-cold sliced tomatoes, cucumbers, baby peas, and pear and cheese salad. We started the meal off with little pan-fried corn cakes, followed by hot biscuits that had been stuck into the oven when we sat down, and served midway through the meal with a jelly called Mayhaw that's known only in southern Georgia. It was something like crab apple, and grew in the swamps and along the river. For dessert, pound cake with something called a Charlotte, mostly made with thick whipped cream; and of course, gallons of iced tea with crushed ice (not cubes), with lemon and mint. Those are bygone days." What a pity!

... Old Fashioned Dinners

   —by Edgar A. Guest

It wasn't too much work for her in days of long ago
To get a dinner ready for a dozen friends or so;
The mother never grumbled at the cooking she must do
Or the dusting or the sweeping, but she seemed to smile it through,
And the times that were happiest, beyond the slightest doubt,
Were when good friends were coming and we stretched the table out.
We never thought, when we were young, to take our friends away
And entertain them at a club or in some swell cafe;
When mother gave a dinner, she would plan it all herself
And feed the people that she liked, the best things on the shelf.
Then one job always fell to me, for I was young and stout,
I brought the leaves to father when he stretched the table out.
That good old-fashioned table, I can see it still today
With its curious legs of varnished oak round which I used to play;
It wasn't much to look at, not as stylish or refined
Or as costly or as splendid as the oval, modern kind,
But it always had a welcome for our friends to sit about,
And though twenty guests were coming, we could always stretch it out.
I learned it from my mother—it is foolish pride to roam,
The only place to entertain your friends is right at home.
Just let them in by dozens, let them laugh and sing and play
And come to love and know them in the good old-fashioned way;
Home's the place for fun and friendship, home's the place where joy may
      shout,
And if you crowd our dining room, we'll stretch the table out.

                        —From *The Passing Throng,* by
                        Edgar A. Guest. Reprinted by permission
                        of Contemporary Books, Inc., Chicago.

... A Puritan Sunday

Puritans toiled hard all week, so they took seriously the admonition to rest on the Sabbath. After sundown on Saturday no one could work at all, except to brush sparks from the hearth. They couldn't even make beds. So a Puritan housewife shined up her house on Saturday, and did a colossal baking. Then after three o'clock on Saturday afternoon, the mood of expectancy began to build up to the pivotal day. These people really believed that Sunday would bring encounter with a living and dependable God who had brought them to this new land and watched over their effort to build His holy commonwealth.

While a large roast cooked all day, to ensure cold meat for Sunday, a great copper tub before the fire held water which was being warmed for baths. Shoes were shined, clothes laid out for the next day, and "modesty pieces" ironed. (These were inserts of lace or velvet that were tucked into the neckline of a Sunday dress. Drafts as much as discretion made them a sensible fashion accessory.) Then on Saturday night the family sang a psalm together, had prayers, and went upstairs to bed with a sense of anticipating drama, as children now do only on Christmas Eve.

—From *Marriage to a Difficult Man,* by Elisabeth D. Dodds.
Copyright © MCMLXXI, The Westminster Press.
Used by permission.

...*My Hope*

It is my hope that the theme of this collection of outstanding recipes and the memories which the title conjures up in each of us will help to keep alive the values of families eating together.

...*My Dedication*

To my daughters-in-law, Carol and Mary Lou, wives of young ministers, who are learning to make the most of Sunday dinner.

...*My Thanks*

Without the encouragement and insistence of my husband, I could never have had the courage to request the help of the scores of men and women who sent me some of their prize recipes . . . and without the testing of a number of these recipes by Aletha Miller, and the editing and production expertise of members of the Nazarene Publishing House staff, the book would still be in the file.

Appetizers & Soups

Shrimply Divine Dip

1 8-ounce package cream cheese, softened
1 cup commercial sour cream
2 teaspoons lemon juice
1 5/8-ounce package Italian salad dressing mix
1/2 cup (1 can) finely chopped shrimp

Blend cream cheese with remainder of ingredients. Chill 1 hour or longer.

"This dip is great with fresh vegetables, chips, or small crackers."

MRS. GORDON T. (RHODA) OLSEN
Eugene, Oregon

Vegetable Dip

1 cup sour cream
1 cup Hellmann's mayonnaise
1 1/2 tablespoons minced onion
1 1/2 tablespoons parsley
1 tablespoon dill weed
3/4 teaspoon Accent salt
3/4 teaspoon Lawry seasoning salt

Mix all ingredients together.

"Excellent dip for fresh vegetables."

MRS. MALCOLM (MARY) DELBRIDGE
Lansing, Michigan

Stateside Guacamole Dip

1 medium to large avocado
½ cup small curd cottage cheese
2 tablespoons finely chopped green peppers
3 tablespoons finely chopped onion
1 tablespoon lime or lemon juice
¼ tablespoon salt
½ teaspoon seasoned salt
2 tablespoons finely chopped chili peppers
chopped parsley sprigs (optional)

Mash avocado to a creamy pulp. Add to cottage cheese, mix until creamy and then add all other ingredients as listed and mix well.

"A very delicious dip with taco flavored chips."

MRS. JERALD R. (THELMA) LOCKE
Bethany, Oklahoma

Dill Vegetable Dip

1 cup mayonnaise
1 cup sour cream
1 tablespoon parsley flakes (I like fresh best)
1 teaspoon Accent
1 teaspoon dill weed
2 tablespoons grated onion

Mix all ingredients together and serve with raw vegetables.

"This dip will keep in the refrigerator for days, we like it because it is not too filling, if I want to do something special, I add jumbo cooked shrimp to the vegetable platter."

MRS. ED (ELLEN) ANDERSON
Long Beach, California

Ginger Dip

1 cup sour cream
1 8-ounce package cream cheese
½ cup chopped chutney
2 tablespoons candied ginger, chopped

Mix together. Serve with fresh fruit.

MRS. RUSSELL (ANNABELLE) KLEPPINGER
Miami, Florida

Spinach Dip

1 box frozen chopped spinach
½ cup chopped green onions
2 cups mayonnaise

Cook spinach according to directions on box. When cool, squeeze out all moisture. Stir into mayonnaise, add green onions, salt and pepper to taste.

"Use with raw vegetables."

MRS. CHARLES (LaVERNE) OLIVER
Helena, Alabama

Life in Christ is life at its best (H. T. Reza).

Broccoli Chili Dip

1 package frozen chopped broccoli
1 can cream of chicken soup, undiluted
3 cups grated cheese
1 7½ ounce can chopped chilies
garlic salt

Cook broccoli according to directions. Drain. Add remaining ingredients. Stir until cheese melts. Serve hot. Makes 30 servings.

"Use 1 can or less of the chilies according to taste. I use less. For a large crowd, I make 4 recipes and used 3 cans. Use this dip with about anything; crackers, taco chips, potato chips, etc. It's even good with fresh vegetables: celery, cucumbers, carrots, etc."

MRS. CRAWFORD (MILDRED) VANDERPOOL
Phoenix, Arizona

They did eat of the old corn of the land on the morrow after the passover, unleavened cakes, and parched corn in the selfsame day. And the manna ceased on the morrow after they had eaten of the old corn of the land; neither had the children of Israel manna any more; but they did eat of the fruit of the land of Canaan that year (Josh. 5:11-12).

Tuna Ball

1 6½-ounce can tuna, drained
2 3-ounce packages cream cheese
1 tablespoon lemon juice
1 tablespoon onion, chopped fine
1 tablespoon dill pickle, chopped fine
⅛ teaspoon salt
chopped pecans or walnuts

Blend all ingredients with electric mixer until smooth. Chill. Roll in chopped pecans or walnuts. Serve with crackers.

MRS. JAY (NORMA) BYBEE
Tyler, Texas

Salmon Party Log

2 cups (16-ounce can) salmon
1 8-ounce package cream cheese, softened
1 tablespoon lemon juice
1 teaspoon prepared horseradish
¼ teaspoon salt
¼ teaspoon liquid smoke
½ cup chopped pecans
3 tablespoons snipped parsley

Drain and flake salmon; remove skin and bones. Combine salmon with next 6 ingredients; combine pecans and parsley. Shape salmon mixture in 8 x 12-inch log; roll in more chopped nuts and fine chopped parsley. Chill well. Serve with crackers.

MRS. RUSSELL (ANNABELLE) KLEPPINGER
Miami, Florida

Sweet 'N' Sour Weiner Bites

1 6-ounce jar (¾ cup) prepared mustard
1 10-ounce jar (1 cup) currant jelly
1 to 2 pounds frankfurters, canned Vienna sausage or
    cocktail wieners

Mix mustard and jelly in saucepan. Heat thoroughly until jelly and mustard are mixed well and smooth. Diagonally slice franks into bite-size pieces. Add to sauce and heat through. Serve in chafing dish. Makes 8 to 12 servings.

"A delightful addition to a buffet or hors d'oeuvres table!"

MRS. BUD (NANCY) TOLLIE
Overland Park, Kansas

Sweet and Sour Ham Balls

Meatballs

1 pound smoked ham, ground
1½ pounds fresh pork, ground
2 eggs
2 cups soda cracker crumbs
1 cup milk

Sauce

2¼ cups brown sugar
¼ cup vinegar
¾ cup water
¾ teaspoon dry mustard

Mix meatball ingredients and shape into small bite-size balls. Arrange on jellyroll pans and bake at 325° for 30-45 minutes. Baste with the sauce during baking. Turn meatballs periodically. Serve with toothpicks.

"An excellent pre-dinner appetizer."

MRS. GORDON T. (RHODA) OLSEN
Eugene, Oregon

Full Moon Cheese Ball

1 3-ounce package cream cheese
1 5-ounce jar pasteurized process cheese spread with bacon
1 can crushed French fried onion rings (not frozen)
1 5-ounce jar pimento pasteurized Neufchatel cheese spread

Combine softened cream cheese and cheese spreads, mixing until well blended. Stir in ⅓ crushed onion rings. Shape into a ball; roll in remaining onions. Garnish with pimento, if desired.

"Easy to prepare. This was especially well liked at our Christmas open house for the church board."

MRS. JARRELL (BERNIECE) GARSEE
Boise, Idaho

Holiday Spread

1 8-ounce package cream cheese
½ cup sour cream
1 small jar dried beef, cut into small pieces
¼ cup chopped green peppers
½ teaspoon garlic salt
1 teaspoon onion salt

Mix all together and top with ½ to 1 cup chopped pecans, sauteed in butter. Bake in 350° F. oven for 20 minutes. Serve on your favorite snack cracker.

"A friend gave us this recipe and it is one of our favorites."

MRS. GENE (ONALINE) FRYE
Youngstown, Ohio

Salmon Ball

1 large can red (or pink) salmon, drained
1 8-ounce package cream cheese, at room temperature
1 teaspoon horseradish
1 tablespoon lemon juice (½ lemon)
2 teaspoons minced green onions (or minced dried onions)
¼ teaspoon salt
¼ teaspoon liquid smoke
1 cup crushed nuts

His love knows no limits; neither will ours as we follow Christ (C. William Ellwanger).

Debone the salmon and flake. Mix ingredients together. Shape into a ball. Roll in chopped nuts, and serve with crackers. It's easier to shape into a ball after it is refrigerated for an hour.

"This is one of the favorite cheese ball recipes I used for our teachers' conferences at school."

MRS. WESLEY (PAULINE) POOLE
Fairfield, Ohio

Meat Balls

With my whole heart have I sought thee (Ps. 119:10).

Meat
¾ pound smoked ham, ground
½ pound raw, lean pork, ground
½ cup milk
½ cup cracker crumbs

Sauce
¾ cup brown sugar
½ cup cider vinegar
½ cup water
6 whole cloves
1 tablespoon powdered mustard

Mix and bring to a boil while stirring.

Mix ingredients and roll into approximately 30 small (cocktail size) meat balls. Place in shallow baking pan, pour brown sugar sauce over. Back 350° for 1 hour. For variation of serving. Wrap in bacon after they are cooked and broil until bacon is done. Serve warm.

"Can make meatballs ahead, then prepare sauce when ready for oven. Serve with toothpicks. This recipe can be multiplied several times. I find it a winning recipe. Never any leftovers!"

MRS. MEL (SHIRLEY) RICH
San Diego, California

Party Meatballs

½ pound ground beef
⅓ cup 7-Up
½ cup Italian bread crumbs
1 egg
½ teaspoon garlic salt
½ teaspoon onion salt
stuffed green olives

Place all ingredients in a mixing bowl and mix thoroughly. Make into small size balls and press a green olive in the middle of each, making sure olive is covered. Place under broiler for 10 minutes or until brown. Makes 18.

"These meatballs are great for open house. I have made more than 200 for Christmas Open House at the parsonage."

MRS. PAL L. (JAN) WRIGHT
Bradenton, Florida

As a bird that wandereth from her nest, so is a man that wandereth from his place (Prov. 27:8).

Progress in the Christian way is not made by "partly" seeking the things above (Margaret Bloom).

Hot Olive Cheese Puffs

½ cup flour
¼ teaspoon salt
½ teaspoon paprika
3 tablespoons soft butter or margarine
1 cup sharp cheese, grated
24 stuffed green olives

Combine flour, salt, and paprika. Add butter and use pastry blender to make crumbs. Add cheese and work with hands to make soft dough. Take about 1 teaspoon of dough in palm of hand and flatten, then wrap around each olive. Freeze in airtight container. Bake at 400° F. for 10-15 minutes or until golden. Do not thaw before baking.

"A real favorite with guests who often ask if they are deep fried."

MRS. J. MARK (CAROLE) CALDWELL
Abbotsford, British Columbia, Canada

Autumn Glory

1½ cups sugar
1 cup pineapple juice
1 10-ounce package frozen sliced strawberries
1 10-ounce can mandarin oranges
1 pound can apricot halves, drained
1 No. 2 can pineapple chunks
2 bananas, chopped

Boil sugar and pineapple juice. Remove from heat. Combine fruits and add to sugar syrup. Stir until well mixed. Pour into 9 x 12 x 2 inch glass pan or freezer container that will hold 6 to 8 cups. Cover and freeze. Thaw for one hour before serving. Serve while still frosty after cutting into squares. The mixture can be broken up for topping. Makes 12 servings.

"Our family likes 'Autumn Glory' as an appetizer or a salad!"

MRS. DEAN H. (ROXIE) WESSELS
Olathe, Kansas

Stuffed Mushrooms

12 medium mushrooms
2 tablespoons margarine
¼ cup finely chopped green pepper
¼ cup finely chopped celery
¼ cup finely chopped onion
¼ teaspoon salt

Preheat oven to 350° F. Wipe mushrooms with damp cloth. Remove stems, chop stems fine. Heat 1 tablespoon margarine in skillet. Saute caps on bottom side only, 2 to 3 minutes, remove. Arrange rounded side down, in shallow baking dish. Saute stems, green pepper, celery, and onions in rest of margarine until tender, about 4-5 minutes. Season with salt and pepper. Spoon mixture into mushroom caps. Bake 15 minutes or until heated through. Makes 6 servings.

MRS. CHARLES (FANNY) STRICKLAND
Olathe, Kansas

Golden Crush Appetizer

1 cup sugar
1 cup milk
½ cup orange juice
¼ cup lemon juice (Realemon may be used)
3 bananas

Crush bananas and mix all together; or put into blender. Pour into ice cube tray, with or without divider. Freeze. When ready to serve, put a chunk of it into each glass or cup. Pour orange juice over it. Or, you might want to try fruit cocktail.

"Keep Gold Crush in the freezer, Tang on the shelf, and you are ready for drop-ins."

Mrs. Lorne (Joyce) MacMillan
Toronto, Canada

Dutch Pea Soup

1 pound green split peas
¼ pound lean pork, or metworst or small sausage balls
3 quarts water
salt and pepper to taste
1½ cups diced celery
3 medium onions, cut fine
3 potatoes peeled and diced
1 or 2 carrots, peeled and sliced
parsley
1 cup milk

Cook peas, water, and meat slowly for 2 hours. Add next 5 ingredients and cook 1 hour. Stir. Add parsley and milk. Cook 10 minutes more and serve.

"It freezes nicely."

Mrs. P. J. (Mary) Zondervan
Grand Rapids, Michigan

Corn Chowder

5-6 slices of bacon, cooked and crumbled (drain all but 2
tablespoons fat)
1 onion (plus chives are pretty for color) and 1 potato
chopped and simmered
2 cups water
1 small green pepper, chopped
1 can creamed corn
½ small jar pimentos
1 cup powdered milk

Season with ½ teaspoon dill weed, salt and pepper to taste. Add
dash of thyme, dash of basil, and dash of chevril, if you have it.
Can be thinned with milk or water to taste.

"A hearty Sunday night supper."

MRS. JOHN (DORCAS) RILEY
Nampa, Idaho

My Favorite Corn Chowder

1 medium onion, diced
¼ pound bacon, diced
2½ cups potatoes, diced
1 No. 2 can (2½ cups) creamed corn
1 cup hot milk (more if desired)
1 teaspoon butter
½ teaspoon salt
dash of pepper

Simmer onion and bacon in saucepan until onion is glassy in
appearance. Add potatoes and enough water to cover. Boil until
potatoes are nearly cooked. Add creamed corn and milk and
butter. Season to taste. Finish cooking on low heat. Stir and
serve.

"I made up this recipe many years ago and my family has never
let me forget it! It was an instant success."

MRS. ALBERT D. (JANET) STIEFEL
Nampa, Idaho

Mo's Clam Chowder

1 pound bacon, diced
½ pound smoked ham, diced
6 cups chopped onion

¼ cup flour
 6 cups minced clams, drained
12 cups diced potatoes
 6 cups milk
salt and freshly ground pepper to taste
butter
paprika

Saute bacon and ham until bacon is brown. Drain off fat, add onion, saute till limp. Stir in flour; add potatoes and clams; cook about 15 minutes until potatoes are soft. Add milk; season to taste. Serve hot with dollop of butter; sprinkle paprika on each serving. Makes 12-14 generous servings.

"This recipe is from Famous Mo's on Newport, Oregon, Wharf. We always take out-of-state visitors to Mo's for this delicious clam chowder. I have enjoyed using this recipe at home."

MRS. CARL (DORIS) CLENDENEN
Salem, Oregon

Spinach Meatball Minestrone

1 10-ounce package frozen chopped spinach, thawed
½ pound lean ground beef
2 tablespoons fine dry bread crumbs
1 egg
¼ teaspoon salt
dash of pepper
1 small onion, finely chopped
1 14-ounce can beef broth
1 8-ounce can stewed tomatoes
1 8-ounce can kidney beans
¼ teaspoon each oregano leaves and dry basil
¼ cup each sliced carrot and celery
¼ cup elbow macaroni
Parmesan cheese

And now I beseech thee, lady, . . . that we love one another (2 John 5).

Squeeze liquid from chopped spinach, mix with ground beef, bread crumbs, egg, salt, pepper, and onion. Shape into 1-inch balls. In a wide frying pan, brown meatballs in butter, if needed, over medium heat; remove from pan as browned. In a 3-quart pan, pour beef broth, tomatoes (breaking up with spoon) and their liquid, beans and their liquid, oregano, basil, carrot, celery, and meatballs. Cover and bring to a boil. Reduce heat and cook over medium heat for 15 minutes or until vegetables are tender and meatballs cooked through; skim off any accumulated fat. Stir in macaroni, cover, cook until tender (about 10 minutes). Sprinkle servings with Parmesan cheese.

Teach the young women to be sober, to love their husbands, to love their children (Titus 2:4).

MRS. JAY C. (BONNIE) BAYNUM
Kankakee, Illinois

Smoked Beef Soup

2 cups shredded raw potatoes
1 cup water
½ stick margarine
3 tablespoons onion
1 tablespoon flour
1 teaspoon beef bouillon
¼ teaspoon celery seed or some chopped celery
4 cups milk
1 can whole corn
1 cup (or more) shredded Hickory Farms Beef Stick

Cook potatoes, margarine, and onion in water until tender. Stir in flour, bouillon, and celery and boil for a few minutes. Remove from heat and stir in milk, corn, and beef. Heat to serving temperature. Salt and pepper to taste.

"This soup is a meal in itself. Also delicious enough for company."

MRS. WAYNE (ALICE) QUINN
Vancouver, Washington

Steak Soup

1 pound or more of ground round steak
1 cup diced carrots
1 cup sliced celery
1 package frozen mixed vegetables
1 cup or 2 medium onions, diced
1 No. 2½-can of tomatoes
salt and 2 tablespoons liquid beef seasoning
1 teaspoon pepper
1 teaspoon Accent
1 cube butter
1 cup flour

Brown meat and add Lawry's seasoning salt. Parboil carrots, celery, and mixed vegetables. Using water from beginning, add enough water to make 2 quarts, and add to beef. Add onions and tomatoes. Add seasonings and butter. Thicken with flour.

"Served with a salad and hot bread, this soup could well be the main course. The seasoning is what makes it so delicious."

MRS. WALTER E. (FAYE) LANMAN
Hastings, Nebraska

Hearty Steak Soup

1½ pounds ground chuck
1 cup chopped onion
1 cup shredded carrots
1 cup diced celery
1 cup shredded potatoes
¼ cup margarine (½ stick)
½ cup plus two tablespoons flour
2 quarts water
1 8½-ounce can peas drained
½ teaspoon salt
½ teaspoon pepper
3 tablespoons liquid beef concentrate

In large soup pot or dutch oven brown ground chuck. Drain thoroughly and discard drippings. Simmer onions, carrots, celery, and potatoes in water to cover till partly cooked. Drain and reserve liquid. Melt margarine in pot used to brown meat, remove from heat, blend in flour to make a smooth paste. Mix in water (use liquid drained from vegetables plus enough water to make two quarts). Stir till paste is smoothly mixed with liquid. Return to heat and bring to a boil, stirring to prevent lumps. Reduce heat to simmer, add browned meat and rest of ingredients, stir well once and simmer about 20 minutes. Taste for seasoning. May be frozen. Makes 8 or 10 servings.

"This is plenty good served with crusty bread and a dish of fruit for dessert."

MRS. HUGH C. (AUDREY) BENNER
Leawood, Kansas

Quick Homemade Chicken Soup

4 chicken breasts
1 large onion
2 potatoes
1 can chicken noodle soup
1 can celery soup
salt and pepper

Cook chicken breasts in quart of water. Bring to boil and simmer. When done take out of broth and cut meat in small pieces. Cut onion and potatoes to cook in broth till done. Salt and pepper to taste. Pour noodle soup and celery soup in and stir.

MRS. L. H. (LUCILLE) ROEBUCK
Georgetown, Kentucky

Hamburger Soup

1 teaspoon salt
1 pound ground beef
2 tablespoons drippings or lard
1 bay leaf
1 large onion, sliced
1 10½-ounce can tomatoes
1½ cups water
1 can consomme
1 package frozen baby lima beans
½ cup celery, sliced

Brown ground beef in drippings. Pour drippings off. Combine ground beef, bay leaf, salt, onion, celery, tomatoes, water, and consomme. Cook, covered, slowly, 2 hours. Add beans, simmer 30 minutes. Discard bay leaf.

"Very good on a cool, fall day!"

MRS. JAMES R. (PAT) COUCHENOUR
Columbiana, Ohio

Swiss Cheese Soup

2 tablespoons butter
3 tablespoons flour
3 cups boiling water
1 package dehydrated onion soup mix
2 cups milk
1½ cups shredded Swiss cheese (6-ounce package)
parsley

In medium-size pan, melt butter. Stir in flour; cook over low heat till mixture bubbles and color starts to turn golden. Remove from heat. Pour in boiling water. Sprinkle onion soup mix on top; return to heat and cook for 15 minutes. Add milk and cheese. Heat just till cheese starts to melt. Garnish with parsley.

MRS. WALTER (IRIS) GRAEFLIN
Bluffton, Indiana

Salads

Alfalfa Sprouts

1 tablespoon alfalfa seed

Pour in a wide-mouth quart fruit jar, with

2 cups lukewarm water

Let stand 12 hours. Be sure seeds go to the bottom and soak up the water. Cover with a damp cloth and set in a dark place (cupboard). Next day, tie a piece of nylon over mouth of jar and pour water out. Set back in the cupboard. Every 4 hours during the day rinse the seeds with fresh water then pour it out. Be sure you drain all the water out of jar after each rinse. After 3 or 4 days of this, your jar will be full of sprouts. Keep refrigerated. Use in a tossed green salad.

Mrs. Winston (Merreta) Ketchum
Vancouver, Washington

It shall come to pass, for the abundance of milk that they shall give he shall eat butter: for butter and honey shall every one eat that is left in the land (Isa. 7:22).

God said, Let the earth bring forth grass, the herb yielding seed, and the fruit tree yielding fruit after his kind . . . and God saw that it was good (Gen. 1:11).

Cranberry Gelatin Salad

1 large or 2 small boxes strawberry gelatin
1 cup boiling water
1 small package frozen strawberries
1 can whole cranberries, drained
2 medium (1 cup) mashed bananas
sour cream for garnish

Have all ingredients ready. Pour 1 cup boiling water in gelatin. Make sure it is dissolved. Add frozen strawberries. Break berries apart, then add rest of ingredients. Pour in mold and chill for 2-3 hours.

Mrs. John (Violet) Wordsworth
Edmonds, Washington

Cranberry Salad

1 quart fresh cranberries
2 3-ounce packages lemon gelatin
½ to 1 cup chopped pecans
2 cups sugar
2 oranges

Put cranberries and orange rind through food chopper. Dissolve gelatin in 2 cups hot water. Add sugar. When thick, add cranberries and orange rind, nuts, and orange sections. Place in refrigerator to congeal.

MRS. BILL (CHARLOTTE) DAVIS
Gadsden, Alabama

Pimento Cheese Salad

1 small jar pimento cheese spread
2 small flat cans crushed pineapple, strained and set aside
2-3 cups miniature marshmallows
1 large (9-ounce) frozen Cool Whip
½ cup chopped nuts

Blend about ¼ of the juice from pineapple with cheese until creamy consistency (you may need more juice). Add pineapple, marshmallows, and nuts. Fold in frozen Cool Whip until mixture is well blended. Pour into 9 x 9 pan and chill until set.

For a slight flavor change, use colored marshmallows. Also ¼ cup of salad dressing gives it a nice flavor change. You may serve this as a frozen salad, too.

MRS. HOYLE (JUANITA) THOMAS
Nampa, Idaho

Choice Salad

1 cup pineapple juice
2 tablespoons cornstarch
½ cup sugar
2 eggs, beaten
1 cup diced pineapple
1½ cups diced pasteurized cheese spread
1 cup miniature marshmallows
nuts (optional)

Combine sugar and cornstarch with pineapple juice. Cook until thick, then add hot mixture to 2 beaten eggs. Cook 2 minutes.

Cool slightly. Pour over the diced pineapple, cheese, and marsh-mallows.

MRS. FLOYD (GRACE) HESS
Coffeyville, Kansas

Pineapple Cheese Salad

1 No. 2 can crushed pineapple
3 eggs
¾ cup sugar
½ cup water
2 heaping tablespoons flour
pinch of salt
¼ pound butter
½ pound marshmallows
longhorn cheese
cherries

Drain pineapple thoroughly and set aside. Beat eggs well. Add sugar, salt, and flour, and add to pineapple juice to which water has been added. Cook until thick and add butter, marshmallows, and pineapple. Pour into a flat dish that you can use as a serving dish. Cool. Before serving, grate longhorn cheese over top of salad and dot with cherries. Could also top with Cool Whip.

MRS. GRANT (JUNE) CROSS
Otisville, Michigan

Warm Pineapple Salad

1 No. 2 can pineapple chunks, drained (save juice)
2 eggs, well beaten
½ pound yellow mild cheese, cubed
½ cup sugar
1 tablespoon flour
1 cup reserved pineapple juice

Combine pineapple juice, flour, and 2 beaten eggs and cook until thick. Add pineapple chunks and cubed cheese. Serve immediately while warm.

"This is so good served with baked ham."

MRS. L. E. (MERRETA) HUMRICH
Muncie, Indiana

Surprise Salad

1 No. 2 can crushed pineapple
¾ cup sugar
2 packages lemon gelatin
2 cups grated cheese
½ pint whipping cream, whipped
¾ cup nuts

Mix crushed pineapple with sugar and bring to boil. Dissolve lemon gelatin in 2 cups of boiling water; add to hot pineapple and sugar. Let them all cool. Then add grated cheese. Just before the gelatin is entirely set, add whipping cream and nuts. Serve in pretty serving dish.

MRS. WENDELL (BONNIE) PARIS
Henryetta, Oklahoma

Carrot Pineapple Salad

1 can crushed pineapple, drained
1 package carrots
salad dressing

Grate carrots, add pineapple with 2 or 3 tablespoons salad dressing and mix. Can be served immediately.

"A delicious easy-to-fix salad that everyone will enjoy. Ingredients can be kept on hand, and quickly put together when emergencies arise."

MRS. DUDLEY (LOIS) ANDERSON
Gallup, New Mexico

Carrot Salad

2 packages carrots
1 green pepper
1 large onion

Dressing
1 can tomato soup
1 cup sugar
⅔ cup salad oil
¾ cup vinegar
1 teaspoon salt
½ teaspoon pepper
1 teaspoon dry mustard

Peel and slice carrots lengthwise in thin slices. Cook until tender. Drain well. Slice green peppers and onions over carrots in a long dish. Cover with the above dressing.

"A great pitch-in dinner salad. Can be prepared the day before."

MRS. MARK L. (VIRGINIA) FRAME
New Castle, Indiana

Molded Carrot Cream Salad

1 6-ounce package orange gelatin
½ cup boiling water
1 8-ounce can crushed pineapple with syrup
2 large carrots, shredded
1 cup sour cream
½ cup mayonnaise
1 tablespoon lemon juice
½ cup cream, whipped

Dissolve gelatin in boiling water. Add pineapple and carrots. Chill until lightly thickened. Mix sour cream, mayonnaise, lemon juice and whipped cream. Fold in mixture. Use 2 quart mold.

MRS. MARK R. (CLARICE) MOORE
Kansas City, Missouri

Raspberry Salad

2 packages red raspberry gelatin
1½ cups applesauce
2⅔ cups hot water
1 8-ounce package frozen raspberries
chopped nuts

Dressing
2 cups small marshmallows
½ pint sour cream

Dissolve gelatin in hot water, then stir in ingredients. Dressing is made by adding 2 cups small marshmallows to ½ pint sour cream. Let set overnight then beat well. Spread over top of gelatin salad.

"Have received many compliments on this recipe. I have even served it with a pancake supper. It is especially good with ham."

MRS. ALECK G. (ETHELYN) ULMET
Louisville, Kentucky

Raspberry Velvet Salad

1 6-ounce box raspberry gelatin
1 3-ounce box vanilla pudding and pie filling
3½ cups water
1 package (12-16 ounces) slightly sweetened, frozen raspberries
1 9-ounce carton frozen whipped topping

Mix gelatin and pudding in saucepan, stirring in the 3½ cups water (slowly to blend well). Continue stirring until mixture comes to a boil, boil 2 minutes. Allow to cool, refrigerate until slightly jelled. Add raspberries and fold in whipped topping. Sets pretty in a cut glass salad bowl.

MRS. WILLIAM (MARGARET) GRIFFIN
Indianapolis, Indiana

Raspberry Tang Salad

1 package raspberry gelatin
2 cups hot water
1 large package cream cheese
¼ cup mayonnaise
1 banana
1 small can crushed pineapple
¼ cup shredded coconut
¼ cup chopped nuts

Dissolve gelatin in water and chill until thickened. Whip until light. Mix cream cheese with mayonnaise. Mash banana. Fold both together with pineapple, coconut, and nuts, then mix all together with gelatin. Mold and refrigerate several hours before serving.

"This is a beautiful pink salad and can be effectively used for buffet suppers or showers as well as a regular meal."

MRS. EUGENE (FAYE) STOWE
Englewood, Colorado

Turkey Salad

5 cups chopped leftover turkey
2 cups chopped celery
½ cup chopped green pepper
2 hard cooked eggs, chopped
1 cup pineapple chunks, drained

1½ cups mayonnaise
1 cup whipped cream
1 7-ounce package macaroni shells, cooked
½ avocado, cut up

Mix all ingredients together just before serving. Season to taste. Makes at least 15 servings.

MRS. FLOYD H. (CAROL) POUNDS
Peoria, Illinois

Broccoli Salad

1 large bunch of broccoli (cooked, chilled, then chopped)
    or 1 large bag of frozen broccoli, cooked and chilled
4 boiled eggs, chopped
¼ cup chopped salad olives
3 dill pickles, chopped
¼ teaspoon celery salt
3 tablespoons mayonnaise (more if necessary for good
    consistency)
2 teaspoons chopped onion

Cook the broccoli and chill. Combine all the other ingredients and serve chilled.

"This is a handy salad because it can be prepared ahead and kept in the refrigerator the day before the dinner."

MRS. WILMER (DONNA) WATSON
Fort Wayne, Indiana

Summer Garden Salad

1 chopped green pepper
1 cup chopped celery
1 bunch green onions, chopped stems and all
1 can French cut green beans
Pimento for color

Dressing
½ cup oil
½ cup vinegar
½ cup sugar
¼ teaspoon salt

Combine vegetables in bowl. Mix dressing until sugar is dissolved. Pour over vegetables and refrigerate overnight.

MRS. KENT (MIMI) ANDERSON
Eugene, Oregon

Sauerkraut Salad

2 pounds sauerkraut, well drained
1 medium green pepper, chopped
¼ cup chopped celery
1½ cups sugar
½ cup oil
1 medium chopped onion
½ cup vinegar
1 large carrot, shredded

Add onion, celery, carrot, green pepper to well drained sauerkraut. Add sugar to oil and vinegar and stir well until blended. Add this mixture to sauerkraut mixture and mix well. Store covered overnight.

"For those who do not like sauerkraut, this recipe tastes nothing like sauerkraut. For those who do like sauerkraut, this recipe still tastes nothing like sauerkraut."

MRS. ROY E. (DORIS) CARNAHAN
Ellicott City, Maryland

Zucchini Salad

Mix together:
2 tablespoons dehydrated onion
⅛ cup wine vinegar
¾ cup sugar
1 teaspoon salt
½ cup chopped green pepper
½ cup chopped celery
½ teaspoon black pepper
⅓ cup salad oil
⅔ cup cider vinegar
5 quartered zucchini, sliced paper thin

Marinate six hours or overnight in the refrigerator. Drain before serving on lettuce bed or top of regular tossed salad. This salad will keep for weeks. Regular white or red onion may be used instead of dehydrated. Red onion gives a little flair to the salad.

MRS. GEORGE (MARTHA) FERGUSON
San Diego, California

Pomegranate Salad

1 diced apple
½ cup raisins

½ cup diced celery
1 large pomegranate, separated

Dressing
1 tablespoon mayonnaise thinned with 2-3 tablespoons
    milk or cream
sugar to your taste

Mix first list of ingredients lightly. Mix in dressing thoroughly. Refrigerate 1-2 hours before serving. Keeps well in refrigerator.

Mrs. George (Wanda) Almgren
Bakersfield, California

Cinnamon Apple Ring

1 can applesauce
2 regular size packages red raspberry gelatin
½ cup red hots (cinnamon) candies
2½ cups hot water

Into boiling water put gelatin and red hots. When candies are melted, stir into applesauce. Pour into large ring mold and chill till set. Also good in hot applesauce: Melt red hots in small amount hot water, then add to applesauce.

Mrs. John (Janet) Hay
Camby, Indiana

Happy living is a project for the entire family (Milo L. Arnold).

Avocado Fruit Salad

3 avocados
3 oranges, peeled and sectioned
small bunch of seedless grapes

Dressing
1 small can frozen concentrate orange juice
¾ cup salad oil
¼ cup cider vinegar
3½ tablespoons sugar
½ teaspoon dry mustard
¼ teaspoon Tabasco
¼ teaspoon pepper

I know whom I have believed, and am persuaded that he is able to keep that which I have committed unto him against that day (2 Tim. 1:12).

Cut avocados in half lengthwise; remove pits. Arrange 6 or 7 orange sections in or around avocado halves and place some green grapes in or around avocado halves. Serve with dressing made by shaking dressing ingredients together (mixing in blender more satisfactory). Makes 6 servings.

Mrs. T. E. (Helen) Martin
Kansas City, Missouri

Banana-Peanut Salad

Dressing
> 1 tablespoon vinegar
> ½ cup sugar
> 2 tablespoons flour
> ½ cup water
> 1½ tablespoons butter
> 2 egg yolks

Mix first 4 ingredients well. Add butter. Cook over low heat until it begins to thicken. Pour beaten egg yolks slowly into mixture and continue cooking until thick and creamy. Cool and refrigerate. Have ready 3 large, cold bananas and 1 cup salted peanuts. Peel and dice bananas. In cold bowl lined with lettuce leaves, layer bananas, peanuts, and dressing until all ingredients are used. Chill ½ hour. This can also be made into individual salads if desired.

"This is really yummy! I have never served this without someone asking for the recipe."

> MRS. JOHN (EUNICE) BULLOCK
> *Great Falls, Montana*

Banana Lemon Salad

Mix together:
> 1 large package lemon gelatin
> 2 cups hot water

Add
> 2 cups cold water

Allow gelatin to partially set, then add
> 3 large bananas, sliced
> 1 cup miniature marshmallows
> 1 can pineapple tidbits, drained (reserve juice for topping)

Topping
> 1 egg
> 1 cup reserved pineapple juice (add water if needed)
> 2 tablespoons cornstarch
> ¼ cup sugar
> squeeze of lemon juice

Cook all topping ingredients until thick. Let cool. Add ½ pint cream, whipped, or 1 package of whipped Dream Whip. Fold together and put on top of gelatin mixture.

> MRS. DALLAS (GERVAYSE) BAGGETT
> *Middletown, Ohio*

Lime Mist

 2 3-ounce packages lime gelatin
 2 cups applesauce
 1 cup chopped celery
 ½ cup chopped nuts
 ¼ cup maraschino cherries, well drained and chopped
 2 cups lemon-lime carbonated beverage
 1 cup undiluted evaporated milk
 2 tablespoons lemon juice
 few drops of green food coloring

Combine gelatin and applesauce in saucepan. Warm over low heat until gelatin dissolves; cool. Stir in celery, nuts, cherries, and carbonated beverage. Chill until syrupy. Chill evaporated milk in freezer until soft ice crystals form around edges of tray. Whip until stiff. Add lemon juice and whip until very stiff. Fold into gelatin mixture. Add green food color. Spoon into 2-quart mold. Chill until firm. Makes 8-10 servings.

He left not himself without witness, in that he did good, and gave us rain from heaven, and fruitful seasons, filling our hearts with food and gladness (Acts 14:17).

"This salad goes well with holiday dinners."

Mrs. Arthur F. (Doris) Tallman
Sparks, Nevada

Chicken Fruit Salad

 3 chicken breasts
 ¾ cup celery, diced
 1 cup seedless grapes, halved
 1 cup mandarin oranges, drained
 ½ cup mayonnaise
 ½ cup sour cream
 2 tablespoons parsley, chopped
 2 tablespoons onion, finely chopped
 1 tablespoon lemon juice
 ½ teaspoon salt
 ½ teaspoon pepper
 ½ teaspoon packaged herb salad dressing mix
 lettuce
 toasted almonds

He that tilleth his land shall have plenty of bread: but he that followeth after vain persons shall have poverty enough (Prov. 28:19).

Steam chicken until tender. Cool and remove skin. Cut chicken into bite-size pieces. Add celery, grapes, and oranges. Chill. Mix mayonnaise, sour cream, parsley, onions, lemon juice, and seasonings. Pour over chicken and fruit. Mix well and cover to chill several hours (could chill overnight). Arrange in lettuce cups, or serve in large salad bowl. Top with toasted almonds.

"Will keep several days."

Mrs. M. L. (Doris) Mann
Prescott, Arizona

Layered Green Salad

1 head lettuce, shredded
4 stalks celery, cut diagonally
1 bunch fresh onions (usually 5 or 6), thinly cut
1 package frozen English peas (tiny ones), washed and
  separated
1 can water chestnuts, sliced
1 cup mayonnaise
2 tablespoons sugar
Romano cheese, grated (1 or 2 ounces to taste)
garnish, crisp bacon bits and boiled eggs

Place the layers in order given in a container that can be tightly sealed, as Tupperware. Refrigerate at least 8 hours or overnight. Stir well just before serving. Garnish individual servings if desired.

MRS. MARK R. (CLARICE) MOORE
Kansas City, Missouri

Layered Salad

1 small head lettuce, chopped
1 cup chopped celery
1 cup chopped green pepper
1 medium size chopped onion
1 package frozen English peas (do not thaw)
2 cups mayonnaise (dab on by teaspoonfuls)
2 tablespoons sugar (sprinkle over mayonnaise)
¼ cup shredded cheddar cheese
bacon bits (optional)

Place as listed in recipe by layers in a large flat dish. Cover and store in refrigerator overnight or several hours. Spoon out. Do not toss. Will keep in refrigerator two to three days. Serves 8 to 10 persons.

"This is the first recipe I have found that enables one to make a green salad ahead and still have the lettuce remain crisp. Do not worry about not cooking English peas, they are delicious that way!"

MRS. FORD (BARBARA) BOONE
Baton Rouge, Louisiana

Seven-Layer Salad

1 small head lettuce
½ cup onion, chopped
1 cup green pepper, chopped
1 cup celery, chopped
1 can green peas, drained
1 jar pimento, chopped
1 tablespoon sugar
salt and pepper to taste

Topping
6-8 slices bacon, crumbled
2 hard-boiled eggs, chopped
grated cheddar cheese

The fruit of the Spirit is love, joy, peace, longsuffering, gentleness, goodness, faith, meekness, temperance (Gal. 5:22-23).

Layer ingredients as listed. Seal with salad dressing ¾ inch thick. Refrigerate overnight. Top with bacon, hard boiled eggs, and grated cheese.

"Delicious! A beautiful salad to make ahead of time for company. Good leftover, too. I serve in a 7 x 7 glass container."

MRS. DONALD (LINDA) CAIN
McCrory, Arkansas

Better is a dry morsel, and quietness therewith, than an house full of sacrifices with strife (Prov. 17:1).

Seven-Layer Salad

1 head lettuce
½ cup chopped celery
¼ cup green pepper
¼ cup chopped spanish onion
1 10-ounce package frozen peas
1 pint mayonnaise
2 tablespoons sugar
4-6 ounces grated Parmesan cheese
8 strips fried bacon, crumbled

Slice lettuce and fill pan half full. Add in layers: green pepper, onion, celery, frozen peas (cooked and drained), sugar (sprinkle on top of mayonnaise). Cover top of salad with Parmesan cheese and sprinkle fried and crumbled bacon over all. Cover with plastic wrap. Refrigerate 8 hours.

"This salad is very good and may be prepared ahead of time."

MRS. EMMA PIERCE
Bethany, Oklahoma

24-Hour Salad

A neighbor is one who lives so near that he can hear the cries of a person in need, whether the cries come from next door or the next town. He always lives near enough to help whether the needy be a sad, sick, sarcastic neighbor around the corner or a heathen around the world (Jim Bond).

layer shredded lettuce
layer finely chopped onion
layer finely chopped celery
1 package frozen peas, uncooked
1 small can baby shrimp
1 small can water chestnuts, sliced

Spread mayonnaise to cover. Refrigerate 24 hours. Garnish with tomato wedges and boiled egg slices.

Mrs. Larry (Pat) Neff
Owosso, Michigan

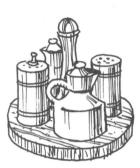

Green Salad and Dressing

Dressing
½ teaspoon salt
dash pepper
2 tablespoons sugar
2 tablespoons vinegar
½ cup salad oil
dash red pepper sauce
1 tablespoon parsley flakes

Salad
¼ cup sliced almonds
1 tablespoon plus 1 teaspoon sugar
¼ head lettuce
¼ head romaine lettuce
1 cup chopped celery
2 green onions with tops, thinly sliced
1 11-ounce can mandarin oranges, drained

Shake dressing ingredients in tightly covered jar and refrigerate. Cook almonds and 1 teaspoon sugar over low heat. Stir constantly until sugar is melted and almonds coated. Cool and break apart. Store at room temperature. Tear lettuce and romaine in bite-size pieces (4 cups). Place greens in plastic bag, add celery, onions. Fasten bag and refrigerate. Just before serving pour dressing into bag, add 1 can drained oranges. Fasten securely and shake until coated. Add almonds and shake. Serve immediately.

Dressing and greens may be made several hours before being served, but do not mix until 5 minutes before serving.

Mrs. J. S. (Velda) Roberts
Alexandria, Indiana

Korean Salad

1 pound of fresh spinach
1 small head of lettuce
2 5-ounce cans water chestnuts, drained and sliced
1 pound can bean sprouts, drained
4 hard cooked eggs, chopped
¾ pound of bacon, fried, drained, and crumbled

Dressing
1 cup oil
½ cup sugar
⅓ cup catsup
¼ cup vinegar
1 tablespoon Worcestershire sauce
2 teaspoons salt

Wash spinach, trim and drain thoroughly. Tear the lettuce and mix with the other ingredients. Mix the dressing ingredients in the blender.

"This makes a really big salad. If there is any chance you think you might not use it all, leave the dressing off part of it. The most important step is to make sure the spinach is thoroughly drained: this will keep the salad from becoming 'weepy.'"

Mrs. Donald (Eleanor) Whitsett
Bethany, Oklahoma

Set your affection on things above, not on things on the earth (Col. 3:2).

Layered Lettuce Salad

1 head of lettuce
1 cup diced celery
4 hard cooked eggs, sliced
1 tablespoon onion, diced
8 slices cooked and diced bacon
½ small head cauliflower
2 cups mayonnaise
2 tablespoons sugar
4 ounces cheddar cheese, grated

Cut lettuce in bite-size pieces. Place on bottom of airtight container. Layer remaining items on top. Add mayonnaise and sugar, spread over vegetables, as you would ice a cake. Top with grated cheese. Cover and refrigerate 8-12 hours. Toss just before serving.

"This is great to make Saturday and have ready for Sunday."

Mrs. James (Mary Lou) Reader
Chrisman, Illinois

Therefore I say unto you, Take no thought for your life, what ye shall eat, or what ye shall drink; nor yet for your body, what ye shall put on. Is not the life more than meat, and the body than raiment? (Matt. 6:25).

Layered Spinach Salad

Dressing:
2 cups sour cream
1 pint Miracle Whip (2 cups)
½ cup Parmesan cheese

Line 4-quart dish with 1 package fresh chopped spinach leaves. Sprinkle 1 pound of crumbled bacon. Over this a layer of chopped crisp lettuce, 8 little green onions (use stems, too, if tender), chopped. Dribble some dressing over this and add generous amount of Parmesan. Add 1 8-ounce package frozen green peas (do not cook). Slice 8 hard cooked eggs over this. Add remaining dressing. Refrigerate 24 hours. 24 servings.

Mrs. Marshall (Edwina) Stewart
Hamlin, Texas

Seafood Salad

2 cups mayonnaise
½ cup catsup
¼ cup chopped green onions
¼ cup chopped dill pickles
2 hard cooked eggs, chopped
1 clove garlic, split and put on a toothpick
½ teaspoon black pepper
1 can shrimp, drained
1 can crab

Mix mayonnaise, catsup, onion, pickles, eggs, and pepper. Add garlic. Cover and refrigerate several hours, or fix before going to Sunday school. When ready to serve, take garlic out and add shrimp and crab. Serve over crisp lettuce.

"This is a good recipe to serve when the weather is hot. All you need with it is cold lemonade and warm rolls."

Mrs. John (Esther) Biggers
Sacramento, California

Lobster Salad

2 cups chopped lobster
1 cup chopped celery
½ cup chopped onion
3 tablespoons mayonnaise
1 teaspoon lemon juice
1 teaspoon salt
⅛ teaspoon ground red pepper
⅛ teaspoon ground cumin

⅛ teaspoon ground turmeric
a sprinkling of paprika

Mix all ingredients thoroughly. Sprinkle with paprika. Serve with your Sunday dinner on lettuce leaves or fill hot-dog rolls with this delicious salad mixture for lunch.

MRS. DAVID (LINDA) AASERUD
Bangor, Maine

Great Spinach Salad

1 pound spinach
½ package of dry garlic salad dressing
½ cup sour cream
2 hard cooked eggs
½ cup celery

Wash and break up spinach. Mix the sour cream and garlic mix. Slice the eggs and chop the celery. Toss all together. Makes 6 to 8 servings.

"This is one of the most delicious and healthy salads I have ever eaten."

MRS. DWIGHT (MARILYN) MILLIKAN
Decatur, Illinois

Six-Layer Tuna Salad

1½ cups prepared Hidden Valley Ranch Original Salad
    dressing
2 cans (6½-ounce each) white tuna, drained and flaked
3 tablespoons finely sliced green onions
2 cups shredded lettuce
2 tomatoes coarsely chopped
½ pound bacon, cooked and crumbled
2 cans (2¼-ounce each) sliced black olives
1 avocado thinly sliced

Combine tuna, 1¼ cups dressing and onion. Mix till dressing is absorbed. In a large glass bowl, layer ingredients as follows: 1 cup lettuce, tomatoes, and olives, ½ of tuna mixture, bacon and avocado, 1 cup lettuce, balance of tuna mixture. Drizzle remaining dressing over top. You may substitute 2 cups cooked chicken in place of the tuna. Makes 4-5 servings.

"This is a beautiful salad—so good with hot bread. I double this for a ladies' luncheon. Fantastic!"

MRS. GERALD (PAULETTE) WOODS
Clovis, New Mexico

I have fed you with milk, and not with meat: for hitherto ye were not able to bear it, neither yet now are ye able (1 Cor. 3:2).

Salad a la Wells

shrimp or crabmeat
celery
slender zucchini
tart apple
lettuce
hard cooked eggs
tomato wedges for garnish

Slice celery, zucchini, about ½ to 1 cup each; dice one apple (peeled), add one small can (4½ ounces) shrimp or crabmeat. Dress lightly with Trader Vic's Japanese dressing. If that touch of herbs and spices is not desired, use Best Foods mayonnaise to taste. An extra can of shrimp adds to the richness. Makes 4 servings.

"Several years ago, I became bored with seafood salad and decided that tart apples added an interesting taste, also zucchini. Guests have since verified this idea."

MRS. SHERWOOD (WINOLA) WIRT
Poway, California

Heavenly Hash

2 cups miniature marshmallows
3 egg yolks, beaten
2 tablespoons sugar
2 tablespoons vinegar
1 can (1 pound, 4 ounces) pineapple chunks
2 tablespoons syrup drained from pineapple
1 tablespoon butter or margarine
⅛ teaspoon salt
1 1-pound can Thompson seedless grapes, drained
1 11-ounce can mandarin orange segments, drained
½ pint heavy cream, whipped

Combine egg yolks, sugar, and vinegar in saucepan. Drain pineapple, reserving 2 tablespoons syrup. Add reserved syrup to mixture in saucepan along with butter or margarine and salt. Cook over medium heat, stirring constantly, until thick and smooth; cool. Fold in pineapple and remaining ingredients in order listed; chill 24 hours. Serve as a salad or dessert. Makes 8 servings.

"I have served this at our Christmas dinner for the church board. Everyone loves it. I add about ½ cup of maraschino cherries for holiday serving."

MRS. DUANE (EVELYN) LANDRETH
Indianapolis, Indiana

Tropical Fruit Salad

1½ cups fresh cranberries, finely chopped
½ cup sugar
1 cup miniature marshmallows
1 cup chopped pecans
3-4 bananas, sliced
2 13½-ounce cans tropical fruits (or fruit cocktail), drained
2 cups whipped topping

Mix cranberries and sugar. Add other ingredients with the exception of whipped topping. Mix well and fold in topping. Sprinkle with coconut and use this as a dessert.

Mrs. Joel E. (Daley) Love
Lakeland, Florida

Big Batch Frozen Fruit Salad

5 cups strawberries
4 cans crushed pineapple
2 1-pound cans of sliced peaches
2 cups fresh white seedless grapes, halved (red can be used
—take out seeds)
1½ cups maraschino cherries, cut in fourths
½ pound small marshmallows
1 envelope unflavored gelatin
¼ cup cold water
1 cup orange juice
¼ cup lemon juice
2½ cups sugar
½ teaspoon salt
2 cups chopped nuts
2 quarts heavy cream whipped or substitute dessert
topping mix
3 cups mayonnaise (for salad)

Drain fruit, save 1½ cups pineapple juice, cut peaches in cubes. Combine fruit, marshmallows. Soften gelatin in cold water. Heat pineapple juice to boiling. Add gelatin, stir to dissolve. Add orange juice, lemon juice, sugar and salt. Stir to dissolve. Chill. When mixture starts to thicken, add fruit juice mixture and nuts, fold in whipped cream. Spoon into quart milk containers, cover and freeze—to serve remove from freezer, tear off carton; cut in 1-inch slices—serve on lettuce or with fresh fruit in season and whipped cream. Makes 9 quarts.

Every plant, which my heavenly Father hath not planted, shall be rooted up (Matt. 15:13).

"This recipe may be used as a dessert or salad. It does not need to be out of freezer too long before serving. It is great to use when something is needed on the spur of the moment."

Mrs. James (Donna) Hetrich
Summerville, Pennsylvania

Fruit Salad

1 16-ounce can fruit cocktail, drained
½ pound small marshmallows
½ pint whipping cream, whipped
1 3-ounce package cream cheese, softened
1 tablespoon salad dressing
½ teaspoon salt
1 16-ounce can cubed pineapple, drained

Combine cream cheese, salt, whipped cream, and salad dressing. Beat until smooth. Fold in fruit and marshmallows. Refrigerate until ready to serve—at least 8 hours.

"A delicious spoon salad."

MRS. RAY (DOROTHY) SHADOWENS
Clarksville, Tennessee

Fruit Salad

1 can pineapple chunks with unsweetened juice
1 can mandarin oranges, drained
1 can fruit cocktail, drained
maraschino cherries (optional)
½ cup coconut (optional)
2 tablespoons of Realemon juice
1 box instant lemon pudding mix

Mix all ingredients together, adding the instant pudding last. Chill. Slice bananas over salad before serving.

"This recipe is very good if you are serving a large number of people. Use a number 10 can fruit cocktail; 3 cans pineapple; 3 cans mandarin oranges; 6 tablespoons real lemon and 4 boxes pudding mix."

MRS. ERNEST (DOROTHY) RHODES
Bulford, Ohio

Refreshing Salad

1 20-ounce can crushed pineapple
2 envelopes unflavored gelatin
1 pint cold water
1½ cups boiling water
1½ cups sugar
1 lemon (juice and grated rind)

2 oranges
2 bananas
1 11-ounce can mandarin oranges
1 small jar maraschino cherries

Soften gelatin in cold water, then heat till warm. Add crushed pineapple, set aside. Dissolve sugar in boiling water, add lemon juice and grated rind. When cool, add cut up orange slices, banana slices, mandarins, and cherries. Add to gelatin-pineapple mixture. Chill well.

MRS. WILLIAM (MAE) MOWEN
Ephrata, Pennsylvania

Heavenly Delight

16 or 20 miniature marshmallows
2 large cans drained fruit cocktail
1 cup chopped nuts (pecans)
extra maraschino cherries, cut in half
1½ pints whipped cream (you may use Cool Whip if you
    prefer)

Sweeten. Mix all together and put in ice tray to harden or serve as it.

MRS. W. E. (DOROTHY) RHODES
San Antonio, Texas

Frozen Fruit Salad

1 8-ounce package cream cheese
¼ cup mayonnaise
1 can fruit cocktail, drained
¼ cup chopped nuts
2 cups miniature marshmallows
¼ cup chopped maraschino cherries (with juice for color)
1 large carton frozen whipped topping

Blend softened cream cheese and mayonnaise together. Add other ingredients in order given and fold in thawed whipped topping. Blend together and freeze in large mold. Serves 12.

"This recipe lends itself to any season, depending on shape of mold and garnishes. At Christmas buffets, I use a round ring mold and fill the center with freshly washed holly.

MRS. DOUGLAS (ELAINE) FARMER
Salem, Oregon

Behold, I stand at the door, and knock: if any man hear my voice, and open the door, I will come in to him, and will sup with him, and he with me (Rev. 3:20).

It's certain that fine women
eat
A crazy salad with meat.
William Butler Yeats

Fruit Salad

Fruit Ingredients (variable)
1 can pineapple chunks
3 medium bananas
1 can peach slices
12 large marshmallows
½ cup nuts, coarsely chopped
1 can Queen Anne cherries

Salad dressing
2 tablespoons flour
2 tablespoons margarine
1 egg yolk, slightly beaten
¼ cup sugar
1 cup pineapple juice
1 cup whipped cream

Melt margarine in skillet, add flour and blend. Remove from heat and blend in pineapple juice and sugar. Return to heat until mixture thickens. Add a small amount of hot mixture to egg yolk, then combine with mixture in skillet. Blend, cook 2 minutes longer. Chill, then fold in whipped cream. Mix salad dressing with drained fruits.

MRS. CHUCK (JEANNIE) MILLHUFF
Olathe, Kansas

As the bridegroom rejoiceth over the bride, so shall thy God rejoice over thee (Isa. 62:5).

Apricot Salad Supreme

2 packages peach gelatin
2 cups boiling water
1 cup miniature marshmallows
1 No. 2½ can apricots
1 No. 2 can crushed pineapple

Topping
1 cup pineapple juice
1 egg
2 cups sugar
3 tablespoons flour
2 tablespoons butter
1 package Dream Whip

Dissolve gelatin and marshmallows in boiling water in a 9½ x 13 baking dish. Drain juice from apricots, adding enough water to make 2 cups. Add this to above mixture and chill till "shaky." Drain pineapple and reserve juice for topping. Add diced apricots and pineapple to gelatin and chill till firm.

Topping: Combine sugar and flour and blend into beaten egg in small saucepan. Gradually stir in pineapple juice (add water to equal 1 cup if needed). Cook over medium heat till thick, stirring constantly. Remove from heat and stir in butter and cool. Whip Dream Whip till stiff. Fold in cooled dressing and spread over gelatin. Sprinkle generously with chopped walnuts or grated cheddar cheese. Chill. Makes 11-12 servings.

"This can be used as a dessert salad, and if so, I serve with nut bread."

MRS. GUNNELL JORDEN
Kankakee, Illinois

Apricot Nectar Mold

1½ cups apricot nectar
¼ cup grapefruit juice
1 package of lemon gelatin
⅛ teaspoon salt
1 cup grapefruit segments
½ cup finely chopped blanched almonds

Drain can grapefruit segments; save the juice. Heat apricot nectar and grapefruit juice together to boiling. In this dissolve lemon gelatin and salt. Remove from heat and chill. When beginning to thicken, beat until light and frothy. Add grapefruit segments and almonds and pour into mold. Serves 6.

A man that flattereth his neighbour spreadeth a net for his feet (Prov. 29:5).

"This is a nice tart and tasty salad that goes well with everything."

MRS. DWIGHT (MARILYN) MILLIKAN
Decatur, Illinois

Apricot Mold

1 large can apricot nectar
1 large can peeled apricots
2 large packages apricot gelatin
1 pint sour cream

Bring to a boil 4 cups of nectar. Add gelatin and stir to dissolve. Add 4 cups cold nectar and juice from apricots. Pour half of mixture in tube mold. Place apricot halves around mold. Let jell partially. Spoon sour cream over surface. Add other half of gelatin mixture.

"You should make the night before using."

MRS. WILLIAM (DORIS) RESTRICK
Wallingford, Connecticut

Apricot Fruit Salad

1 can apricot pie filling
1 can mandarin oranges
1 can pineapple tidbits
1 can grapefruit sections
1 cup miniature marshmallows
2 or 3 bananas

Drain canned fruits. Then combine all ingredients and chill in the refrigerator. For variety, try other fruit fillings and fruit combinations. Can be made ahead. Keeps well.

MRS. HARRY (ADELINE) REIMER
Fairbanks, Alaska

Apricot Gelatin Salad

1 large package apricot gelatin
2½ cups pineapple juice
1 cup miniature marshmallows
2 cups cold water
1 large can crushed pineapple, drained
2 bananas
½ cup sugar
2 tablespoons flour
1 egg, beaten
2 teaspoons butter
1 3-ounce package cream cheese
1 9-ounce carton Cool Whip

Heat 2 cups pineapple juice to boiling, stir in marshmallows to dissolve. Add gelatin; then cold water, crushed pineapple, and sliced bananas. Let stand in refrigerator to congeal. In saucepan mix ½ cup pineapple juice, sugar, flour, egg, and butter for topping and cook until thick (about 5 minutes). Add cream cheese. When cool, add Cool Whip. Cover congealed salad with this topping. Make this recipe in a 9 x 13 inch dish.

MRS. ROBERT (BEVERLY) ALLEN
Louisville, Kentucky

Bing Cherry Salad

2 packages cherry gelatin
1 3-ounce package cream cheese
1 tablespoon lemon juice
2 tablespoons mayonnaise
1 No. 2 can pitted cherries (dark sweet or bing)
½ cup pecans

Prepare gelatin as directed using cherry juice as part of liquid. Pour 1 cup of gelatin mixture into mold. Allow to set firm in refrigerator.

Combine cream cheese, lemon juice, mayonnaise and cream well. When gelatin in bowl begins to set, put half of above mixture in it. Mix well. Add the cherries and pecans. Put half of this mixture in mold that has clear gelatin in it. Also add remaining cheese mixture. When firm add remaining gelatin mixture.

MRS. FRED (GRACE) BERTOLET
Lake Worth, Florida

Be not conformed to this world: but be ye transformed by the renewing of your mind (Rom. 12:2).

Frozen Bing Cherry Salad

1 can black sweet pitted cherries, drained
2 cups sour cream
2 tablespoons lemon juice
½ cup sugar
8 ounces crushed pineapple, drained
1 banana, sliced
¼ cup nuts
dash of salt
1-2 drops of red food coloring

A word fitly spoken is like apples of gold in pictures of silver (Prov. 25:11).

Mix all ingredients, and put into 8 x 10 or 8 x 8 pan. Freeze overnight. Thaw 15 minutes before cutting. Serve on lettuce.

MRS. ORVILLE (JOY) MAISH, JR.
Mason, Michigan

Frozen Cherry Salad

1 16-ounce can cherry pie filling (or other flavor)
1 14-ounce can crushed pineapple
1 14-ounce can condensed milk
1 13½-ounce container whipped topping

Mix all ingredients. Freeze in 9 x 13 pan. Cut in squares and garnish to serve.

MRS. ROY T. (SUE) NIX
Birmingham, Alabama

New England Cole Slaw

chopped cabbage
pineapple tidbits, or other fruit
seasonings: celery seed
drizzle of honey
tarragon vinegar
few chopped chives and/or green pepper
chopped pimento for color
2 shakes dill weed
2 shakes Italian seasonings

Mix all ingredients and enjoy good eating!

MRS. JOHN (DORCAS) RILEY
Nampa, Idaho

Cabbage Slaw

3 cups cabbage
¼ cup green pepper, chopped
1 teaspoon red pepper, chopped
½ tablespoon grated onion
3 tablespoons salad oil
⅓ cup vinegar
1 teaspoon salt
¼ teaspoon black pepper
½ teaspoon dry mustard
1 teaspoon celery seed
2 tablespoons sugar

Grate cabbage—small or medium grater, only. Mix other ingredients, in order, as listed above. This should be made a day in advance. It is much more tasty if allowed to set in refrigerator over night. Will keep for several days. Cover well in plastic container.

"Very good with vegetable dinner, is very tasty with your roast, chicken, or whatever kind of meat you choose to have."

MRS. MEL (DOT) THOMPSON
Hammond, Indiana

Freezer Slaw

1 medium head cabbage, shredded
1 carrot, grated
1 green pepper, grated

1 cup vinegar
¼ cup of water
1 teaspoon mustard seed
1 teaspoon celery seed
2 cups sugar
1 teaspoon salt

Cover cabbage with water, add 1 teaspoon salt. Let stand one hour. Drain. Squeeze out excess moisture. Add grated carrot and green pepper. Boil vinegar and water for 1 minute. Add mustard seed, celery seed, and sugar. Cool to lukewarm. Pour over cabbage mixture. Freeze.

MRS. FORREST W. (BELLE) NASH
Bourbonnais, Illinois

Six-Weeks Slaw

3 pounds shredded cabbage
1 finely chopped green pepper
1 medium onion, grated
2½ cups sugar
2 cups white vinegar
1½ teaspoons prepared mustard
½ teaspoon celery seed
1½ teaspoons salt

Mix sugar, vinegar, mustard, salt, and celery seed. Boil. Pour over vegetables while hot. Store in refrigerator.

MRS. FORREST W. (BELLE) NASH
Bourbonnais, Illinois

Raw Cauliflower Salad

1 large head fresh cauliflower
1 small can sliced black olives
1 jar sliced stuffed olives
¼ pound sliced fresh mushrooms
1 small jar of pimentos
1 green pepper, sliced

Mix altogether and marinate overnight in Italian Wishbone dressing. Serve on lettuce. Serves 10-12.

"This always receives a lot of compliments and is great for the cook since it is better made a day ahead."

MRS. WILBERT (MARGUERITE) EICHENBERGER
Santa Ana, California

Until we put our trust in the Lord, we are like the gentleman who testified "to show that crowd he was just as good as they were." An empty barrel will make a lot of noise, but it does no one any good. They that trust the Lord find many things to praise Him for. Praise follows trust (Lily May Gould).

Fresh Cauliflower Salad

It is true that we have great responsibilities in our own land to spread the gospel, but millions are dying untold around the world. It is also true that the light that shines the farthest out, shines the brightest at home (John W. May).

Salad
  1 head cauliflower
  ½ cup chopped green pepper
  1 cup chopped celery
  ½ cup chopped green onion
  2 ounces green olives, sliced

Salad Dressing
  1 teaspoon sugar
  1 teaspoon salt
  1 teaspoon pepper
  ⅓ cup mayonnaise
  ¼ cup Otts French Dressing (If you cannot locate Otts
      Dressing, use any French dressing that contains horse-
      radish.)

Break the flowerette portion of the cauliflower into small bite size pieces. Add the remaining salad ingredients. Marinate in salad dressing four or five hours before serving. Salad dressing preparation: Simply mix together and add to salad.

"A favorite with the boys at my house."

MRS. JAMES (BEVERLY) SMITH
Olathe, Kansas

Orange Salad

The earth shall be full of the knowledge of the Lord (Isa. 11:9).

  1 large package lemon gelatin
  1 large can crushed pineapple, not drained
  2 cups boiling water
  1 small frozen orange juice
  1 can mandarin oranges, drained

Heat 2 cups water to boiling, mix with gelatin to dissolve. Add 1 can frozen orange juice, stirring until completely blended. Add crushed pineapple and 1 can oranges. Mix thoroughly. Put in refrigerator to congeal.

Topping:
Mix 1 package vanilla instant pudding with 1½ cups cold milk. Mix until it begins to thicken. Stir in 1 large container Cool Whip until well mixed. Pour over top of gelatin and let stand a few hours. Makes large salad.

MRS. IRA L. (CAROLYN) EAST
Wilmington, Ohio

Orange Almond Salad

crisp lettuce, chopped
2 oranges, peeled and diced
⅔ cup slivered almonds, broiled in butter
1 cup Cool Whip
2-3 tablespoons thawed orange juice concentrate

Ahead of time (or day before) "broil" slivered almonds in small amount of butter, stirring until lightly browned. Cool. Toss lettuce, diced oranges, and broiled almonds in individual salad dishes and top with orange whip.

Orange Whip: Stir the Cool Whip and thawed orange juice together. If too thick, thin with small amount of milk. Makes 4 good servings.

Mrs. B. Edgar (Kathryn) Johnson
Olathe, Kansas

Orange-Pineapple Salad

1 20-ounce can chunk pineapple, drained
3 apples, cut up
2 bananas, sliced
1 cup chopped walnuts

Sauce
juice of 2 oranges
juice of half of the pineapple
1 egg, beaten
1 tablespoon cornstarch, dissolved in a little water
½ cup sugar

Bring sauce ingredients to boil and let cool. Mix with other ingredients.

Mrs. Willis (Evelyn) Whitling
Seneca, Pennsylvania

God, who commanded the light to shine out of darkness, hath shined in our hearts, to give the light of the knowledge of the glory of God in the face of Jesus Christ (2 Cor. 4:6).

Mandarin Orange Salad

1 6-ounce package of orange gelatin
2 cups hot water
2 tablespoons lemon juice
½ pint orange sherbet
2 cans mandarin oranges, drained

Mix gelatin in hot water. Add lemon juice, sherbet, and oranges. Chill until firm.

Mrs. James (Thelma) Cullumber
Tucson, Arizona

Mandarin Orange Salad

2 egg yolks or 1 egg, well beaten
1 tablespoon flour
⅓ cup sugar
1 3-ounce box orange gelatin
1 can mandarin oranges
1 No. 2 can crushed pineapple
½ package miniature marshmallows
1 small carton Cool Whip

In small saucepan, combine and boil 1 minute: eggs, flour, sugar, and juices from oranges and pineapple. Add orange gelatin and chill. In large mixing bowl, put drained oranges and pineapple, and miniature marshmallows. Fold in chilled dressing and Cool Whip. Put in serving dish and chill 3 to 4 hours. Reserve 5 mandarin oranges and 5 miniature marshmallows for decoration on top of salad.

MRS. BYRON (CAROLYN) BUKER
Bedford, Indiana

Polynesian Salad

⅓ cup salad dressing
½ teaspoon curry powder
1 tablespoon chopped onion
1 cup cooked small sea shell macaroni
1 can tuna, drained (or 6 ounces of cooked tiny shrimp)
1 20-ounce can of pineapple chunks, drained
1 cup sliced celery
½ green pepper

Combine salad dressing, curry powder, and chopped onion and let stand. Meanwhile combine other ingredients. Toss with the dressing and serve on lettuce. Makes 6 luncheon servings.

MRS. PAUL K. (EMILY) MOORE
Mount Pleasant, Michigan

Fonduloha Salad

2 fresh pineapples
2½ cups cooked and chopped shrimp or chicken
¾ cup chopped celery
¾ cup salad dressing
1 teaspoon curry powder
1 sliced banana
½ cup coconut
1 can mandarin oranges, drained
½ cup salted peanuts

Surely the churning of milk bringeth forth butter, and the wringing of the nose bringeth forth blood: so the forcing of wrath bringeth forth strife (Prov. 30:33).

Cut each pineapple in half, lengthwise, right through green tops, then in half again to make 4 pieces. Remove fruit from shell. Drain shells upside down. Combine cubed pineapple and the shrimp or chicken. Cover and chill. Mix dressing with curry powder and chill. Just before serving, drain fruit mixture, toss with the dressing, banana, and nuts. Fill the shells, sprinkle with coconut, and garnish with mandarin oranges. Makes 8 servings.

MRS. C. WILLIAM (TWYLA) ELLWANGER
Bourbonnais, Illinois

Chinese Chicken Salad

1 chicken breast, cooked and cut into small pieces
2 green onions, diced
½ cup nuts, chopped
1 head lettuce, shredded
Chinese noodles (when fried, 2-3 cups)

Salad dressing
2 tablespoons sugar
½ tablespoon salt
1 teaspoon seasoning powder
½ teaspoon black pepper
¼ cup vegetable oil
1 tablespoon sesame oil
3 tablespoons vinegar

French fry in oil the Chinese noodles putting in a small amount at a time. They only hit the oil then turn. Put on paper to drain and cool. Combine other ingredients and toss just before serving.

"This is the first salad to go at any church social. All ages like it."

MRS. JAMES (WILMA) SHAW
Concord, California

Mexican Chef Salad

4 tomatoes
1 medium onion (optional)
1 head lettuce
1 bag Dorito Taco chips or Fritos, rolled fine
1 pound ground beef, browned
1 can kidney beans, drained
6 ounces mild cheese (cheddar or longhorn), shredded
1 8-ounce bottle of Kraft Thousand Island Dressing

Cut up tomatoes, onion, lettuce, browned beef, and add kidney beans and heat. Remove from heat. Add rest of ingredients—cheese, taco chips, and salad dressing, beef and beans. Toss together. Makes 6-8 servings for big eaters.

"Always a hit at any social gathering."

Mrs. Phillip (Shirley) Riley
Jamestown, North Dakota

Taco Salad

1 pound hamburger, browned and drained
1 head shredded lettuce
½ cup cheddar cheese, shredded
3 medium tomatoes, chopped
¾ cup celery, chopped
¼ cup green pepper, chopped
1 small package Doritos
1 can chili or red kidney beans, well drained
Italian dressing to taste

Brown hamburger and drain well. Cut lettuce in thin shreds and combine other ingredients. Add dressing when you are ready to serve.

"This is very good to take to a potluck and as a leftover, served with sandwiches."

Mrs. Delbert (Frances) Remole
Potomac, Illinois

Mexican Salad

1 can kidney beans, drained
1 large onion, diced
1 large tomato, diced
1 10-ounce package of sharp cheddar cheese, shredded

1 8-ounce bottle of Kraft Spicy Sweet Catalina French
Dressing (may take a little more)
1 head of lettuce, torn into bite-size pieces
1 9-ounce bag Fritos, slightly crushed

Mix the first 5 ingredients and marinate for 12-15 minutes. Add the lettuce and the Fritos just before serving.

MRS. J. TED (GENEVA) HOLSTEIN
Roanoke, Virginia

Crisp Cucumber Salad

2 medium cucumbers, peeled and sliced thin
1 small onion, sliced thin
½ cup sour cream
1 tablespoon minced parsley
2 tablespoons sugar
3 tablespoons cider vinegar
¾ teaspoon salt
¼ teaspoon each dry mustard and pepper

In serving dish, gently toss cucumber and onion to mix; chill until serving time. Beat sour cream, sugar, vinegar, salt, mustard, and pepper until well blended. Pour over cucumber, onion mixture, sprinkle with parsley; serve at once. Makes 4 to 6 servings.

Drink waters out of thine own cistern, and running waters out of thine own well (Prov. 5:15).

MRS. DON (FAITH) BELL
Olathe, Kansas

Cucumbers and Sour Cream Dressing

2 medium cucumbers
1¼ teaspoons salt
1 cup sour cream
2 tablespoons vinegar (I use white)
1 tablespoon minced onion
¼ teaspoon sugar

Pare and slice cucumbers and sprinkle with 1 teaspoon of the salt. Chill for about 30 minutes. Press out any excess water (after chilling) in a towel. Combine remaining ingredients and add to cucumbers and mix gently. Chill for 30 minutes. Pepper is optional. Garnish with paprika or parsley.

"Our family liked this salad served with beef or fish. It can be made a day ahead, so was a good addition to the Sunday dinner."

MRS. WALTER H. (ETHEL) SMYTH
Boynton Beach, Florida

Cucumbers in Sour Cream

Thinly slice 1 large cucumber; sprinkle with one teaspoon salt; let stand 30 minutes. Drain. Combine ½ cup sour cream, 1 tablespoon vinegar, 1 to 2 drops Tabasco sauce, 2 tablespoons chopped chives, 1 teaspoon dill seed, and dash of pepper; pour over cucumbers. Chill about 30 minutes.

MRS. GARY (RAEDEAN) HENECKE
Olathe, Kansas

Blueberry Salad

1 can blueberry pie filling
1 large package raspberry gelatin
½ cup nuts
1 package Dream Whip
1 or 2 bananas

Prepare gelatin. Put it in refrigerator until almost jelled. Stir in blueberry pie filling. Chill until set. Add prepared Dream Whip, chopped nuts, and sliced bananas. Mix slightly and serve. Makes 10 servings.

"Goes well with ham and potato salad. Makes enough for our family and at least one more. Easy to fix on Saturday."

MRS. CHARLES E. (BARBARA) JONES
Nacogdoches, Texas

Blueberry-Pineapple Salad

2 regular boxes of grape gelatin (or 1 large)
2 cups boiling water
1 20-ounce can crushed pineapple
1 can blueberry pie filling

Topping
1 8-ounce package cream cheese
1 pack Dream Whip
½ cup milk
½ cup sugar
1 teaspoon vanilla
sprinkle of coconut for top (optional)

Mix together: grape gelatin, water, pineapple, blueberry pie filling. Refrigerate until firmly congealed. Topping: Combine in a mixing bowl; 1 pack Dream Whip, ½ cup milk, ½ cup sugar. Beat until stiff. Add: cream cheese (room temperature), vanilla flavoring. Spread on top of your congealed salad. Makes 15-18 servings.

"This salad can be served with a big meal, or just sandwiches. Can be used as salad or a dessert."

MRS. C. L. (MARY) THOMPSON
Richmond, Virginia

Pretzel Salad

2 cups twisted pretzels, broken up
1 stick melted butter
3 tablespoons white sugar
2 packages Dream Whip
1 8-ounce package cream cheese
1 can pineapple pie filling
½ cup sugar

Melt butter in 9-inch square pan. Stir in 3 tablespoons sugar and broken pretzels. Bake 10 minutes at 350° F. Cool and break loose from pan. Mix together Dream Whip, cream cheese, ½ cup sugar, and spread on pretzel mix. Top with pineapple pie filling.

MRS. C. DEXTER (SUSANNA) WESTHAFER
Huntington, Indiana

Return to thine own house, and show how great things God hath done unto thee (Luke 8:39).

Strawberry Salad

1 large package strawberry gelatin
2 cups boiling water
1 large package frozen strawberries
3 mashed bananas
1 can crushed pineapple
1 cup nutmeats (walnuts)

Mix gelatin in hot water. Thaw frozen berries in hot gelatin. This also quick-cools the gelatin. Add all ingredients. Spread half of mixture in 7 x 11 inch glass baking dish. Freeze about 5 minutes. Refrigerate other half. Spread one-half pint sour cream over frozen gelatin mixture. Add balance of mixture and refrigerate. Serve on lettuce leaf.

"Our family has been enjoying this salad for 15 years."

MRS. MILTON (LILLIAN) MOUNTAIN
Flint, Michigan

Strawberry Pretzel Salad

First step
 2 cups pretzels, crushed
 3 tablespoons sugar
 ¾ cup margarine, melted

Second step
 1 8-ounce package cream cheese
 1 9-ounce container Cool Whip
 ½ cup sugar

Third step
 2 3-ounce packages strawberry gelatin
 2 cups boiling water
 2 10-ounce packages frozen strawberries

First step: mix and put in 9 x 13 pan. Bake at 350° F. for 10 minutes. Let cool. Second step: cream softened cream cheese. Beat in sugar and Cool Whip. Put on cooled crust. Third step: dissolve gelatin in boiling water, add thawed strawberries, pour on top of cheese layer. Chill. Cut in squares.

"I put the pretzels in blender to crush."

MRS. WILLIS (EVELYN) WHITLING
Seneca, Pennsylvania

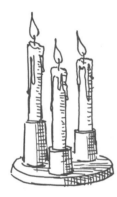

Frozen Strawberry Salad

1 9-ounce container Cool Whip
1 can Eagle Brand milk
1 large (or 2 small) packages frozen strawberries
1 large can crushed pineapple
3 bananas, diced

Mix milk, Cool Whip; add thawed strawberries including juice, pineapple, and bananas. Freeze in 9 x 13 dish. Set out about 5 to 10 minutes before serving.

MRS. RONALD (DONNA) PEACH
Kingsport, Tennessee

Strawberry Gelatin Salad

1 3-ounce package strawberry gelatin
1 3-ounce package cherry gelatin

1 cup hot water
2 cups cold water
1 16-ounce package strawberries
1 8-ounce package cream cheese
1 cup chopped pecans

Dissolve strawberry and cherry gelatin with one cup of hot water. Add two cups of cold water. Chill. Thaw strawberries and allow cream cheese to soften at room temperature. Fold strawberries into gelatin. Form the cream cheese into small balls and roll them over the chopped nuts. Fold into gelatin. Refrigerate.

MRS. D. MOODY (NINA) GUNTER
Columbia, South Carolina

Potato Salad

4 or 5 cooked potatoes
5 or 6 hard-boiled eggs
1 whole bunch green onions (tops, too, cut fine)
1 small jar pimentos
1 heaping tablespoon mayonnaise
1 heaping tablespoon salad dressing (add more if desired)
salt and pepper

This keeps very well for days.

"Our favorite potato salad."

MRS. P. J. (MARY) ZONDERVAN
Grand Rapids, Michigan

But thou, when thou fastest, anoint thine head, and wash thy face; that thou appear not unto men to fast, but unto thy Father which is in secret: and thy Father which seeth in secret shall reward thee openly (Matt. 6:17-18).

Sour Cream Potato Salad

⅓ cup Italian salad dressing
6 cups potatoes cooked in skin, peeled and sliced
¾ cup sliced celery
½ cup sliced green onion
4 hard cooked eggs
1 cup mayonnaise
½ cup sour cream
1½ teaspoons horseradish mustard

Pour Italian dressing over warm potatoes; chill 2 hours. Add celery, onion, and chopped egg whites. Sieve yolks and mix with mayonnaise, mustard, and sour cream. Fold into salad. Add salt and celery seed to taste. Chill 2 hours. Makes 8 servings.

MRS. BOB (MARY JO) KETCHUM
Shawnee, Oklahoma

Glazed Almond Salad Dressing

Dressing
½ teaspoon salt, dash of pepper
  2 tablespoons sugar
½ cup plus 2 tablespoons Italian dressing
dash red pepper sauce
  1 tablespoon snipped parsley

Mix and shake well. Store ahead of time. Shake before using.

Glazed Almonds
½ cup sliced almonds
  1 tablespoon plus 2 teaspoons sugar

Cook almonds and sugar until sugar melts and coats. Cool on waxed paper and break apart.

¼ head iceberg lettuce
¼ head romaine lettuce
  1 cup chopped celery
  2 green onions plus tops finely chopped
  1 can mandarin oranges, drained

Mix lettuce, celery, and onions ahead of time and store. Just before serving, add dressing, mandarin oranges, and then almonds.

"This salad has won me compliments every time I serve it."

MRS. WALTER E. (FAYE) LANMAN
Hastings, Nebraska

Celery Seed Salad Dressing

¾ cup vinegar
⅛ cup water
  1 egg
  2 teaspoons salt
  1 cup sugar
  1 teaspoon powdered mustard
1-2 teaspoons grated onion
  2 cups salad oil
  1 tablespoon celery seed

Mix ingredients in electric mixer at high speed for 20 minutes. In a blender, use medium speed about 15 seconds (no need to grate onion if using blender).

"This is very much like the 'house dressing' in many Amish restaurants."

MRS. PAUL (MARY ELLEN) MERKI
Alliance, Ohio

French Salad Dressing

¾ cup sugar (or substitute)
¾ cup vinegar
1 can tomato soup
1 medium onion, grated
1 teaspoon dry mustard
1½ cups salad oil
2 tablespoons Worcestershire sauce
1 tablespoon salt
garlic (optional)

Beat ingredients well. Keep refrigerated.

"This is a favorite dressing for our family and for company."

MRS. IRVING (BEVERLY) LAIRD
Nampa, Idaho

Unto you therefore which believe he is precious (1 Pet. 2:7).

Sweet-Sour French Dressing

1 cup sugar
1 cup tomato catsup
½ onion, chopped fine
1 teaspoon dry mustard
½ teaspoon pepper
½ teaspoon salt (garlic, if desired)
1 teaspoon lemon juice (garlic juice adds flavor)
½ teaspoon Worcestershire sauce
1 cup vinegar

Blend all together and let season in refrigerator.
"This is so delicious that I could eat it with a spoon."

MRS. WILMER (EVALEEN) LAMBERT
Syracuse, New York

Lend, give, yield God everything you have today, and then watch the interest pile up in all your tomorrows (C. William Fisher).

Meats, Poultry, & Fish

Labour not for the meat which perisheth, but for that meat which endureth unto everlasting life, which the Son of man shall give unto you: for him hath God the Father sealed (John 6:27).

Liver Stroganoff

    1 pound liver
    flour
    salt, pepper
    ½ stick (¼ cup) butter or margarine
    ½ cup sliced onion
    ½ cup sliced mushrooms
    1 cup sour cream, at room temperature

Cut liver into ½-inch strips; dip in flour; season with salt and pepper. Melt butter in large, heavy skillet. Lightly saute onions and mushrooms; add liver. Brown on all sides quickly. Cover; cook over low heat about 10 minutes. Blend in sour cream; serve immediately. Makes 4 servings.

"Serve stroganoff over rice or noodles, accompanied by broccoli or asparagus, and a tart salad of fresh orange and grapefruit sections and avocado wedges."

MRS. L. THOMAS (LOIS) SKIDMORE
Medina, Ohio

Baked Coon

    2 back legs of coon
    ½ cup cranberries

1 apple, quartered
¼ cup sugar

All the meat offering that is baken in the oven and all that is dressed in the frying-pan, and in the pan, shall be the priest's that offereth it (Lev. 7:9).

Cut off all exposed fat from the meat. Cover meat with water in a heavy saucepan. Boil for 5 minutes. Drain water; rinse. Place legs in baking pan; sprinkle with salt; cover with cranberries and apples. Cook 1½ hours in a 325° F. oven. Remove fruit from pan and place in blender, add sugar. Remove meat from bone and spread fruit sauce over top. Serve while hot.

"Married to a hunter, I learned to enjoy wild game. This is one of our family's favorites."

MRS. WALTER (IRIS) GRAEFLIN
Bluffton, Indiana

Venison Stroganoff
(Men's Fellowship Dinner)

8-10 pounds of venison meat
    Bone venison quarter and cut into slices or strips ½ inch
        by 3 to 6 inches long
8 slices bacon
2 cups minced onion
4 cups boiling water with 4 beef bouillon cubes added
2 teaspoons salt
3 teaspoons Worcestershire sauce
1 teaspoon rosemary
3 cups sour cream
4 cups sliced mushrooms

Fry bacon until very crisp. Remove bacon from pan and brown venison in bacon drippings. Remove venison from pan and place strips in pressure cooker for 10 minutes for each batch of meat. When pressure cooking is completed, set meat aside. Saute sliced mushrooms and minced onions in bacon drippings until lightly browned. Add beef bouillon dissolved in boiling water, salt, Worcestershire sauce, and rosemary. Return the venison strips and any juice to this pan. Slowly stir in sour cream; warm, but do not bring to a boil. Serve over noodles, cooked according to package directions. Sprinkle with paprika. Serve with plenty of hot French bread, tossed green salad, and a green vegetable. Makes 16-20 man-size servings.

And Jesus said unto them, I am the bread of life: he that cometh to me shall never hunger; and he that believeth on me shall never thirst (John 6:35).

"Sometimes you are given a venison quarter, or the great hunter-pastor brings home the game. Here is a way to prepare a delicious, no wild taste, main dish."

JOHN FABRIN
Selma, California

Swedish Meat Balls

½ *pound ground beef*
½ *pound ground sausage*
½ *cup fine graham cracker crumbs*
　1 *egg*
⅛ *teaspoon pepper*
　1 *teaspoon nutmeg*
　1 *teaspoon allspice*
　1 *teaspoon ginger*
½ *cup cream*
¼ *cup dry bread crumbs*
1½ *teaspoons salt*
½ *cup water*

Combine all ingredients except water. Form into balls. Brown slightly in small amount of butter. Add water. Cover: simmer for 30 minutes. Pour into casserole. Bake at 300° F. for 1 hour.

Mrs. Roger (Mary Lou) Parrott
Upper Marlboro, Maryland

Sweet-Sour Meatballs

¾ *cup dry bread crumbs*
　1 *tablespoon instant minced onion*
　2 *teaspoons salt*
½ *teaspoon pepper*
just enough water to soften
　3 *pounds ground beef*
　1 *pound of bulk pork sausage*
　3 *eggs slightly beaten*
cooking oil
　1 *bouillon cube*
1½ *cups water*
　4 *carrots*
　3 *green peppers*
¾ *cup cider vinegar*
　1 *cup light brown sugar*
¼ *cup soy sauce*
⅓ *cup cornstarch*

Combine bread crumbs, onion, salt and pepper with water and let stand a few minutes. Add to this the ground beef and pork sausage, eggs, and mix well. Shape into small balls and brown in a heavy skillet containing a small amount of oil. Remove to roasting pan; pouring off fat in skillet, add water and bouillon cube; heat and strain—pour this liquid over the meatballs. Cover and bake in preheated oven. Cut carrots into strips and cook until almost tender; cut green peppers into wedges and cook for a few minutes. Make sauce by combining 4 cups water, vinegar, sugar and soy sauce. Bring to a boil; thicken with cornstarch, cook until thick and clear. Pour liquid off meatballs and discard; add carrots and green peppers to meatballs. Pour soy sauce mixture over all and return to oven to heat gently. Bake in oven for approximately 50 minutes at 350° F. Makes 12 servings.

"The recipe above is great served with rice or potatoes. Also good for a large group and, because it improves with reheating, the dish can be prepared ahead of time."

MRS. LeROY (BEVERLY) WRIGHT
Reddick, Illinois

Korean Barbecue Short Ribs

6 lbs. short ribs
1¼ cups soy sauce
1 clove garlic, finely minced
1 teaspoon ginger, finely minced
¼ cup raw sugar
2 tablespoons sesame oil
½ tablespoon sesame seed
¼ teaspoon black pepper
2 tablespoons chopped green onion
¼ teaspoon tenderizer (if necessary)

Slice meat into ½ inch cuts to within 1 inch of bones. The cut meat should resemble a fan. Combine remaining ingredients and pour over the ribs, let soak overnight. Broil in oven or over charcoal, about 10 minutes to the side.

MRS. MIYOJI (NATSUKO S.) FURUSHO
Hanapepe, Kauai, Hawaii

Brisket of Beef

5-6 pounds beef brisket
Lawry's seasoning salt
heavy duty foil

On Saturday night, wash meat and pat dry. Rub Lawry's seasoning salt in with fingers, 2 or 3 times. Wrap in 2 sheets of heavy duty foil. Bake at night, 400° F., first half hour, 250° for 8-10 hours in shallow baking dish. Take out in morning. Place in refrigerator to solidify fats—6-8 hours. Remove all fat—slice ¼ inch and place in juice at 400° F. for ½ hour. To heat through or juice starts to boil.

MRS. JOHN (VIOLET) WORDSWORTH
Edmonds, Washington

For whosoever hath, to him shall be given, and he shall have more abundance: but whosoever hath not, from him shall be taken away even that he hath (Matt. 13:12).

Sauerbraten Supreme

3-4 pounds top round roast cut in 1-inch thickness
2 tablespoons vegetable oil
2 medium onions, sliced
½ cup water
¼ cup cider vinegar
1 tablespoon packed brown sugar
1 bay leaf
4 whole cloves
¼ teaspoon ground allspice
2 celery stalk tops
6 gingersnaps

Sprinkle beef with salt. Brown on both sides in hot oil in 6-quart Dutch oven, over medium heat. Top with onions. Place water, vinegar, brown sugar, bay leaf, cloves, allspice, and celery tops in medium saucepan, and bring to boil. Pour vinegar mixture over meat. Simmer covered until meat is tender, about 2½ hours. Add more water if necessary. Remove roast to serving platter, keep warm. Strain liquid, discard vegetables and spices. Return liquid to Dutch oven, spoon off excess fat. Thicken gravy with crushed gingersnaps. Season to taste. Makes 8 servings.

Mrs. Harold (Merry) Little
Modesto, California

Barbecued Brisket

5 or 6 pounds brisket (request from butcher)
3 ounces liquid smoke
celery salt, onion salt, garlic salt
salt, pepper
Worcestershire sauce
6 ounces barbecue sauce

Place brisket on baking sheet. Pour liquid smoke over meat and sprinkle generously with celery salt, onion salt, and garlic salt. Cover pan with foil, place in refrigerator and marinate overnight or at least 8 hours. Before baking, pour off liquid and sprinkle with salt, pepper, and Worcestershire sauce. Replace foil. Bake 5 to 7 hours in a 275° F. oven. Remove from oven; pour barbecue sauce over meat, and bake one more hour. Allow to cool before slicing in thin slices.

"This recipe can be prepared in advance, then, before serving, reheat the meat, making sure the foil is tightly closed so the delicious juices do not escape."

Mrs. Clarence (Sue) Kinzler
Nampa, Idaho

Barbecued Brisket

1 large brisket
1 bottle liquid smoke
celery salt
garlic salt
onion salt

Marinate brisket with liquid smoke overnight. In morning, sprinkle with the various salts and wrap in foil. Bake 6 hours at 250° F. or 275° F. Open foil at top; pour barbecue sauce over it and continue baking for 30 minutes, uncovered. Cool 30 minutes before slicing.

"This is very easy to prepare and ready to eat when we return from church. I usually bake potatoes at the same time. Children love this for Sunday dinner."

One can become a cook, but one is born a roaster of meat (Anthelme Brillat-Savarin).

MRS. HARRY (MARION) RICH
Kansas City, Kansas

Oven Barbecued Steaks

3 pounds round steak, ¾" thick
2 tablespoons vegetable oil
½ cup chopped onion
¾ cup catsup
½ cup vinegar
1 tablespoon brown sugar
1 tablespoon mustard
1 tablespoon Worcestershire sauce
½ teaspoon salt
⅛ teaspoon pepper
½ cup water

The discretion of a man deferreth his anger; and it is his glory to pass over a transgression (Prov. 19:11).

Heat oven to 350° F. Cut meat in serving pieces, brown steak in oil on both sides. Put steaks in roasting dish; add onion to oil and brown; add rest of the ingredients to make a barbecue sauce. Simmer 5 minutes. Pour sauce over steak in dish and bake 2 hours or until meat is tender and sauce has thickened.

"This can be prepared the day before, refrigerated, and put in oven just before going to church."

MRS. HOYLE C. (JUANITA) THOMAS
Nampa, Idaho

He that passeth by, and
meddleth with strife belong-
ing not to him, is like one
that taketh a dog by the ears
(Prov. 26:17).

Fast Pepper Steak

1 ½ pounds chuck steak
2 tablespoons oil
1 package dry onion soup mix
½ pound fresh mushrooms, thinly sliced
1 green pepper, thinly sliced
1 large can tomatoes
1 teaspoon salt
1 teaspoon soy sauce
1 teaspoon Worcestershire sauce
1 teaspoon pepper

Cut meat in narrow strips and brown in oil. Add all other ingredients and simmer 30 minutes. Serve over hot rice. Makes 4
servings.

"Serve this with your favorite salad, hot French bread. And
share Jesus with a brand-new couple. You'll love the evening."

MRS. GERALD (PAULETTE) WOODS
Clovis, New Mexico

Stew Meat Special

1 package stew meat
1 can cream of mushroom soup
1 can beef consomme soup
1 can pearl onions, drained

Place meat in heavy Dutch oven. Pour onions on top of meat. Stir
in condensed soups. Place covered in 250° F. oven before breakfast and forget about it until after church. Serve over rice or
egg noodles. Makes 6 servings.

"Do not add salt or water (until you have tried it)! You can
use meat other than stew meat—like round steak, etc., cut
into pieces."

MRS. ALAN (SHARON) RODDA
Portland, Oregon

Depart from evil, and do
good; seek peace, and pur-
sue it (Ps. 34:14).

Roast Beef

1 chuck or arm roast of a suitable size
1 can mushroom soup, undiluted
potatoes
carrots

Pour mushroom soup over roast; place potatoes and carrots around meat. Cover with aluminum foil. Cook 4 hours at 325° F.

"This is very simple, but it is our typical Sunday dinner, as it can be cooking while we are at church and it takes only a few minutes to fix a salad and maybe another vegetable and we can be eating Sunday dinner in a very short time."

MRS. RAY (DOROTHY) MARLIN
Indianapolis, Indiana

Country Steak and Cream of Onion Gravy

2 pounds round steak, cut in serving pieces
1 teaspoon salt
¼ teaspoon pepper
½ cup vegetable oil
2 cans Campbell's cream of onion soup
1 cup water

Trim all fat from steak; roll in flour and brown in oil in skillet. Add seasoning. When browned, put in "slow-cooker," then add cream of onion soup and water. Let cook slowly for 3-4 hours.

What man is there of you, whom if his son ask bread, will he give him a stone? Or if he ask a fish, will he give him a serpent? (Matt. 7:9-10).

"What a quickie meat and gravy dish! Serve with baked potato or mashed. We really like it. You may substitute venison steak instead of beef—works just as well!"

MRS. HARLAN (RUBY) HEAP
Ainsworth, Nebraska

Old English Prime Rib

standing rib roast
ice cream rock salt
pepper
Accent
Worcestershire sauce

Rub meat with pepper, Accent, and lots of Worcestershire sauce. Layer bottom of roaster pan with ice cream salt. Set roast on top of salt. Cover meat with mountains of salt. Bake in oven. Cook 12 minutes per pound at 500° F. with no lid for rare; 17 minutes per pound at 500° F with no lid for medium; 22 minutes per pound at 500° F with no lid for well done.

Garnish with spiced apples, parsley, mandarin oranges, and/or apricots.

MRS. BUD (NANCY) TOLLIE
Overland Park, Kansas

Beef or Veal Paprika

2 pounds meat
1 package Lipton vegetable soup mix
1 can mushrooms
1 large onion
2 teaspoons cayenne pepper
2 teaspoons salt, pepper, and paprika
½ cup flour
a little grease
1½ cups water
1 cup sour cream

Cut meat into strips. Mix flour and spices in paper bag. Shake meat in mixture and brown in pan. Make a thick meat layer in casserole dish. Cut onions up and spread on top of meat. Pour mushrooms over it. Cook vegetable soup in 1½ cups water for about 10 minutes. Let cool. Stir in sour cream. Pour over meat and bake in 350° F. oven for 1 hour or until meat is done.

"Good served over cooked rice."

MRS. WALLY (GINGER) LAXSON
Athens, Alabama

Sugar Cured Ham Rolls

6 slices boiled ham (⅛ inch thick)
1 cup cooked wild and white rice
½ cup slivered chicken
2 cups mushroom sauce

Mushroom sauce
1 cup sliced mushrooms
4 tablespoons butter
4 tablespoons flour
salt
¾ cup chicken stock
½ cup cream

Mix rice and chicken. Place about 3 tablespoons on center of ham slice. Roll up carefully and place in a well buttered baking dish. Cover with foil and heat in moderate oven. Serve with mushroom sauce. I allow 2 ham rolls per serving.

MRS. MELVIN (GENEVA) McCULLOUGH
Colorado Springs, Colorado

Savory Pot Roast

1 3-pound pot roast
⅛ cup oil
¼ cup catsup
¼ cup wine vinegar
2 tablespoons soy sauce
2 tablespoons Worcestershire sauce
1 teaspoon crushed dried rosemary
½ teaspoon garlic powder
½ teaspoon dried mustard

Flour, salt, and pepper roast. Braise in hot oil in Dutch oven or heavy skillet. Combine remaining ingredients and pour over roast. Simmer until tender. When done, thicken juice for gravy.

"This recipe works best with inexpensive cuts of beef and done on the top of stove over low heat. It also can be prepared in the oven at 300° F. for 3-4 hours. Leftover roast makes delicious cold meat sandwiches."

MRS. ROY E. (DORIS) CARNAHAN
Ellicott City, Maryland

If when we suffer we are inclined to self-pity, we will be impoverished rather than enriched by the investment of pain. If, however, our suffering makes us more understanding of others, more sympathetic, more humble, and more mature, we will find that the touch of pain can produce the enkindling of inspiration (Milo L. Arnold).

Sukiyaki American Style

1¼ pounds steak (sirloin tip sliced on No. 20)
¼ cup sugar
¾ cup soy sauce
¼ cup water
1½ cups carrots, sliced diagonally
1 cup celery, sliced diagonally
2 onions, sliced in thin rounds
1 green pepper, sliced in strips
1 bunch green onions, sliced in 1-inch strips
1 can whole string beans, drained
optional: mushrooms, water chestnuts, bamboo shoots,
     canned or fresh tomatoes

Cut meat in strips and brown in oil. Mix sugar, soy sauce, and water; add to meat; simmer for about 25 minutes. Add carrots; cook 10 minutes. Add balance of vegetables and cook 2-3 minutes. Serve over rice or chow mein noodles, or half of each.

"Ooh's and aah's from my guests make it a most delightful dish for special people."

MRS. DORIS McDOWELL
Walnut Creek, California

Jesus answering said unto him, Suffer it to be so now: for thus it becometh us to fulfill all righteousness. Then he suffered him (Matt. 3:15).

Dilly Pot Roast

2 tablespoons flour
1 teaspoon salt
¼ teaspoon pepper
2½ pound beef pot roast
1 tablespoon shortening
¼ cup water
1 tablespoon vinegar
1 teaspoon dill weed
5 small potatoes, pared
5 carrots, quartered
½ teaspoon salt
1 pound zucchini squash, quartered
½ teaspoon salt

Mix flour, 1 teaspoon salt, and the pepper; rub meat with flour mixture. Brown well in hot shortening in large heavy skillet or Dutch oven. Add water and vinegar. Sprinkle ½ teaspoon dill weed over meat; turn meat and sprinkle with remaining ½ teaspoon dill weed. Cover; simmer 1½ to 2 hours. Add potatoes and carrots; sprinkle with ½ teaspoon salt. Cover and simmer 40 minutes. Add zucchini; sprinkle with ½ teaspoon salt. Cover and simmer 20 minutes or until vegetables are tender. Remove meat and vegetables to a platter while making sour cream gravy.

Sour Cream Gravy

Measure meat broth. (If necessary, add enough water to make 1 cup liquid.) Mix 1 cup dairy sour cream, 1 tablespoon flour, and 1 teaspoon dill weed in skillet; gradually stir in meat broth. Heat just to boiling, stirring constantly.

MRS. VERNON (CAROLYN) LUNN
Farmington Hills, Michigan

Gourmet Pork Chops

6 pork chops
2 tablespoons flour
1 teaspoon salt and dash of pepper
2 tablespoons shortening
1 10½-ounce can condensed cream of mushroom soup
½ teaspoon ground ginger
¼ teaspoon dried rosemary, crushed
1 3½-ounce can French fried onions
½ cup sour cream

Coat chops with a mixture of salt, flour, and pepper. In skillet, brown on both sides in hot shortening. Place in 11 x 7 x 1½-inch baking dish. Combine soup, ¾ cup water, ginger, and rosemary.

Pour over chops. Sprinkle with half the onions. Cover and bake at 350° F. for 50 minutes, or till meat is tender. Uncover; sprinkle with remaining onions and continue baking 10 minutes. Remove meat to platter. Blend sour cream into soup mixture; heat. Serve with meat.

MRS. CHARLES (CHRISTIANA) PICKENS
Dodge City, Kansas

Spareribs and Sauerkraut

3-4 pounds country style spareribs
1 large can sauerkraut
1 tablespoon brown sugar
1 apple sliced and cored

Cook spareribs in boiling water until tender. Allow to sit overnight, in the refrigerator. Remove the fat over top the spareribs before heating the next morning. Add large can of sauerkraut with brown sugar and sliced apples. Simmer for 45 minutes.

"Usually spareribs are very greasy. Cooking them the day before one uses them, eliminates this problem."

MRS. JOHN (REBA) WOODRUFF
Eau Claire, Wisconsin

Sweet and Sour Spareribs

2 pounds spareribs
1½ cups brown sugar
½ cup vinegar
1 cup water
1 teaspoon soy sauce
2 tablespoons cornstarch
2 tablespoons cold water
1 tablespoon soy sauce

Cut spareribs into 1-inch pieces. Roll in flour and brown in skillet in small amount of oil. Place browned ribs into saucepan and add the mixture of brown sugar, vinegar, water, 1 teaspoon soy sauce. Simmer for 1 hour, or until tender. Thicken with 2 tablespoons cornstarch and 2 tablespoons cold water. Add 1 tablespoon soy sauce. Serve with steamed rice.

"This recipe is easy to make, yet delicious. I always receive compliments whenever I serve it."

MRS. GLENN FOLLIS
Edmonton, Alberta, Canada

Behold, the days come, saith the Lord God, that I will send a famine in the land, not a famine of bread, nor a thirst for water, but of hearing the words of the Lord (Amos 8:11).

Pork Chop Orange

6 pork chops, ½-inch thick
1 teaspoon salt
1 large onion, cut into 6 slices
1 6-ounce can frozen orange juice concentrate, partially
    thawed
¾ cup water
2 pounds sweet potatoes or yams, pared and cut into
    ½-inch slices
1 orange, cut into 6 thick slices
¼ cup brown sugar, packed
½ teaspoon allspice
3 tablespoons lemon juice

Trim excess fat from chops. Grease skillet and brown chops on both sides; salt lightly. Drain off excess fat. Top each chop with onion slice. Mix orange juice concentrate, sugar, allspice, lemon juice, and water; pour into skillet. Heat to boiling; reduce heat. Arrange sweet potato slices under pork; cover and simmer until pork and potatoes are done (30-45 minutes). Add orange slices 10-15 minutes before serving.

"I like to serve with a green vegetable."

MRS. CHARLES (MARJORIE) BLAKE
Wyckoff, New Jersey

Baked Salmon Fillets

Salmon fillets cut in serving-size pieces
1 tablespoon brown sugar per fillet
1 tablespoon butter or margarine per fillet
1 teaspoon lemon juice
salt and pepper

Place salmon fillets in buttered casserole. Sprinkle brown sugar on pieces. Melt butter, add lemon juice, salt, and pepper. Pour over salmon fillets. Bake 20 minutes at 400° F.

"This is a recipe I adapted from the recipe used for a tourists' Salmon Barbecue in Juneau."

MRS. ROBERT (EVA) SHEPPARD
Anchorage, Alaska

Fillets Elegante

1 pound frozen fish fillets (sole, haddock, halibut, or cod)
fresh ground pepper
  2 tablespoons butter or margarine
  1 can frozen condensed cream of shrimp soup, thawed
      (regular shrimp soup can be substituted)
¼ cup shredded Parmesan cheese
paprika

Thaw fish fillets enough to separate. Arrange in buttered 9-inch pie pan. Dash with pepper and dot with butter or margarine. Spread shrimp soup over fillets and sprinkle with Parmesan cheese and paprika. Bake at 400° F. for 25 minutes. Serve with lemon wedges. Makes 4 servings.

MRS. ALEX (GREETA) CUBIE
South Windsor, Connecticut

We remember the fish, which we did eat in Egypt freely; the cucumbers, and the melons, and the leeks, and the onions, and the garlick (Num. 11:5).

Shrimp Creole

½ cup cooking oil
  2 cups finely chopped onions
  1 cup chopped green pepper
  1 cup finely chopped celery
  2 teaspoons finely chopped garlic
  2 medium-size bay leaves
  4 cups finely chopped Italian plum tomatoes
  1 cup hot water
  1 tablespoon paprika
½ teaspoon cayenne pepper
  1 tablespoon salt
  3 pounds medium shrimp, cleaned, rinsed, and dried
  2 tablespoons cornstarch
¼ cup cold water

Heat the oil in a heavy pan and saute the onions, green pepper, celery, and garlic. Stir in the bay leaves, tomatoes, hot water, paprika, cayenne pepper, and salt; bring to a boil. Cover, reduce heat to low and let simmer 25 minutes. Stir in shrimp and continue to simmer about 5 minutes or until shrimp are hot and firm to the touch. Mix cornstarch and cold water until thoroughly blended. Add to the shrimp mixture and gently stir till the sauce slightly thickens. Remove bay leaves and serve over long-grain rice. Serves 4.

MRS. DEAN (KAY) WILDER
Liberty, Kansas

Fish Supreme

5-10 small panfish (bluegill, perch, etc.)
  Clean; cut off head, fins, and tail. Leave skin on.
1 gallon boiling water, to which you add:
1 cup vinegar
1 bay leaf
10 peppercorns
½ cup salt

Boil fish about 5 minutes, or until the skin slips off easily. Remove from water, skin, and serve covered with melted butter, garnished with dried parsley. The backbone and small bones can be removed before serving if desired.

JOHN FABRIN
Selma, California

The children of Israel did eat manna forty years, until they came to a land inhabited; they did eat manna, until they came unto the borders of the land of Canaan (Exod. 16:35).

Chicken Diván

4 chicken breasts, halved
2 10-ounce packages frozen broccoli spears, or 2 to 3
  pounds fresh broccoli
2 tablespoons butter
2 tablespoons flour
1 cup chicken broth, fresh or reconstituted
  (I always use the broth from cooking the chicken)
1 teaspoon Worcestershire sauce
1½ cups grated mild cheddar cheese
1 cup (½ pint) sour cream, at room temperature
paprika

Simmer chicken in lightly salted water to cover for 25 minutes or until cooked through. Skin and bone cooked chicken. Cook broccoli and drain. Over medium heat, melt butter in stainless steel, glass, or enamel saucepan. Stir in flour and cook until bubbly. Add broth and Worcestershire sauce: cook, stirring, until thickened. Reduce heat and stir in 1 cup of the cheese, heating gently until melted. Empty sour cream into medium bowl: gradually add cheese sauce, stirring constantly. Salt to taste. Arrange broccoli in 8 portions in baking dish. Top each with half a chicken breast, pour sauce over all. Sprinkle with remaining cheese and paprika. Bake at 325° F. about 25 minutes or until heated through. Makes 8 generous servings.

MRS. ROSS (HARRIETTE) HAYSLIP
Tucson, Arizona

Chicken Diván

He brought quails, and satisfied them with the bread of heaven (Ps. 105:40).

2 bunches of broccoli
3 whole chicken breasts
2 cans cream of chicken soup
1 cup mayonnaise
1 teaspoon lemon juice
½ teaspoon curry powder
½ cup shredded cheese

Cook broccoli. Cook and debone chicken breasts. Place broccoli on the bottom of casserole that serves six. Arrange chicken on top of broccoli. Combine the other ingredients except the cheese. Pour on top of the chicken and broccoli. Sprinkle with cheese and bake ½ hour at 350° F.

"Can easily be made the day before and refrigerated; then bake 45 minutes instead of 30."

MRS. EARL (HAZEL) LEE
Pasadena, California

Unto you it is given to know the mystery of the kingdom of God (Mark 4:11).

Chicken Elegant

1 chicken
1 small jar peach jam
1 small jar apricot jam (optional)
1 bottle clear Italian dressing
1 package Lipton onion soup mix
½ cup water

Clean chicken, cut in serving pieces, and skin. Place in greased, shallow baking dish. Combine remaining ingredients in a bowl, mix thoroughly, and pour over chicken. Bake for one hour in 350° F. oven. (If sauce is saved in a jar and kept cold it can be reused at a later date.)

"We were introduced to this 'feast' in my sister-in-law's kitchen in Winslow, Maine. It has become an instant hit with our family!"

MRS. ALBERT D. (JANET) STIEFEL
Nampa, Idaho

Parmesan Chicken

3 cups crushed corn flakes
½ cup grated Parmesan cheese
1 teaspoon garlic powder
2 teaspoons salt
½ teaspoon coarsely ground pepper
melted butter or margarine (amount depending on
    quantity of chicken)
meaty chicken pieces

Dip pieces of chicken in melted butter or margarine, then in the mixture of dry ingredients listed above. Bake 45 minutes on a cookie sheet at 350° F. You may make all preparation early in the morning and put in the oven after church. The chicken does not need to be turned, it will brown on all sides.

"I like this recipe because all preparation can be done ahead and the kitchen cleaned up."

MRS. C. DEXTER (SUSANNA) WESTHAFER
Huntington, Indiana

Curry Chicken

chicken pieces (we usually use 12 thighs)
flour
salt and pepper
   1 can cream of chicken soup
   1 cup sour cream (small carton)
1½ teaspoons curry powder
   1 small can of button mushrooms
   2 cups uncooked white rice

Wash chicken pieces then coat with a mixture of salt, pepper, and flour. Fry chicken until brown, and put in a casserole dish. Mix cream of chicken soup and curry powder, and pour over chicken. Bake in covered casserole at 350° F. for 1 hour. Take chicken out of casserole and put on a platter, keep chicken warm in oven. Mix sour cream and mushrooms with sauce in casserole and heat until thickens like gravy (add a little milk if too thick).

Serve sauce over chicken and cooked white rice.

MRS. PAUL (VERNELL) PRICE
Eureka, California

Chicken Something Different

4 chicken breasts, halved, boned, and skinned
8 slices uncooked bacon
2 3-ounce packages chipped smoked dried beef
2 cans mushroom soup
1 pint sour cream

Line bottom of greased oblong glass baking dish with layers of dried beef. Wrap each breast with bacon strips. Place breasts in two rows of four each on top of beef. Mix together soup and sour cream and pour over chicken, spreading to completely cover. Bake at 250° F. for three hours, uncovered.

"The dish may be assembled and frozen, thawed and baked when needed. The soup makes good gravy over rice. A delicious Sunday main dish, that will bake while you're at church."

MRS. MILTON (LILLIAN) MOUNTAIN
Flint, Michigan

Martha was cumbered about much serving, and came to him, and said, Lord, dost thou not care that my sister hath left me to serve alone? bid her therefore that she help me. . . . Jesus answered and said unto her, Martha, Martha, thou art careful and troubled about many things (Luke 10:40-41).

Sunday Chicken

2 young chickens, cut up
salt, pepper, flour
4 tablespoons salad oil

Sauce
1 large onion
1 small can mushrooms
1 small green pepper
1 teaspoon garlic powder
1 small can tomato juice and 1 can water
1 teaspoon salt
1 teaspoon sugar

Sprinkle cut-up chicken with flour, salt, and pepper. Brown lightly in salad oil.

Sauce: cook vegetables in shortening until almost brown. Add tomato juice, water, seasoning. Pour sauce over chicken, cover and cook slowly until chicken is tender; about 35-40 minutes.

"I often fed this to 10-12 young people who had missed their Sunday dinner at the college cafeteria. I cooked it on Saturday, heated it Sunday while the vegetables were cooking. I used 3 chickens for 10-12 people."

MRS. ALEXANDER (MARGARET) ARDREY
Calgary, Alberta, Canada

Batter Crisp Chicken

2 broiler-fryers (about 2 pounds each), cut into serving-size
pieces
2 teaspoons salt
1 teaspoon rosemary
½ cup water
ginger batter
shortening or salad oil for frying

Ginger Batter
1 ¼ cups sifted regular flour
1 teaspoon baking powder
1 teaspoon salt
½ teaspoon ground ginger
1 egg
1 cup milk
¼ cup salad oil

The rib, which the Lord God had taken from man, made he a woman, and brought her unto the man. And Adam said, This is now bone of my bones, and flesh of my flesh: she shall be called Woman, because she was taken out of Man (Gen. 2:22-23).

Wash chicken pieces, pat dry. Place in a single layer in a large shallow baking pan; sprinkle with salt and rosemary; add water; cover. Bake in moderate oven (350° F.) for 1 hour. Remove chicken from pan; pull off skin. You may wish to remove small rib bones. Thoroughly drain chicken over paper towel. While chicken cooks, prepare Ginger Batter. Melt enough shortening or salad oil to provide a 2-inch depth in an electric deep-fat fryer or large saucepan; heat to 350° F. Dip pieces 2 or 3 at a time, into ginger batter; hold over bowl to catch excess. Fry in hot shortening 3 minutes, or until golden-brown. Lift out with a slotted spoon; drain well. Keep hot until all pieces are cooked.

Ginger Batter
Sift flour, baking powder, salt, and ginger into a medium size bowl. Add remaining ingredients all at once; beat with a rotary beater until smooth.

Make prayer a top priority rather than a last resort (Jackson D. Phillips).

"An electric deep fat fryer is not absolutely necessary. You can fry chicken in a skillet with very deep oil. The Puffy-golden jacket and a smidgen of spice enhances the flavor of this chicken."

MRS. GERALD L. (KAY) MORGAN
Marietta, Ohio

Cream Chicken

1 fryer, or
6 chicken breasts
1 can undiluted cream of chicken soup
1 small carton sour cream
45 Ritz crackers, crushed
1 stick melted margarine

Boil chicken with a couple of bay leaves and a piece of celery until tender. Bone chicken and place in oblong pyrex dish. Add cream of chicken soup and sour cream—fold together. Add melted margarine to cracker crumbs and place on top of casserole. Bake in oven 15 to 20 minutes at 350° F. Makes 12 servings.

MRS. RUBY HOLLAND
North Little Rock, Arkansas

Hardening of the heart is much more devastating in the long run than hardening of the arteries (Donald R. Peterman).

Grandma Fisher's Southern Fried Chicken

1 2½- to 3-pound fryer (may use larger chicken)
flour
salt
pepper
paprika
oil for frying
Karo syrup (light brown)

Put flour, salt, pepper, paprika into paper bag. Wash and dry chicken, and put into bag and shake well. Fry chicken in hot oil until nice and brown on both sides. After turning, right before finishing, drizzle Karo (lightly, not too much). Chicken will crisp up.

"Favorite with preachers and PKs too!"

MRS. D. E. (WAVALENE) CLAY
Mount Vernon, Ohio

Chicken Supreme

2 whole chicken breasts
2 tablespoons cooking oil
1 can chicken or mushroom soup
⅓ cup milk
1 can mixed vegetables, drained
1 tablespoon chopped parsley
¼ teaspoon thyme

A gracious woman retaineth honour: and strong men retain riches (Prov. 11:16).

The house of the wicked shall be overthrown: but the tabernacle of the upright shall flourish (Prov. 14:11).

Brown chicken, pour off fat. Stir in soup, milk, and thyme. Simmer 30 minutes. Stir, add other ingredients, cook another 20 minutes. Serve with cooked rice. Makes 4 servings.

MRS. MELVIN (MARCY) SHROUT
Olathe, Kansas

Sunday Chicken

1 chicken, cut-up, or ½ breast per person
1 can cream of mushroom soup
1 can cream of chicken soup
1 cup uncooked rice
2 cups diced celery
1 can water

Mix all ingredients and bake at 250°-275° F. until you return from church.

MRS. ALAN (SHARON) RODDA
Portland, Oregon

Russian Chicken

1 small bottle Russian salad dressing
1 small (10-ounce) jar apricot preserves
1 package instant onion soup mix
1 chicken, cut up
flour

Roll chicken pieces in flour and place in a baking dish. Mix all other ingredients together and pour over the chicken. Bake at 350° F. for 1 hour.

"This is very good fixed with a rice dish."

MRS. ROY (MARY) SHUCK
Greencastle, Indiana

Pineapple Chicken

2 boneless chicken breasts
3 slices pineapple
diced bell pepper
2-3 garlic buttons
1 tablespoon oil

Marinade
1 teaspoon cornstarch
2 teaspoons soy sauce
1 tablespoon oil
½ teaspoon salt

Sauce
3 teaspoons cornstarch
3 teaspoons soy sauce
3 tablespoons water
6 tablespoons pineapple juice

2 teaspoons vinegar
1-2 tablespoons brown sugar

Cut chicken in strips ½" wide and 1" long. Mix marinade and add to chicken. Let stand for 15 minutes. Cut pineapple in ½" wedges. Reserve juice. Crush, peel, and mince garlic. Mix sauce ingredients. Heat 1 tablespoon oil (none if using Teflon pan) until very hot in skillet. Add chicken and stir-fry for 3 minutes. Add pineapple and bell pepper, lower heat, cover, and cook 3 minutes. Remove and set aside. Clean skillet, if greasy. Add garlic and stir-fry few seconds. Add cornstarch mixture and cook; stir until thickened. Add chicken and mix. Serve over rice.

"A very quick dish. Especially if you mix the marinade and sauce ahead of time. In fact, chicken, pineapple, etc., can all be cut up ahead, and stored in refrigerator."

Mrs. B. Edgar (Kathryn) Johnson
Olathe, Kansas

Irene's Chicken Pie with Savory Pastry

12 large mushroom caps, sliced
¼ cup butter
¼ cup flour
1 teaspoon salt
¼ teaspoon pepper
2 cups chicken stock
⅔ cup cream
2 cups chicken cut in large chunks

Savory Pastry
⅓ cup shortening
1 cup flour and ½ teaspoon salt
1 teaspoon celery seed
½ teaspoon paprika
2 tablespoons water

In him was life; and the life was the light of men (John 1:4).

Boil chicken with favorite seasonings to make stock. Sauté mushroom caps in a little butter. Melt butter, blend in flour and seasonings. Add chicken stock and cream. Stew chicken with favorite seasonings for an hour or more. (I have used patty shells or made just one large chicken pie.)

Pastry
Cut shortening into flour and salt. Add celery seeds, paprika, and water. Mix well with fork until dough clings together. Round into smooth ball and roll pastry fairly thin. Cut in circles or shape of baking dish. Bake 30 minutes, in 425° oven. Makes 6 servings. Or divide chicken and mushrooms among 6 individual baking dishes. Pour on hot sauce. Top with pastry.

Every good gift and every perfect gift is from above, and cometh down from the Father of lights, with whom is no variableness, neither shadow of turning (Jas. 1:17).

Mrs. James E. (Flora) Hunton
Springfield, Illinois

Sweet 'n' Sour Chicken

1 8-ounce can pineapple chunks
2 pounds chicken breasts
2 tablespoons butter or margarine
½ cup chicken bouillon
2 large carrots, sliced
¼ cup firmly packed brown sugar
2 tablespoons cornstarch
¼ cup vinegar
2 tablespoons soy sauce
1 medium onion, sliced and separated into rings
1 8-ounce can water chestnuts, thinly sliced
½ green pepper, cut in strips
hot rice

Drain pineapple, set aside juice. Bone chicken breast, cut into slivers; saute in butter until no longer pink. Add bouillon and carrots, cover and cook until carrots are tender. Combine reserved juice, brown sugar, cornstarch, vinegar, and soy sauce and add to chicken and carrots. Cook until mixture thickens. Just before serving, add pineapple, onion, green pepper, and water chestnuts. Cook just until heated. Serve over hot rice.

MRS. ROBERT (FRANCES) SPEAR
Boca Raton, Florida

Herb Chicken

2 2½-pound chickens, quartered
½ cup lemon juice
2 cloves garlic, crushed
2 teaspoons dried thyme leaves
1½ teaspoons salt
1 teaspoon black pepper
lemon pepper seasoning, scant
ginger, scant
¼ cup butter or margarine, melted
¼ cup chopped parsley

Soak chicken in cold water at least ½ hour. Dry well and arrange chicken in baking dish. Combine all seasoning with lemon juice, mix well. Spoon over chicken, to coat well. Refrigerate in marinade 3-4 hours. Turn chicken several times during this process. Preheat oven to 425° F. Remove chicken, drain on paper towel, arrange in baking dish, brush with melted butter. Bake uncovered until done, brushing occasionally with marinade. Serve over rice, garnish with chopped parsley. Makes 8 servings.

MRS. CHARLES (FANNY) STRICKLAND
Olathe, Kansas

Chicken Cheese Elegant

  5 whole chicken breasts
  4 green onions, bottoms only
1½ cups grated cheddar cheese
  1 can cream of celery soup, undiluted
  2 cans cream of chicken soup, undiluted

Cut chicken breasts in half and skin. Place skinned chicken in large casserole dish, bone side down. Do not stack. Use 2 pans if necessary. Sprinkle chicken generously with paprika. Slice the green onions over chicken. Sprinkle grated cheese over chicken. Mix together celery and chicken soups. Spoon over chicken. Cover with foil and bake at 325° F. for 2 hours. Makes 5 servings.

"This is delicious served with chicken Rice-a-Roni which has been prepared according to package directions. It's a great recipe for Sunday because it can be put in the oven when you go to church and is ready when you come home."

MRS. ALPIN (BETTY) BOWES
Prairie Village, Kansas

So ought men to love their wives as their own bodies. He that loveth his wife loveth himself (Eph. 5:28).

Even so must their wives be grave, not slanderers, sober, faithful in all things (1 Tim. 3:11).

Chicken or Turkey a la King

  1 6-ounce can sliced mushrooms, drained
½ cup diced green pepper
½ cup butter or margarine
½ cup flour (regular or Wondra)
  1 teaspoon salt
¼ teaspoon pepper
  2 cups chicken broth*
  2 cups light cream
  2 cups cubed cooked chicken or turkey
  1 4-ounce jar pimento, chopped
patty shells, tart shells, or toast cups may be used for
      serving.

Cook and stir mushrooms and green pepper in butter for 5 minutes. Remove from heat. Blend in flour, salt, and pepper. Cook over low heat, stirring until mixture is bubbly. Remove from heat. Stir in broth and cream. Heat to boiling, stirring constantly. Boil 1 minute. Add chicken and pimento; heat through. Serve hot in patty shells. Makes 8 servings.

*Chicken broth may be made by dissolving 2 chicken bouillon cubes in 2 cups boiling water, or use canned chicken broth.

"Excellent for crowds, served in chafing dish."

MRS. R. J. (MAUDIE) CLACK
Madison, Wisconsin

Crispy Baked Chicken

5 or 6 pounds chicken pieces
1 cup enriched self-rising flour
1 tablespoon paprika
1 teaspoon seasoned salt
½ teaspoon pepper
½ teaspoon parsley flakes
½ teaspoon crushed thyme
¼ cup oil or melted butter

Wash and dry chicken. Stir together flour and spices, and place in plastic bag. Shake chicken, 3 pieces at a time, in mixture. Coat large pan with oil or butter. Place chicken, skin side down, in pan and bake at 425° F. for 15 minutes. Turn chicken and bake 30 minutes more. Makes 8 or 10 servings.

MRS. JOHN (VENITA) HANCOCK
Bradley, Illinois

Baked Chicken

8-10 chicken breasts, thighs, or drumsticks
1 package dried onion soup mix
1 cup water
8 ounces French dressing
8 ounces apricot jam

Mix last 4 ingredients together in a blender. Skin chicken and put in flat pan. Pour ½ mixture over chicken. Bake ¾ hour at 325° F. Turn pieces and pour rest over and bake another ½ hour or until tender.

"Easy! Delicious! Handy to serve with oven-fried potatoes and a vegetable casserole."

MRS. DANIEL J. (JOYCE) DERKSEN
Burnaby, British Columbia, Canada

Chicken Rice Casserole

1 cup raw rice
1 can each cream of chicken, celery, and mushroom soup
½ cup orange juice
12 chicken pieces—thighs, legs, breasts
sliced or slivered almonds
Parmesan cheese
melted butter

Mix together raw rice, soups, and orange juice. Place in lightly buttered casserole about 9 x 13" size. Place chicken pieces on rice mixture and pour over ¼ pound melted butter. Sprinkle nuts and cheese over all, cover and bake at 275° F. for 2 hours. Uncover and bake ½ hour longer to brown.

"This is a favorite of many of my friends. It is delicious and can be baking while we are attending church."

MRS. WILBERT (MARGUERITE) EICHENBERGER
Santa Ana, California

Baked Chicken Pieces

1 cup buckwheat cereal
1 cup Rice Krispies, soda crackers, or corn flakes
½ cup flour
2 tablespoons Hidden Valley Ranch powdered seasoning
    (or Lawry's Seasoned Salt)
1 large fryer chicken, salted and cut up

Mix together first three ingredients, rolled fine; add seasoning. Roll chicken pieces in dry mixture. Place in 9 x 13" pan after dotting bottom of pan with margarine. Cover with foil. Bake 300° F. for 2 hours (or higher temperature for less time). Take lid off last ½ hour.

"This works well for Sunday dinner. Leftover dry mixture may be kept on hand and added to as needed for future dinners. Very tasty."

MRS. DONALD E. (JANICE) TYLER
Ottawa, Illinois

Go to the ant, thou sluggard; consider her ways, and be wise: which have no guide, overseer, or ruler, provideth her meat in the summer, and gathereth her food in the harvest (Prov. 6:6–8).

Apricot Chicken

1 cut-up chicken (fryer)
salt and pepper
1 bottle French dressing
1 jar apricot jam
1 package onion soup mix
dash of Tabasco sauce

Salt and pepper chicken and put in casserole. Mix remaining ingredients and pour mixture over chicken and bake at 350° F. for 55 minutes.

MRS. ALEX (GREETA) CUBIE
South Windsor, Connecticut

Parmesan Oven-Fried Chicken

2-3 pounds frying chicken, cut in serving-size pieces
  1 cup flour
  2 teaspoons salt
  ¼ teaspoon pepper
  2 teaspoons paprika
  2 eggs
  3 tablespoons buttermilk
  ⅔ cup grated Parmesan cheese
  ⅓ cup fine dry bread crumbs
  2 tablespoons butter
  2 tablespoons shortening

Heat oven to 400° F. (moderately hot). Coat chicken with mixture of flour, salt, pepper, and paprika. Dip in mixture of egg and buttermilk which has been slightly beaten. Roll in Parmesan cheese and bread crumb mixture. Let stand 5 to 10 minutes. Melt butter and shortening in shallow baking pan in heated oven. Place coated chicken, skin side down, in pan. Bake 30 minutes. Turn skin side up and continue baking, until tender, about 30 minutes. Makes 6 servings.

MRS. PAUL (JERRI) MANGUM
West Chester, Pennsylvania

And he commanded the people to sit down on the ground: and he took the seven loaves, and gave thanks, and brake, and gave to his disciples to set before them; and they did set them before the people (Mark 8:6).

Special Accompaniments

Hot Sweet Meat Sauce

  1 gallon tomato pulp
  1 pint chopped onion
  1 pint chopped sweet pepper
  ½ cup chopped garlic or ¼ cup garlic flakes
  ¼ cup ground ginger
  ¼ cup ground mustard
  ½ cup black pepper
  1 tablespoon allspice
  1 tablespoon nutmeg
  1 tablespoon cinnamon
  2 pints sugar
  2 pints vinegar
  1 tablespoon salt

Mix and cook until thick, about two hours. Makes about six pints.

MRS. D. E. (WAVALENE) CLAY
Mount Vernon, Ohio

Cranberry Casserole for Poultry

2 cups fresh cranberries washed and drained
3 cups unpeeled apples, diced
¾ cup white sugar

Mix and place in buttered casserole.

Then mix:
1 cup quick oats, uncooked
½ cup chopped nuts
⅓ cup flour
½ cup brown sugar
1 stick melted butter or margarine

Pat second mixture on top of first mixture. Bake uncovered 1 hour at 325° F. Makes 6-8 servings.

"A nice side dish with turkey, chicken, or pork. Our boys love it with the meal and also with vanilla ice cream as a dessert. It is delicious!"

MRS. ROBERT (MIRIAM) WILFONG
Kennett Square, Pennsylvania

If thy oblation be a meat offering baken in the frying-pan, it shall be made of fine flour with oil (Lev. 2:7).

Hot Curried Fruit

1 No. 1 can pear slices
1 No. 1 can apricot halves
1 14-ounce can pineapple chunks
1 small jar maraschino cherries
2 tablespoons butter, room temperature
2 tablespoons dark brown sugar
1 teaspoon curry powder
2 teaspoons cornstarch
½ teaspoon grated lemon peel

Drain all fruit and turn out into a 1½ quart casserole and mix together lightly. Blend together soft butter, brown sugar, curry, cornstarch, lemon peel. Sprinkle over fruit. Let mixture stand for several hours to drain out juices. Bake uncovered in 325° F. oven for 1 hour. Baste often. Serve while hot.

"To be served with meal, maybe in place of vegetables or with casserole."

MRS. CLIFF (CAROL) COWLEY
Portland, Oregon

The Divine Presence speaks to us, not only in death, but in life. We may be washing dishes, riding along the highway, performing some task, and not be consciously thinking about Him. But on an ordinary day He sometimes breaks in upon our common task to remind us He is with us, like a human friend who has stopped in to say hello (Alice Spangenberg).

Remoulade Sauce

3 cups mayonnaise
4 garlic buttons, pressed
3 tablespoons dark mustard
3 tablespoons horseradish sauce
2 tablespoons Worcestershire sauce
4 tablespoons vinegar
4 hard cooked egg yolks, sieved
2 tablespoons paprika
dash Tabasco sauce
4 heaping tablespoons chopped parsley

Salt and pepper to taste. Chill and serve over boiled shrimp, or chip shrimp and add to sauce for dip.

Mrs. Erwin (Ruth Elizabeth) Davis
Austin, Texas

Baked Pineapple for Ham

1 No. 2 can pineapple chunks
1 egg yolk
2 tablespoons lemon juice
⅓ cup sugar
1 tablespoon butter
2 tablespoons cornstarch

Cook juice, thickening, sugar, yolk, and butter in double boiler (or over low heat) until it thickens slightly. Pour into buttered casserole over pineapple chunks. Top with marshmallows and bake in oven at 350° F. until lightly browned.

"This is especially delicious served with ham, but can be used with any meat meal."

Mrs. Eugene (Faye) Stowe
Englewood, Colorado

Cranberry Ice

1 pound cranberries (1 quart)
5 cups boiling water
2½ cups sugar
1 tablespoon gelatin dissolved in ½ cup cold water
4 tablespoons lemon juice

Cook cranberries and water until tender. Put through sieve. Add sugar. Add gelatin dissolved in water 15 minutes. Add lemon juice. Freeze in ice-cube trays for easy serving.

"Serve with main course in small sherbet glasses, delightful for Thanksgiving turkey, or chicken, or fish. For eye appeal, save out enough raw cranberries to string for the turkey's necklace."

MRS. ROBERT H. (EVELYN) SUTTON
Eugene, Oregon

Corn Bread Dressing

These may be prepared day before:
1 skillet of cornbread, cooled
1 cookie sheet of toasted stale bread, crisp

Cook in skillet:
1 package hot sausage with 1 large onion; drain off fat.

In large bowl:
Crumble corn bread, crisp bread, and drained sausage.

Add to this:
3 cans of cream of chicken soup

If more liquid is needed, you may add some bouillon with water. Pour into iron skillet or casserole and bake in oven 1 hour at 350° F.

MRS. BOB (PEGGY) BENSON
Nashville, Tennessee

"Be not overcome of evil, but overcome evil with good" (Rom. 12:21).

Butter and honey shall he eat, that he may know to refuse the evil, and choose the good (Isa. 7:15).

Main-Dishes, Casseroles, & One-Dish Meals

Beerock or Kraut Biscuits

Dough
   1 cup boiling water
   1 tablespoon shortening
   ¼ cup sugar
   ½ teaspoon salt
   1 package yeast, dissolved in ½ cup warm water
   flour for soft dough

Pour boiling water over shortening, sugar, salt. Let cool. Dissolve yeast in warm water. Add enough flour for soft dough. Knead well and let raise till light. Roll out to ¼ inch thick. Cut in 6-inch squares. Put on filling, press edges together. Put on greased cookie sheet. Let raise until light and bake in moderate oven.

Filling
¾ pound hamburger
onion, small amount
shortening, small amount
salt and pepper
6 cups shredded cabbage

Brown hamburger with onion and shortening, salt and pepper. Then add shredded cabbage and simmer until cabbage is done, cool and place on squares.

MRS. JAMES (VERNETTA) CORBETT
Billings, Montana

They shall hunger no more, neither thirst any more; neither shall the sun light on them, nor any heat. For the Lamb which is in the midst of the throne shall feed them, and shall lead them unto living fountains of waters: and God shall wipe away all tears from their eyes (Rev. 7:16-17).

Chop Suey Roll

Who can find a virtuous woman? for her price is far above rubies (Prov. 31:10).

Use leftover

ground cold meat
mashed potatoes
vegetables
gravy

Make a mix of
2 cups all-purpose flour
2 tablespoons sugar
1 teaspoon baking powder
½ teaspoon salt
1 egg
⅔ cup milk
½ cup margarine, butter, or oil

Blend egg, milk or light cream, with margarine, butter or oil. Add all at once to dry ingredients, stir only to moisten, then roll out as for cinnamon rolls. Spread with butter or margarine, spread potatoes, meat, and then the vegetables, roll up and bake 400° F. for 15 minutes or until done. Serve with leftover gravy or make new with bouillon cubes.

"A good way to use leftovers, I have used for years especially during a revival meeting."

Mrs. H. T. (Vera May) Stanley
Grand Rapids, Michigan

She will do him good and not evil all the days of her life (Prob. 31:12)

Her children arise up, and call her blessed; her husband also, and he praiseth her (Prov. 31:28).

Green Rice

2 tablespoons finely chopped onion
2 tablespoons butter
2 cups boiled rice (or cooked "instant" rice)
½ cup finely chopped parsley
1¼ cups milk
2 eggs
1 teaspoon salt
1 cup grated cheddar cheese

Sauté onion in butter. Add rice, parsley, and milk. In small bowl, beat eggs slightly, and mix in salt and cheese. Combine the two mixtures and pour into a buttered casserole. Place casserole in a pan of hot water in a 350° F. oven and bake for about 40 minutes or until mixture is firm. May be completely mixed the night before; just adjust baking time to make up for the extra coldness.

Mrs. Bud (Maxine) Goble
Winamac, Indiana

Veranika

To overcome any tendency toward the lukewarmness of neutrality, we must boldly throw ourselves into the swift stream of devotion and service to our Lord (Ross W. Hayslip).

2 cups of dry cottage cheese
1 dash of pepper
1 tablespoon onion greens chopped fine
1 tablespoon cream
1 egg yolk
½ teaspoon salt

Mix all ingredients well.

Dough
2 cups flour
1 teaspoon salt
½ cup milk (part cream)
1 whole egg and the egg white
½ teaspoon baking powder

Roll out dough on floured board and cut circles with a large cup. Put 1 teaspoon full of cheese mixture in center of circle and moisten edges and fold dough over and press edges together. Drop veranika into boiling water and cook until they rise from bottom. Then carefully lift out of water and fry them until browned in butter.

Sauce: Fry slices of ham or diced pieces of bacon and use fat to fry 1 small onion. Add sour cream or cream and serve veranika with this hot cream sauce.

"This is a German dish more commonly known as Cheese Buttons."

MRS. JAMES (VERNETTA) CORBETT
Billings, Montana

Cheese Pudding

The angel of the Lord encampeth round about them that fear him, and delivereth them (Ps. 34:7).

10 slices frozen white bread
¾ pound sharp New York cheese
2½ cups milk
1 teaspoon salt
3 eggs

Butter slices of bread, then cut off crusts, and cut in cubes. Grate the cheese, and layer the bread and cheese alternately in a casserole dish. Beat the milk, salt, and eggs together and pour over the bread and cheese. This can be put together the day before and refrigerated. Should stand at room temperature for 2-3 hours before baking at 300° F. for 45 minutes.

"This is unbelievably simple, but so good. Almost like a souffle, but much easier. Great with ham dinner."

MRS. CLIFF (BILLIE) BARROWS
Greenville, South Carolina

Macaroni Casserole

1 8-ounce package small elbow macaroni, cooked until
    tender in salted water
8 or 9 ounces sharp cheddar cheese, grated
5 eggs
1 tall can evaporated milk
salt and pepper
butter

In one large casserole dish or two small ones (with cover), place a layer of macaroni and then a layer of grated cheese ending with cheese on top (should be at least two layers of each in small bowls). Beat eggs, milk, dash salt, pepper, and pour over cheese and macaroni. This mixture will come to top of cheese. Place several slices of butter on top. Bake in oven at 425° F. until brown and done.

"In the south we call this 'Macaroni Pie.'"

MRS. J. R. (THELMA) HUCKS
Chester, South Carolina

Spam and Rice Dish

1 can Spam luncheon meat or Treet, cubed
1 onion, chopped
2 tablespoons butter
1 can cream of celery soup
⅔ soup can of milk
¼ cup cashew nuts, chopped (optional)
salt and pepper to taste

Brown onion and Spam in butter. Add remaining ingredients and simmer 10-15 minutes. Serve over rice.

MRS. ED (KITTY) BAKER
Pittsburgh, Pennsylvania

Corned Beef Sandwiches

1 cup cheddar cheese (shredded)
1 can corned beef
¼ cup chopped onions
½ cup olives
2 tablespoons Worcestershire sauce
½ cup catsup

Mix all ingredients and put in 8 to 10 hamburger buns; wrap in foil. Heat 15 minutes at 375° F.

MRS. GARY (RAEDEAN) HENECKE
Olathe, Kansas

Cheddar Spinach Quiche

1 10-ounce package frozen chopped spinach
2 cups (8 ounces) shredded sharp cheddar cheese
2 tablespoons flour
1 can milk
2 eggs, beaten
3 crisply cooked bacon slices, crumbled
½ teaspoon salt
dash of pepper
1 9-inch unbaked pastry shell

After cooking, drain spinach well on absorbent paper. Toss cheese with flour. Add spinach, milk, eggs, bacon, and seasonings; mix well. Pour into unbaked pastry shell. Bake 1 hour. Garnish with additional bacon, if desired.

"Ideal for brunch or luncheon."

MRS. MAXINE RUDDLE
Dearborn Heights, Michigan

Impossible Quiche

3 eggs, whipped
1 cup grated Swiss cheese
1½ cups milk
¼ teaspoon salt
dash of pepper
½ cup biscuit mix
ham cubes
mushrooms
¼ cup melted margarine

Mix together eggs, milk, salt, pepper, biscuit mix, margarine. Pour in pie plate greased with oil. Pat in ham, Swiss cheese, mushrooms. Bake at 350° F. for 45 minutes to 1 hour.

MRS. JAY (BONNIE) BAYNUM
Kankakee, Illinois

Omelette

1 pound sausage
6 slices bread (remove crust and cube)
6 eggs
2 cups milk
1 teaspoon salt
1 teaspoon dry mustard
1 cup grated cheddar cheese

Brown sausage and crumble in separate dish; beat eggs and add other ingredients. Place bread in baking dish, place drained and browned sausage over bread. Pour egg mixture over sausage and bread. Bake 350° F. for 45 minutes. Prepare in baking dish 9 x 13. Makes 6 to 8 servings.

"This may be made up the night before and refrigerated and then baked the next morning. Ideal for overnight guest."

MRS. THAREN (MAXINE) EVANS
Crawfordsville, Indiana

Egg Puffs

5 eggs
6 pieces of buttered bread
dash of salt

Separate yolks from whites. Beat whites till stiff. Fold in yolks and dash of salt. Spoon lightly onto buttered bread. Place on cookie sheet. Pop into preheated oven (400° F.) for 15 minutes or until peaks are golden brown.

For larger quantity use 6 eggs for 8 pieces of bread or 9 eggs for 12 pieces of bread.

MRS. BOB (DODIE) SMEE
Visalia, California

Bacon and Cheese Oven Omelet

12 slices bacon
6 slices cheese
8 eggs, beaten
1 cup milk

Cook bacon. Drain. Chop 4 slices and leave others as whole slices. Cut cheese slices in halves, arrange in bottom of lightly buttered 9-inch pie pan. Beat together eggs and milk with fork. Add chopped bacon. Pour over cheese and bake in preheated oven 350° F. for 30 minutes. Arrange whole bacon slices on top. Bake 10 minutes longer. Let stand 5 minutes before cutting. Makes 5-6 servings.

"This is great for company, too, and is so easy. Substitutions: Ham cubes, different cheeses."

MRS. IRVING (BEVERLY) LAIRD
Nampa, Idaho

Egg Bake

8 slices of bread
1 pound of bacon
2 4-ounce packages of cheddar cheese
1 small can of mushrooms
1 dozen eggs
1 teaspoon salt
¼ teaspoon dry mustard
1 cup milk

Grease a 9 x 13" glass baking dish with margarine. Remove the crust from the bread and butter both sides, place in baking dish. Fry one pound of bacon crisp and crumble over bread, sprinkle the cheddar cheese on top of the bacon. Beat the eggs and add salt, dry mustard, and milk; pour over the bread, bacon and cheese. Garnish with the mushrooms on top. Let stand in refrigerator overnight. Bake the next morning, in 325° F. temperature for 50-60 minutes.

"This is a great way to save time when you have guests for Sunday morning breakfast."

MRS. ROY (MARY) SHUCK
Greencastle, Indiana

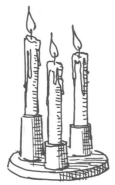

Egg and Sausage Loaf

9 slices bread
1 pound sausage
cheddar cheese
9 eggs
2½ cups milk

Cube nine slices bread and place in large loaf cake pan, 9 x 13". Brown one pound sausage in frying pan and drain. Place a layer of sausage, cooked and drained, on top of bread cubes—then add a layer of grated cheddar cheese. Mix 9 eggs and 2½ cups of milk (beat) and pour on top of the above mixture. Leave all night in the refrigerator. Bake at 350° F. for 45 minutes. Cut and serve. Makes 12 generous servings.

"This is an outstanding recipe for breakfast or brunch, or snack. Also good as a main dish. Easy to serve to large groups of people, since it can be prepared ahead."

MRS. WILLIAM (ESTHER) DAMON
Haslett, Michigan

Pizza Crescents

1 pound hamburger
1 6-ounce can tomato paste
1 tablespoon chopped onion
1 teaspoon sugar
½ teaspoon oregano leaves
⅛ teaspoon pepper
2 cans Pillsbury crescent rolls
½ cup shredded Mozzarella cheese
milk
sesame seeds

Brown hamburger in skillet, chopping fine, salt, and drain off fat. Add next 5 ingredients and cool. Make 8 rectangles from dough and place ¼ cup meat mixture on each. Place 1 tablespoon cheese on top of each meat mound. Fold over and seal with a fork. Brush tops with milk and sprinkle with sesame seeds. Bake: 400° F. for 15-20 minutes. Makes 8 servings.

"Serve for lunch with a good salad."

MRS. MILTON (NORMA) HARRINGTON
Walla Walla, Washington

Observation on improper food: A group of teenagers, happy, hot, and tired arrived for a singing engagement at their Midwest destination on an unusually hot and humid day in July. Upon arrival they were told by their hostess to wash up for lunch because their meal was ready. Apparently the hostess knew little about teenage likes and dislikes or needs. They were served hot chili with crackers and not-too-cold milk. They longed for something cool. The hospitable lady was willing, but her menu was inappropriate. Sixty teens still talk about it because it just wasn't very neat.

Easy Chili

Section 1
3 pounds hamburger
2 tablespoons minced onion
salt and pepper to taste
2 teaspoons chili powder
sprinkle of garlic salt

Section 2
2 cans cream of mushroom soup
1 quart tomato juice
2 No. 2 cans kidney beans
⅓ cup sugar (rounded)
5 tablespoons Heinz steak sauce

Mix section 1 in skillet, and brown. Add section 2, and simmer.

MRS. AUSTIN (MARGARET) WRIGHT
Warren, Ohio

Chilies Rellenos Casserole

1 cup half-and-half (or diluted canned milk)
2 eggs
⅓ cup all-purpose flour
3 whole green chilies (Ortega, 4-ounce can)
½ pound Monterey Jack cheese, grated
½ pound sharp cheddar cheese, grated
1 8-ounce can tomato sauce

Preheat oven to 375° F. Beat half-and-half with eggs and flour until smooth. Split open chilies, rinse out seeds and drain on paper towels. Mix cheeses together on sheet of waxed paper and reserve ½ cup for topping. Make alternate layers of cheese, chilies, and egg mixture in deep 1½-quart casserole. Pour tomato sauce over top and sprinkle with reserved cheese. Bake one hour, or until done in center. Serve with hot corn bread, refried beans, and green salad. Makes 4 servings.

Mrs. Frances L. (Eileen) Smee
Visalia, California

Chili Cheese Jubilee

(For Microwave)

1½ pounds lean ground beef (cooked 5 minutes in microwave)
1 10-ounce bag Dorito chips
1 package sliced Monterey Jack cheese
1 pint sour cream

Sauce ingredients
2 tablespoons butter, melted
1 small can tomato sauce
1 package chili seasoning mix
½ cup water
2 eggs
1 cup half-and-half
2 tablespoons minced onions

Make sauce, add minced onion to melted butter, add tomato sauce, the chili seasoning mix, add ½ cup water. Slightly beat the two eggs, add the cup of half-and-half. Mix sauce and egg mixture together and cook one minute in microwave. Layer in baking dish, half bag of chips, half ground beef, half sliced cheese, half sauce mixture. Repeat layers. Top with sour cream and sprinkle with cheddar cheese. Cook 7 minutes in microwave.

Mrs. M. L. (Doris) Mann
Prescott, Arizona

Mexican Chili

1 can kidney beans
2 onions, chopped fine
few stalks celery, chopped fine
2 tablespoons fat
1 pound ground beef
¼ teaspoon cinnamon
1 teaspoon salt
¼ teaspoon pepper
½ teaspoon dry mustard
⅛ teaspoon cloves
1-2 tablespoons chili powder
1 quart canned tomatoes
parsley, garlic cloves

Brown meat, onion, celery, garlic in 2 tablespoons fat; add other ingredients. Make well in advance of serving. Makes 4 servings.

Mrs. Bob (Ardis) Gray
South Portland, Maine

Behold, how good and how pleasant it is for brethren to dwell together in unity! (Ps. 133:1).

Chili Supreme

2 No. 2½ cans tomatoes
1 quart tomato juice (or 46-ounce can)
2-3 pounds ground beef
2 large onions
1 5-ounce bottle Heinz "57" sauce
3 tablespoons prepared mustard
1 can mushrooms (stems and pieces)
1 can mushroom soup
3 No. 2 cans red kidney beans
3-4 tablespoons sugar
salt and pepper to taste
chili powder to taste

Sauté onions and ground beef. Drain well (this is very important). Combine all ingredients in large kettle and simmer slowly for at least an hour. Makes 12-15 servings.

"Here's a dish that's good for a cold winter day. This chili recipe was given to me by the late Rev. Clayton Bailey, during a revival in our church in Parkersburg, West Virginia. He called it 'Greaseless Chili.' I have served it to dozens and dozens of guests."

Mrs. Harvey (Maxine) Hendershot
Nashville, Tennessee

Whatever thy hand findeth to do, do it with thy might; for there is no work, nor device, nor knowledge, nor wisdom, in the grave, wither thou goest (Eccles. 9:10).

Five-Hour Stew

1½ pounds stew meat
6 potatoes, cut in half
3 carrots, cut in 2" pieces
1 large onion, sliced
1 can mushroom soup, undiluted
1 can tomato soup, undiluted
1 can peas, juice and all
salt and pepper to taste

Put in layers starting with meat into casserole dish or pan. Bake 5 hours at 325° F., covered.

MRS. DON (FAITH) BELL
Olathe, Kansas

Spanish Stew

2 pounds beef, cut in 1-inch cubes
1 8-ounce bottle Catalina brand French dressing
2 cups water
1 cup sliced stuffed green olives
8 small onions
8 small whole potatoes

Brown meat in ¼ cup dressing; add remaining dressing and water. Cover and cook slowly 2 hours. Add olives, onions, and potatoes; cook 45 minutes or until meat and vegetables are tender. Thicken liquid for gravy, if desired. Makes 6 to 8 servings.

MRS. LEON (DORIS) DOANE
Olathe, Kansas

Western Goulash

1 pound ground beef
1 small can Green Giant Mexicorn
1 can of plain Franco-American Spaghetti O's
salt, pepper

Brown ground beef. Add Mexicorn and Spaghetti O's. Season to taste with salt and pepper. Simmer about ten minutes. Makes 6 to 8 servings.

Delicious and very quick to prepare. Serve with hot bread and tossed salad and you have a delicious and quick meal."

MRS. LEON (ELIZABETH) WYSS
San Diego, California

Baked Chipped Beef Casserole

1 cup cheddar cheese
3 tablespoons chopped onion
1 cup elbow macaroni, uncooked
1 cup dried beef
1 can mushroom soup
1½ cups milk

Mix together all ingredients. Place in well-buttered casserole dish and refrigerate overnight, or at least 5 hours. Bake 1 hour in 350° F. oven.

"While we were holding a revival in Kansas City, the pastors' wife, Mrs. E. E. Reep, served this dish. It was so good, I came home with her recipe and have used it many times. It is fun to try variations by adding something new, or using celery soup, etc."

MRS. ROBERT (MARJORIE) GOSLAW
Santa Ana, California

Strips of Beef Casserole

Brown in large skillet, stirring constantly:
1 pound round steak, cut in ½-inch strips
¼ cup shortening

Stir in:
1½ cups chopped onion
2 tablespoons flour

Cook until onions are tender, stirring.
Add:
1 cup canned tomatoes
1 cup water
1 6-ounce can tomato paste
1 tablespoon sugar
1½ teaspoons salt
¼ teaspoon pepper
½ teaspoon Worcestershire sauce

Man did eat angels' food: he sent them meat to the full (Ps. 78:25).

Cover and simmer for 1½ hours, or until meat is tender. Stir occasionally. Add ¾ to 1¼ cups of mushrooms, fresh or canned, and ¾ cup sour cream. Continue cooking five minutes. Place mixture in 2 quart casserole and cover with canned biscuits. Bake uncovered at 425° F. for 20-25 minutes or until biscuits are golden brown.

MRS. JACOB (HELEN) BLANKENSHIP
Houston, Texas

Bean Casserole with Meatballs

1 ½ pounds lean ground beef
1 medium onion, chopped fine
2 tablespoons oil
1 teaspoon salt
1 cup catsup
½ cup water
¼ cup brown sugar
2 teaspoons vinegar
2 teaspoons dry mustard
1 16-ounce can kidney beans, drained
2 small cans pork and beans
1 large can chunk pineapple (save ½ cup for top)

Mix beef, onion, and salt. Roll meat into small balls and fry in oil until brown. Add to meat: catsup, water, sugar, vinegar, and mustard. Bring to boil. Reduce heat and simmer 10 minutes. In large casserole, place both beans and pineapple chunks. Add meatballs and rest of pineapple. Bake uncovered at 375° F. for 45 minutes. Makes 8-10 servings.

"Good for potluck or picnic."

MRS. NEAL (EVA) DIRKSE
Corvallis, Oregon

Mock Lasagna

1 8-ounce package medium noodles
1 can spaghetti sauce
1 pound ground beef
½ teaspoon salt
1 large chopped onion
1 pound Mozzarella cheese

Cook noodles and drain. Brown the ground beef and onion and add the spaghetti sauce, ½ teaspoon salt. Stir noodles and sauce mixture together. Place in 9 x 13 inch loaf pan and top with the sliced Mozzarella cheese. Bake at 350° F. for 15 or 20 minutes till cheese melts and browns a little. The noodles and sauce mixture should be very hot before placing in oven.

"This is a quickie supper dish and satisfies the family that craves lasagna."

MRS. WILMER (DONNA) WATSON
Fort Wayne, Indiana

Lasagna

1 ½ pounds hamburger
1 ½ teaspoons salt
⅛ teaspoon pepper
1 onion, diced
¼ teaspoon garlic salt or fresh garlic
1 32-ounce bottle Ragu Spaghetti Sauce with Mushrooms
1 15-ounce can tomato sauce
1 6-ounce can tomato paste
1 pound small-curd cottage cheese
2 eggs
¾ cup Parmesan cheese
1 package Mozzarella cheese
lasagna noodles

Brown meat with onion, spices, and sauces. Simmer for two hours, stirring occasionally. While sauce is simmering boil noodles, drain, and rinse in cold water. Mix 2 eggs beaten with cottage cheese, Parmesan cheese. In oblong casserole, layer meat sauce, noodles, cottage cheese mixture, meat, Mozzarella cheese, noodles, meat. Bake until good and hot.

"This casserole may be made ahead of time and refrigerated until baking time. Makes 10 or more servings."

MRS. HAROLD B. (BETTIE) GRAVES
San Antonio, Texas

Baked Potato Burger

selected 12-ounce potatoes
3 ounces of ground round per potato (20 percent fat)
cheddar cheese
All Seasoning
2 ounces cream cheese

Bake potatoes, then slice off about 25 percent of potato, the long way. Scrape out potato and place in mixing bowl. This leaves a nice jacket with an open top. Braize meat medium; drain fat and add to potato with cream cheese and mix. Add seasoning. Stuff mixture in potato jackets. Add cheddar cheese on top of potato and place under heat to melt cheese. Serve with sour cream, sliced onion, bacon bits, and other garnish to suit.

"You can make these up ahead, cook and wrap in foil and store in your freezer. Excellent for a quick tasty dinner. All you have to do is reheat and then put cheese on top and melt. This is the newest item on our menu. Very popular!"

LEO T. QUALLS
Hi-Ho Restaurants, Inc.
Salem, Oregon

Some hae meat, and canna eat,
And some wad eat that want it;
But we hae meat and we can eat,
And sae the Lord be thankit.
Robert Burns

Zaleveri
(Church Builder Casserole)

1½ pounds ground round
1 onion
1 large green pepper
1 can corn, drained
1 large can tomatoes
1 can olives, drained
1 cup grated cheddar cheese
1 10-ounce package noodles
½ teaspoon seasoned salt
¼ teaspoon pepper
¼ teaspoon oregano

Cook noodles in salted water as per directions on package. Brown ground round, onions, sliced green pepper in a little oil with the seasonings. Combine ground round mixture, drained corn, cut up tomatoes (do not add the juice), drained noodles, and olives. Place in casserole dish and cover with grated cheese. Bake for 20 minutes in a 350° F. oven.

"This dish has been served to men at 'work days' at three different churches. The men often request this dish for their lunch."

MRS. JOHN (JOYCE) FABRIN
Selma, California

Wild Rice and Hamburger Casserole

1½ pounds hamburger
2 medium onions, chopped (or dehydrated onions)
1 8-ounce can mushroom pieces
1 package wild rice mix (use both packages in box)
2 tablespoons butter
2 cups sour cream
½ cup grated cheese

Sauté onions in butter. Sauté meat until no longer red. Add mushrooms. Cook 3 minutes. Mix meat, onions, sour cream, and cooked wild rice. Put in a 2-quart casserole. Grate cheese on top. Bake 350° F. for ½ hour. Makes 8 servings.

"Be sure and use the entire box of wild rice, 2 packages in each box. Get this ready first, set aside. Can prepare a day ahead and bake it when ready to use it."

MRS. DAVID L. (ESTHER) GRANGER
Celina, Ohio

Supper-on-a-Loaf

1 ½ pounds ground beef
1 egg
1 ½ teaspoons salt
⅛ teaspoon pepper
½ cup cracker meal
1 tablespoon mustard
½ cup onion, chopped
1 cup shredded cheese (cheddar or colby)
⅔ cup canned milk

Combine above ingredients. Slice a loaf of French bread lengthwise and scoop out the bread to form a boat or indentation. Put half of the meat mixture in each half of loaf. Wrap bottom of loaf with aluminum foil, leaving meat uncovered. Bake 25 minutes at 350° F. Slice to serve.

Two tablespoons of meat mixture can be put on half of a hamburger bun for individual servings. These can be frozen and baked later. Bake for 20 minutes. Recipe will make 18 individual buns.

MRS. BYRON (CAROLYN) BUKER
Bedford, Indiana

O the depth of the riches both of the wisdom and knowledge of God! how unsearchable are his judgments, and his ways past finding out! (Rom. 11:33).

Tamale Bake

¼ cup diced onion
¼ cup diced green pepper
½ cup diced celery
½ pound ground beef
1 tablespoon fat
¼ cup cornmeal
1 ¾ cups canned tomatoes
1 cup whole kernel corn
½ cup ripe olives
1 ½ teaspoons salt
1 ½ teaspoons chili powder
1 ½ teaspoons Worcestershire sauce
½ cup grated cheese

Brown onion, green pepper, celery, and ground beef in fat. Cook cornmeal in tomatoes, 5-10 minutes; add meat mixture. Stir in corn, olives, and seasonings. Pour into 1 ½-quart casserole and top with grated cheese. Bake at 325° F. approximately 30 minutes.

"This is a favorite of family and friends. It's excellent for potlucks."

MRS. ROBERT (JEWEL) FERRIS
Redlands, California

Tamale Pie

1 ½ pounds ground meat, good grade
1 onion
1 clove garlic
1 green pepper
4 tablespoons butter
1 large can tomatoes, chopped
1 can cream style corn
cayenne pepper
1 tablespoon chili powder
salt
1 ½ cups yellow cornmeal
2 cups tomato juice
1 can pitted ripe olives
grated sharp cheese

Cook ground meat until all red is gone, pour off any excess grease. Sauté onion, garlic, green pepper in butter, add to meat. Add chopped tomatoes, cream corn, cayenne pepper, chili powder, salt to taste. Mix the above and simmer for about 30 minutes. Add very slowly: yellow cornmeal, tomato juice, pitted ripe olives, stirring constantly. Pour into buttered casserole dish, top with grated cheese, and cook 30 to 45 minutes at 350° F.

"Great for a crowd."

MRS. LEWIS (BERTHA) SHINGLER
Pasadena, California

Sicilian Meat Roll

2 beaten eggs
¾ cup soft bread crumbs
½ cup tomato juice
2 tablespoons parsley
½ teaspoon dried oregano
¼ teaspoon salt and ¼ teaspoon pepper
1 small clove garlic, minced
2 pounds ground beef
8 slices boiled ham
1 6-ounce package Mozzarella cheese

Combine eggs, bread crumbs, tomato juice, parsley, oregano, salt, pepper, and garlic. Mix in ground beef. On large sheet of foil, pat meat mixture into a rectangle. Arrange ham slices on top of meat, leaving slight margin around edges. Arrange cheese over ham (save a few slices for top of meat loaf). Starting on one end, roll meat carefully (as a jelly roll). Seam side down, seal edges and, using foil to lift, place in baking pan. Bake for 1 hour and 15 minutes, at 350° F. Center will be pink from ham.

Place rest of cheese over top of roll and return to oven till cheese melts.

MRS. MARVIN (GARNET) BEAM
Xenia, Ohio

Jack Pot Casserole

1 pound ground beef
1 large onion, chopped
1 cup cream-style corn
1 can tomato soup
1 can tomato paste
1 6-ounce package noodles
1 cup grated sharp cheese
1 cup sliced olives
1 tablespoon soy sauce
seasoning to taste

Sauté onion in oil or butter. Crumble meat and brown. Add salt and pepper and ¼ teaspoon chili powder. In another pan, put tomato soup and tomato paste and 2 cans water. Bring to a boil, and cook noodles until tender. Mix meat, noodles, and add corn and olives. Pour into greased casserole. Cover with grated cheese. Cook 45 minutes in 375° F. oven.

MRS. BUD (MARION) JONES
South Portland, Maine

Supper Casserole

1 pound ground beef
2 tablespoons parsley flakes or savory
1 small onion
1 19-ounce can vegetable soup
1 19-ounce cream of chicken soup
1½ cups milk
salt and pepper

Brown ground beef in frying pan and put in casserole. Add parsley flakes, 1 onion diced, and soup, milk, salt, and pepper. Make a baking powder biscuit dough and cut out as for biscuit and put over the top and bake in 350° F. oven for 1½ hours or until biscuits are cooked.

MRS. CLARENCE (JOAN) EDGAR
Summerside, P.E.I., Canada

Hamburger Casserole

2 pounds hamburger meat
1 can condensed celery soup
1 medium onion, chopped
1 package frozen tater tots

Cook hamburger meat with onion in frying pan until meat is no longer red. Drain off fat. Put in baking dish 9" x 14". Cover with condensed celery soup. Place tater tots on top. Bake 25 minutes in 350° F. oven.

"This makes an excellent dish for church dinners. I have never had any left. Many ask about it if I fail to take this meat dish. It is very simple to make."

Mrs. L. G. (Phyllis) McArthur
Ardmore, Oklahoma

Enchilada Pie

¼ cup salad oil
1 medium onion, chopped
1 or 2 minced cloves of garlic
1 pound ground beef
2 tablespoons flour
1 8-ounce can tomato sauce
1 teaspoon salt
¼ teaspoon pepper
1 cup beef stock or water
2 tablespoons vinegar
1 cup chopped olives
2 tablespoons chili powder
6 tortillas
1 cup grated sharp cheese
1 small can Las Palmas chili sauce

Heat oil in large skillet, add onion and garlic, and sauté until golden brown; add beef and cook until brown. Sprinkle flour over meat and stir until well blended. Add tomato sauce, stock or water, vinegar, olives, chili powder, salt, and pepper. Simmer for 20 minutes, stirring frequently. Line a greased casserole with sauce, make a layer of tortillas, top with cheese and mixture and repeat layers until casserole is full. Bake in moderate oven, 325° F. to 350° F. for about 45 minutes.

"This may be made before going to Sunday school and when returning just put into oven and it will be finished by the time the rest of the meal is finished."

Mrs. John (Esther) Biggers
Sacramento, California

Cheeseburger Pie

2 packages of Pillsbury crescent refrigerator rolls
1 4-ounce can of tomato sauce
1 pound of lean hamburger
seasonings
1½ cups of grated sharp cheese
milk
sesame seeds

Fry hamburger and drain well. Add sauce and seasonings to the meat, mixing well. Lay roll dough all around the edge of a pizza pan (point side out) so that half of the roll hangs over the edge of the pan (sunburst style). Reserve 3 rolls to cover the center of the pan. Pinch and stretch rolls together in the center of the pan so that it's filled in with dough. Spoon hamburger mixture in the center, and cover with grated cheese. Bring points up over the mixture so they meet in the center. No dough should be extended over the edge of the pan when completing this step. Brush lightly with milk and sprinkle entire pie with sesame seeds. Bake at 375° F. for 15 minutes or until browned. Cut in wedges.

Out of the eater came forth meat, and out of the strong came forth sweetness (Judg. 14:14).

"Be prepared for rave comments. It's truly a delicious dish for Sunday evenings."

MRS. ROLAND (REBA) DUNLOP
Owego, New York

Ham and Green Bean Casserole

3 cups cooked ham cubed
3 cups drained green beans
1 tablespoon minced onions
3 hard boiled eggs, coarsely chopped
¾ cup grated cheese
⅛ teaspoon nutmeg
pepper to taste
1 cup dry bread crumbs
2 tablespoons butter
1 can mushroom soup

Combine above ingredients (ham usually supplies enough salt), except crumbs and butter. Place in a greased casserole. Blend butter and crumbs and sprinkle on bean mixture. Bake at 350° F. for 30 minutes.

"Prepare the day before, if more convenient, refrigerate, then bake when desired. The nutmeg makes the difference."

MRS. G. H. (HAZEL) SAFFELL
Sheridan, Wyoming

Cheese Enchilada Casserole

1 can cream mushroom soup
1 can cream of chicken soup
1 can mild enchilada sauce
1 small can chopped green chilies
1½ pounds hamburger meat
1 pound grated Mozzarella cheese
1 package tortillas

Brown meat, add soups, sauce, chilies, until heated through. Cut tortillas into bite-size pieces. Alternate meat sauces, tortillas, and cheese in casserole dish. Cook in 300° F. oven until heated through and cheese melted.

MRS. GENE (EVELYN) FULLER
Lubbock, Texas

Toad in the Hole

1 pound pork sausage
2 eggs
1 cup milk
1 cup sifted flour
¼ teaspoon salt

Lightly grease a skillet. Add sausages and cook gently, until lightly browned on all sides. Heat oven to 450° F. Beat eggs well, add milk, flour, and salt. Beat until smooth and pour over sausages in skillet. Bake 25 minutes until batter is browned and set. Makes 4 servings.

"An interesting, greaseless way to eat sausages, a real hit with children."

MRS. DANIEL (BONNIE) GALES
Medicine Hat, Alberta, Canada

Ham and Cheese Crepes

2 cups finely chopped ham
2 tablespoons minced green onion
2 tablespoons chopped ripe olives
3 eggs, hard boiled and chopped
2 tablespoons sweet pickle relish
½ teaspoon seasoned salt
¾ cup mayonnaise

10 crepes (make according to standard recipe)
10 slices cheese

Mix ingredients together, use 3 tablespoons mixture per crepe.

Roll and place in baking dish with a slice of cheese over each. Leave in oven until heated through and serve with your favorite cheese sauce.

"This is nice for ladies' luncheons or Sunday night suppers."

MRS. MARLEN (MARY) ANDERSON
Tigard, Oregon

Texas Hash

1 pound hamburger (ground chuck)
2 cups tomatoes
½ cup rice, uncooked
1 bell pepper, minced
1 large onion, minced
3 tablespoons cooking oil (with chuck)
1 teaspoon chili powder
2 teaspoons salt
1 teaspoon black pepper

Brown onion, pepper, and beef. Stir in tomatoes, rice, and seasoning, pour into 1½-quart casserole dish. Bake 1 hour at 350° F. Cover dish with foil while baking.

MRS. HAROLD (BETTIE) GRAVES
San Antonio, Texas

Swedish Spaghetti

1 package Italian spaghetti
1 large can tomatoes
1 can mushrooms
½ green pepper, cut fine
1 clove of garlic, cut fine
1 tablespoon flour
½ pound Velveeta cheese
½ pint of cream
½ pound ground ham

He poured out his soul to death, and was numbered with the transgressors, yet he bore the sin of many, and made intercession for the transgressors (Isa. 53:12, RSV).

Make sauce by cooking strained tomatoes, flour, garlic, green pepper, cheese, ham, mushrooms—add cream last. Serve as a sauce over drained spaghetti cooked in salted water. Makes 8-10 servings.

MRS. PAUL (EDITH) REES
Boca Raton, Florida

Spaghetti Sauce

4 16-ounce cans tomato sauce
1 12-ounce can tomato paste
1 pint tomato juice
1 large onion, chopped
3 garlic cloves
½ teaspoon rosemary
½ teaspoon oregano
1 bay leaf
½ teaspoon thyme
2 teaspoons parsley flakes
¼ teaspoon pepper
1 teaspoon salt
1 teaspoon sugar
1 pound ground beef

Brown meat, onion, garlic. Add other ingredients. Prepare well in advance. Makes 12 servings.

Mrs. Bob (Ardis) Gray
South Portland, Maine

Ham Rolls

6-7 cups ground cook ham
2 pounds whole hog sausage
3 cups graham cracker crumbs
2 cups undiluted evaporated milk
3 eggs, slightly beaten

Use hands to mix thoroughly. Use ½ cup mix for each roll. Place in pan so they touch but are not too crowded. Makes 24 rolls. Pour sauce over and bake one hour at 400° F. Baste occasionally with sauce. These freeze well and slice nicely for sandwiches.

Sauce

2 cups undiluted tomato soup
¾ cup vinegar
2 cups brown sugar, packed
2 teaspoons dry mustard

Mix mustard with brown sugar before adding to liquid. Stir thoroughly. Spoon over rolls.

"This is a recipe from Robert Troutman at Headquarters, so I cannot really claim it, but it is a delicious and different main dish."

Mrs. Richard (Carol) Parrott
Corvalles, Oregon

Party Casserole

2 cups chicken, diced or flaked tuna, or crab meat
1 can cream of mushroom soup
2 tablespoons milk
1 cup diced celery
¼ cup minced onion
1 or 2 cans button mushrooms with liquid
1 can water chestnuts, sliced (optional)
1 can Chinese noodles
1 package cashew nuts
grated cheese

Prepare chicken or seafood by cutting into bite-size pieces or flaking. Mix soup with milk. Add remaining ingredients, except cheese. Pour into buttered casserole. Sprinkle cheese over top. Bake in moderate 350° F. oven for about 30 minutes, until cheese is melted and bubbly. Serve hot. Makes 4 to 6 servings.

"With this casserole it is nice to serve a crisp, tossed salad and hot blueberry muffins. This tasty casserole also makes a good main dish for spring luncheons and buffets."

MRS. W. H. (MYRTLE) DEITZ
Fresno, California

With most of us it isn't a question of turning away from wealth and living a simple life. But we are confronted with the same issue on a small scale. If we aren't faithful with one dollar we wouldn't be with a million (M. Lunn).

Chicken Artichoke Skillet Meal

1½ cups sliced mushrooms
1 tablespoon butter or margarine
2 tablespoons flour
1 teaspoon seasoned salt
2 whole chicken breasts, skinned, boned, and halved (4 pieces)
2 tablespoons salad oil
1 cup chicken broth (I use broth soup)
⅛ teaspoon red hot pepper sauce or freshly ground pepper (optional)
1 9-ounce package frozen artichoke hearts

Saute mushrooms in butter in 9-inch skillet. Remove from pan and set aside. Combine flour and salt; roll chicken in this mixture. Add butter and oil to skillet, add chicken and brown. Add broth and optional pepper or pepper sauce. Cover and simmer about 25 minutes or until chicken is just tender. Add mushrooms and artichokes, spooning sauce over them. Continue cooking, covered, about 10-15 minutes, or until artichokes are tender. Makes 4 servings.

MRS. JOHN (EUNICE) KING
Turlock, California

Sour Cream Chicken Enchiladas

2 cans cream of chicken soup
1 chicken, deboned
1 pint sour cream
1 small can diced green chilies
½ teaspoon salt
2 cups grated cheddar cheese
½ cup chopped green onion or chives
1½ dozen corn tortillas

Mix together: chicken soup, chicken, ¾ pint of sour cream, green chilies, salt, onions. Soften tortillas in hot cooking oil for just a few seconds. Drain on paper towel. Put a portion of the filling in the middle of each tortilla with a small amount of grated cheese on each. Roll. Place in long baking dish that has been lined with small amount of filling. After all enchiladas are assembled, add remaining sauce on top, then add rest of sour cream and any grated cheese remaining. Bake in 350° F. oven for 20-30 minutes.

"Delicious! Can be made ahead of time except for the baking. Serve with a salad and Spanish-style pinto beans."

Mrs. Stanley (Patty) McElrath
Tempe, Arizona

Delicate Chicken Loaf

1 large frying chicken
4 cups soft white bread crumbs
2 cups cooked rice
¼ cup melted butter
¼ cup chopped bell pepper
¼ cup chopped pimento
1 teaspoon paprika
6 beaten eggs
1 quart milk

Boil chicken, bone and cut into chunks; reserve broth. To chunked chicken add remaining ingredients. Mix well and pour into 9 x 13" baking dish. Bake 50-60 minutes at 350° F. Make sauce with broth and giblets (or mushrooms). Makes 8-12 servings.

"Ingredients can be prepared ahead (Saturday), mixed and baked for serving (Sunday). This recipe always brings complimentary remarks."

Mrs. Robert (Carolyn) Scott
Orange, California

Barbecue Chicken Casserole

1 2½-pound chicken or special pieces
1½ cups raw rice
1 onion
1 green pepper
1 hot pepper (optional)
1 small can tomato sauce
Kraft barbecue sauce

Brown chicken slightly in 2 tablespoons shortening or margarine. Take off heat. In a 9 x 13 x 2" pan, place raw rice on bottom, add onion, peppers, tomato sauce, 2⅓ cups water, salt and pepper to taste. Dip chicken or brush with barbecue sauce. Place on top of mixture. Pour drippings over the chicken, sprinkle with a little salt if desired. Place tinfoil tightly around dish. Cook at 325° F. for at least 2 hours. Lower heat can be left longer.

MRS. D. W. (MUZETTE) THAXTON
Spring, Texas

Chicken Rice Casserole

1 fryer (2½ to 3 pounds)
¼ cup oil
1 cup uncooked instant rice (regular needs to be partially
    cooked)
1 cup chicken broth
¼ cup sliced ripe olives
1 medium green pepper sliced in rings
1 medium onion, sliced
2 8-ounce cans tomato sauce (shred a little cheese into
    tomato sauce)
1 teaspoon Worcestershire sauce
½ teaspoon oregano

Brown chicken in oil in a large skillet. Pour off oil. Sprinkle with salt and pepper. Stir in rice, chicken broth and olives. Arrange green peppers and onions on top. Combine tomato sauce and cheese, Worcestershire sauce, ½ teaspoon salt, oregano, and heat. Pour over chicken and rice. Simmer covered for 45 minutes in oven at 325° F. Makes 4 or 5 servings.

In the Lord's Prayer, the first petition is for daily bread; no one can worship God or love his neighbor on an empty stomach (Woodrow Wilson).

"I use this casserole often, and people love it!"

MRS. ROY (RUTH) GREEN
Eugene, Oregon

Rice and Chicken Casserole

1 can of chicken soup
1 can of celery soup
1 can of mushroom soup
2 cups water
1 6-ounce package Uncle Ben's Long Grain and Wild Rice
chicken pieces
1 stick butter

Mix soups, water, and rice. Pour into 9 x 13" baking dish. Put chicken pieces on top. Dot with butter. Bake 275° F. for 3 hours uncovered. Makes 6 servings.

MRS. RAY (IRENE) HORTON
Sciotoville, Ohio

If you want your dinner, don't offend the cook (Old Chinese Proverb).

Hot Chicken Salad

3 cups cubed chicken or turkey
2 cups celery, sliced diagonally
¾ cups salad dressing
1 can chicken soup
1 tablespoon lemon juice
4 hard-boiled eggs
salt and pepper
3 cups crushed potato chips, topping
1 cups shredded cheese, topping

Combine all of above. Add last two ingredients to the top. Bake 20 minutes, or until hot, about a 350° oven.

"I have served large groups with this recipe, by cooking, boning, cubing the chicken or turkey ahead, and freezing.

MRS. GRADY (DOROTHY) CANTRELL
Walnut Creek, California

This bread of life dropt in thy mouth doth cry:
Eat, eat me, soul, and thou shalt never die.
William Butler Yeats

Chicken Enchiladas

1 chicken, boned and chopped
1 package tortilla chips
1 cup grated cheese
1 can cream of chicken soup
1 can cream of mushroom soup
1 cup chicken broth
¼ cup piquant sauce

Blend soups and broth. Layer chips, chicken, soup mixture, and cheese in casserole dish. Repeat layers until all is used, topping with grated cheese. Bake at 350° F. for 30 minutes.

MRS. MELVIN (REBECCA) PIERCE
Arlington, Texas

Chicken-Celery Casserole

1 cup cooked diced chicken
1 cup cooked diced celery
1 cup or 1 can sliced, drained water chestnuts
½ cup sliced almonds
1 cup cooked rice
1 cup cream of chicken soup
2 tablespoons chopped onion
¾ cup mayonnaise

Topping
1 cup crushed cornflakes or bread crumbs
½ stick melted butter

Mix together the above ingredients and put into a greased casserole and add topping.
Topping: mix together: crushed cornflakes or bread crumbs and melted butter. Bake 45 minutes at 350° F.

MRS. DALLAS (GERVAYSE) BAGGETT
Middletown, Ohio

And he said unto her, Give me, I pray thee, a little water to drink; for I am thirsty. And she opened a bottle of milk, and gave him drink, and covered him (Judg. 4:19).

Chicken Stew'n Dumplings

2-3 pound chicken, cut up
2 tablespoons butter or margarine
½ cup water
1 cup sliced onion
¼ teaspoon poultry seasoning
1 can cream of chicken soup
1 10-ounce package frozen mixed vegetables
1 cup packaged biscuit mix
⅓ cup milk

Sprinkle chicken with ½ teaspoon salt, dash of pepper, brown in butter in large, heavy pan. Add water, onion, poultry seasoning. Cover; simmer 30 minutes. Stir in soup, vegetables. Bring to boil; cover; simmer 10 minutes more. Stir now and then. Combine biscuit mix and milk; spoon dumplings onto stew. Cook uncovered 10 minutes. Cover; cook 10 minutes longer. Makes 4 servings.

"This is a nutritious and stupendous meal in one!"

MRS. ROY (MARGARET ANN) RAYCROFT
Monroe, Michigan

Hot Chicken Bake

2 cups cooked diced chicken
2 cans cream of chicken soup
4 teaspoons diced onions
2 cups cooked rice (not instant)
1 teaspoon salt
1 ½ cups mayonnaise
4 ounces slivered almonds
6 hard-boiled eggs, cut up
2 cups diced celery
Rice Krispies

Combine all ingredients and top with Rice Krispies. Bake in pre-heated oven at 375° F. for 30 minutes. Celery will still be crisp. Makes 10-12 servings.

MRS. LEWIS (ERMA) CURTISS
West Chester, Ohio

Chicken-Broccoli Bake

1 10-ounce package frozen chopped broccoli
1 4-ounce package medium noodles
2 cups chopped cooked chicken
1 cup (½ pint) sour cream
1 can (10¾ ounces) condensed cream of chicken or
    mushroom soup
¼ cup diced pitted ripe olives
2 tablespoons chopped pimentos
1 tablespoon instant minced onion
1 teaspoon salt
½ teaspoon Worcestershire sauce
1 tablespoon butter or margarine, melted
½ cup soft bread crumbs
1 cup grated Swiss cheese

Prepare broccoli as directed on package; drain. Cook noodles as directed on package; drain. Combine chicken, sour cream, soup, olives, pimento, onion, salt, and Worcestershire sauce. Add butter to bread crumbs and mix well. Place noodles in a greased shallow 2-quart baking dish. Sprinkle with one third of the cheese. Add broccoli; sprinkle with half of the remaining cheese. Pour on the chicken mixture. Sprinkle with the remaining cheese and then with bread crumbs. Bake at 350° F. for 1 hour, or until golden brown. Makes 6 servings.

MRS. WILLIAM (EVELYN) PRINCE
Butler, Pennsylvania

Broccoli Casserole

2 chicken breasts
2 packages frozen broccoli (Green Giant brand, frozen in
    butter sauce)
2 cans cream of chicken soup
1 cup mayonnaise
½ teaspoon curry powder
1 tablespoon minced onion
1 tablespoon lemon juice
½ cup grated cheddar cheese
cornflake crumbs

Steam chicken breasts until bones are easily removed. Place broccoli, cooked according to directions, in greased baking dish 7½ x 11½". Cut into bite-size pieces. Top with diced chicken. Cover with warm sauce consisting of cream of chicken soup, mayonnaise, curry powder, minced onion, and lemon juice. Then cover with grated cheese and cornflakes. Bake at 350° F. for 30 minutes.

MRS. JOHN Q. (DORIS) DICKEY
Birmingham, Michigan

For the Lord thy God bringeth thee into a good land. A land of wheat, and barley, and vines, and fig trees, and pomegranates; a land of oil olive and honey (Deut. 8:7-8).

Chicken n' Rice Delight

1 cup cooked white rice
1 cup cooked wild rice
2 cups (2½ to 3 pounds) chicken, cooked, boned and diced
2 cups (16 ounces) drained French style green beans
1 10¾-ounce can condensed cream of mushroom soup,
    undiluted
½ cup mayonnaise
½ cup slivered almonds
1 cup (2½ ounces) sliced mushrooms, drained
2 tablespoons chopped pimento
2 tablespoons chopped bell pepper
2 tablespoons chopped onion
¼ teaspoon salt
pepper to taste

Wine that maketh glad the heart of man, and oil to make his face to shine, and bread which strengtheneth man's heart (Ps. 104:15).

Combine rice and chicken with other ingredients. Bake in 2½-quart casserole dish at 350° F. for 30 to 45 minutes. Makes 8 generous servings.

"Wild rice gives this casserole a very special flavor and texture, but it also raises its cost considerably. For a budget meal, try it with 1 cup brown rice or 2 cups all white rice, in place of the wild rice."

MRS. C. R. (TERRY) SAWRIE
Little Rock, Arkansas

Chicken Almond Casserole

2 pounds pork sausage
2 large onions, cut up
1 green pepper, chopped
1 small stalk celery, chopped
3 packages Lipton chicken noodle dry soup mix
9 cups water
2 cups uncooked rice
1 cup almonds
salt to taste

Fry sausage, pour off part of grease. Add onions, green pepper, and celery, and fry lightly. Bring water to a boil and add soup mix and rice. Put all ingredients together. Put in very large casserole or small roaster pan and add almonds. Bake uncovered, for at least one hour in 350° F. to 375° F. oven. Stir a few times during baking time. Makes 20 servings.

MRS. CLIFF (CAROL) COWLEY
Portland, Oregon

Chicken Casserole

1 2-pound fryer (reserve 1 cup stock for thinning)
1 stick butter
1 cup chopped green pepper
1 cup diced celery
1 cup chopped onion
½ pound Velveeta cheese
1 can cream of mushroom soup
1 small jar cut stuffed olives
1 can mushrooms, drained (or fresh)
1 small package noodles
sliced almonds

Cook fryer and reserve 1 cup stock for thinning. Saute in butter, green pepper, diced celery, chopped onion. Add cheese, cream of mushroom soup, stuffed olives, and mushrooms. Boil noodles in chicken broth. Remove chicken from bones and remove skin. Add chicken pieces and noodles to mixture and place in 9 x 13 x 2" casserole. Add sliced almonds. Bake 20 to 30 minutes at 350° F. Do not add salt when cooking chicken. Can be frozen and baked when ready to use. Add the 1 cup stock for thinning before freezing.

"This recipe was given me by my friend, Doris Klein, many years ago and has been a favorite. If you are in a rush just bring it out of the deep freeze into the oven."

MRS. JOHN (RUTH) STOCKTON
Olathe, Kansas

Barbecups

¾ pound hamburger
½ cup Kraft barbecue sauce
1 tablespoon instant minced onion
2 tablespoons brown sugar
1 8-ounce can Pillsbury Refrigerator Tenderflake Biscuits
¾ cup shredded cheddar cheese
salt

Brown hamburger in pan; chop fine while cooking; drain off grease; salt. Mix barbecue sauce, onion, and brown sugar with hamburger. Place 12 biscuits in ungreased muffin cups, pressing dough up sides to edge of cup. Spoon meat mixture into cups. Sprinkle cheese over tops. Bake: 400° F. for 10-12 minutes.

"Serve for lunch with a salad."

MRS. MILTON (NORMA) HARRINGTON
Walla Walla, Washington

Meat and Wild Rice

1 cup all-purpose flour
1 stick margarine
4 cups chicken broth (use water for other meats)
¼ teaspoon pepper
1 teaspoon salt
½ teaspoon hot sauce
1 cup sliced onions
1 cup chopped green peppers
1 cup chopped mushrooms (fresh or canned)
2 tablespoons Worcestershire sauce
1 6¼-ounce package "Uncle Ben's long grain and wild rice" (prepare as directed)
1 cup cooked white rice
1 cup cooked meat (chicken, hamburger, minute steak, round steak, shrimp)

In large pot (3 inches deep x 11 inches wide), saute onions, peppers, mushrooms, and margarine. When tender, add flour and stir often; add broth, stir and simmer 2 minutes. Add remaining ingredients and stir till well mixed. Spoon into two greased, shallow 2-quart casseroles. Bake at 300° F. for 45 minutes or until bubbling.

"This makes up a good beforehand dish. Cover to reheat. Two nonstarch vegetables and a salad make a good meal."

MRS. CLARENCE (EVANGELINE) COLEMAN
Lexington, South Carolina

History shouts to the top of her lungs that one of the telltale signs of a decaying civilization is the lack of authority in the home (Dallas Baggett).

God is my King of old, working salvation in the midst of the earth (Ps. 74:12).

Chicken Spaghetti

1 hen (3 ½ to 4 pounds)
2 teaspoons salt
2 medium onions
2 teapsoons butter or margarine
1 3-ounce can mushrooms
1 10-ounce package spaghetti (elbow type)
½ pound grated cheddar cheese
4 cups chicken broth
4 teaspoons Worcestershire sauce
1 teaspoon Tabasco
2 teaspoons black pepper
1 cup chopped celery
1 6-ounce can tomato paste
1 cup tomato soup
½ cup slivered almonds

Cook chicken in boiling water till tender. Bone and pull apart into small pieces. Heat chicken broth to boiling. Add spaghetti, cook 15 minutes. Saute minced onions in butter till tender. Add mushrooms, sauces. Combine chicken, onions, mushrooms, sauces and seasonings with soup and celery. Add almonds. Place in shallow, long casserole dish and top with shredded cheese. Bake in 350° F. oven, about 20 minutes or until bubbly. Makes 20 servings.

"This dish may be frozen before or after cooking, served with Hawaiian vegetables, tossed green salad, and hot rolls, it is a plan-ahead meal."

MRS. CLAYTON (WANDA) KING
Nashville, Tennessee

Ritz Chicken Casserole

6 chicken breasts
2 cans of cream of chicken soup
1 8-ounce carton sour cream
1 tube of Ritz crackers
1 teaspoon celery seed
1 ½ sticks of margarine

Boil chicken breast until tender. Bone and cut in small pieces. Spread over buttered casserole dish. Mix the two cans of cream of chicken soup and sour cream. Spread over chicken. Crush tube of Ritz crackers, mix with celery seed, and spread over soup—melt the margarine and sprinkle over casserole eveningly. Cook 40 minutes at 350° F.

MRS. RALPH W. (RUBYE) MARLOWE
Albertville, Alabama

Chicken Tortilla

4 whole chicken breasts
1 dozen corn tortillas
1 can of cream of mushroom soup
1 can cream of chicken soup
1 cup milk
1 onion, grated
1 cup green chili salsa
1 pound cheddar cheese, grated

Wrap chicken breasts in foil and bake at 400° F. for 1 hour or until done. Cut tortillas into 1-inch strips. Mix soups, milk, onion, and salsa. Butter a large, shallow baking dish. Put a tablespoon or two of juice from chicken or bouillon or water in bottom of dish. Place a layer of tortillas in dish, then chicken, then soup mixture. Top with cheese. Let stand in refrigerator 24 hours. This is important to allow flavors to blend. Bake for 1 to 1½ hours at 300° F. Makes 8 servings.

"Perfect dish to prepare ahead of time, especially for company. Very tasty!"

MRS. TALMADGE (GENELL) JOHNSON
Jackson, Mississippi

The basic motivation for giving is not that we are helping the church, but rather that we are keeping the way clear between our souls and the Savior through this obedience (Raymond C. Kratzer).

Chaney's Chicken Casserole

2 cups cooked chicken
4 hard-boiled eggs, chopped
2 cans mushroom soup
1 3-ounce package slivered almonds
2 cups rice cooked in chicken broth
1½ cups chopped celery
1 small onion, chopped
1 cup mayonnaise
1 teaspoon salt
2 tablespoons lemon juice (fresh or Realemon)

Topping
*1 cup bread crumbs (can substitute Pepperidge Farm
    dressing mix)*
2 tablespoons butter or margarine

Mix all ingredients except bread crumbs and butter. Place in buttered 9 x 12" pan or casserole. Brown crumbs lightly in butter, sprinkle over top of casserole. Refrigerate overnight. Remove from refrigerator one hour before baking. Bake 40 to 50 minutes at 350° F. Makes 8 to 10 servings.

MRS. REEFORD (BARBARA) CHANEY
Richmond, Virginia

Happy the household in which the children follow the parents' footsteps as Isaac followed Abraham (Albert J. Lown).

Round-Up Casserole

3 eggs, beaten
1½ teaspoons salt
¼ teaspoon pepper
1 teaspoon Accent
1 teaspoon paprika
2 cups finely chopped, cooked chicken
1⅓ cups milk
⅔ cup chicken broth
3 tablespoons finely chopped onion
2 tablespoons minced parsley
1 cup cooked rice
1 cup dry bread crumbs

Blend eggs, salt, pepper, Accent, and paprika. Add all remaining ingredients, mix thoroughly. Spoon into greased 1½-quart shallow casserole; set dish in a pan of hot water. Bake in moderate oven at 350° F. about 45 minutes or until a knife inserted near the center comes out clean. Remove casserole promptly from the pan of hot water, let stand about 5 minutes before cutting into serving pieces. Makes 6 servings.

I am come into my garden, my sister, my spouse: I have gathered my myrrh with my spice; I have eaten my honeycomb with my honey; I have drunk my wine with my milk: eat, O friends; drink, yea, drink abundantly, O beloved (Song of Sol. 5:1).

"If desired, serve with chicken gravy or mushroom sauce. Cranberry sauce makes an especially nice relish contrast."

Mrs. Bob (Elmyra) Rimington
Calgary, Alberta, Canada

Hot Chicken Salad Souffle

6 slices sandwich bread
2 cups cooked chicken, diced
½ cup chopped onion
½ cup chopped green pepper
½ cup chopped celery
½ cup mayonnaise
¾ teaspoon salt
dash pepper
2 eggs, beaten
1½ cups milk
1 can mushroom soup
½ cup shredded cheese

Cube 2 slices of the bread; place in a lightly greasted 8 x 8 x 2" baking dish. Saute onion and green pepper in a little butter. Combine chicken, vegetables, mayonnaise, seasonings; spoon over cubed bread. Trim crusts from remaining 4 slices of bread. Arrange atop the chicken mixture. Combine beaten eggs and milk; pour over all. Cover and chill at least one hour or overnight. Spoon soup over the top. Bake at 325° F. about one hour or until it is set. Sprinkle the cheese over the top for the last few minutes of baking time. Makes 6 generous servings.

"This is a good put-together-on-Saturday casserole. It can be taken from the refrigerator on Sunday morning and put in the timer oven to bake while the family is at church. It's chief value is the 'make ahead' convenience."

MRS. DONALD (ELEANOR) WHITSETT
Bethany, Oklahoma

Five-Can Casserole

1 can chicken with rice soup
1 can cream of mushroom soup
1 can crispy chow mein noodles
1 small can evaporated milk
1 can chicken or 2 cups cooked chicken, cut in pieces

Put all together in a buttered casserole. Top with crushed potato chips. Bake uncovered for 30 minutes in a 350° F. oven.

MRS. FLETCHER (ARLENE) WRIGHT
Cape Elizabeth, Maine

Oregon Shrimp Bake

2 cups shrimp
½ cup chopped black olives
¾ cup chopped green onion
¾ cup diced green pepper
1 small jar chopped pimento
1 cup chopped celery
½ cup sliced mushrooms
2 tablespoons chives
season with salt and pepper

Cheese Sauce
2 cups medium white sauce
2 cups shredded cheddar cheese
1 teaspoon dry mustard
½ teaspoon salt
¼ teaspoon pepper

Prepare cheese sauce. Add remaining ingredients. Bake in 2-quart casserole dish at 350° F. for 25-30 minutes.

"Can be served over rice or baked and served in individual casserole dishes."

MRS. KENT (MIMI) ANDERSON
Eugene, Oregon

Chicken Biscuits

1 package brown and serve rolls (cut the center out of each
*   and save)*
1 stick margarine
1 can cream of chicken soup
1 can boned chicken
dash of nutmeg

Melt margarine in saucepan, add the bread centers from your
rolls (break them into little pieces). Add cream of chicken soup,
boned chicken, nutmeg. Mix this together and fill the center of
your rolls. Bake in oven until brown. 400° F. for 20 minutes or
until brown.

"I have served this so many times and received so many comments. Easy to prepare ahead and pop in oven right before serving. It is best to serve hot."

MRS. C. L. (MARY) THOMPSON
Richmond, Virginia

Toasted Crab Muffins

1 3-ounce package cream cheese
1 tablespoon milk
2 teaspoons lemon juice
several dashes of hot pepper seasoning
2 chopped green onions
1 8-ounce can crab meat
3-4 English muffins

Mix cream cheese with milk, lemon juice, hot pepper sauce, and
onion. Split, butter, and toast muffins and spread cheese filling
over the toasted sides. Put crab meat on top of cheese and broil
until top browns slightly. Makes 6 or 8 open sandwiches.

MRS. CHARLES (MARY) OGDEN
Whittier, California

Shrimp a la Golden

1½ pounds shrimp
1 stick margarine
½ medium onion, diced fine
½ green pepper, diced fine

Saute above ingredients slowly in margarine about 10 minutes.
Add garlic salt to taste, 3 hard-boiled eggs, 1 pint half-and-half.

Add thickening (flour and water). Stir gently. Add ⅓ pound (more or less to taste) grated sharp cheddar cheese. Cook slowly until cheese melts. Add savory salt, rosemary, and thyme to taste.

"This is one of my old standbys. It can be made two or three days ahead. Delicious over rice for main meal, on English muffin or toast for lunch or snacks."

MRS. ELVIN (LOIS) HICKS
Edmonds, Washington

Shrimp Casserole

1 pound shrimp, deveined
1 cup raw rice
1 can cream of chicken soup
1 can cream of celery soup
½ cup chopped onions
½ cup chopped bell pepper
½ can Ro-tel tomatoes
½ stick butter or margarine
½ cup water
½ cup cheddar cheese (optional)

It was as true . . . as turnips is. It was as true . . . as taxes is. And nothing's truer than them (Charles Dickens).

Combine all ingredients and bake at 350° F. for 1 hour.

MRS. JOHN A. (JUSTINE) KNIGHT
Bethany, Oklahoma

Shrimp Casserole

1 pound shrimp (fresh or frozen)
1 can cream of chicken soup
1 can celery soup
½ cup chopped onions
½ cup chopped bell pepper
1 cup raw rice
¾ stick margarine
½ can Ro-tel tomatoes
½ cup water
salt and pepper to taste

Combine all ingredients in a large baking dish. Cover with foil and bake in oven for one hour at 350° F.

MRS. JAY (NORMA) BYBEE
Tyler, Texas

Crab Souffle Casserole

8 slices white bread
2 large cans crab (or 2 packages frozen crab)
¾ cup mayonnaise
1 onion, chopped fine
1 cup celery, chopped fine
1 cup pepper, chopped fine
pimento (optional)
3 cups milk
4 eggs, beaten
1 teaspoon salt
1 cup grated cheese
1 can mushroom soup
paprika

'Tis not meat, but 'tis the
appetite
Makes eating a delight.
Sir John Suckling

Grease a 16-inch baking pan, and put in 4 slices of diced bread plus the crusts from other 4 slices, diced. Mix crab, mayonnaise, onion, green pepper, pimento, and celery. Place on diced bread. Place remaining 4 slices of bread with crusts removed on top of crab mixture. Mix beaten eggs, milk, salt and pepper to taste, and pour over all. Let sit in the refrigerator overnight. Next day, pour on undiluted soup (do not mix in), sprinkle with cheese and paprika, and let stand at room temperature for one hour. Then bake one hour at 350° F. Makes 8 to 10 servings.

MRS. PONDER (FLOY) GILLILAND
Bethany, Oklahoma

Crab Supper Pie

1 cup (4 ounces) shredded Swiss cheese
1 unbaked 9-inch pastry shell
1 7½-ounce can crab meat, drained and flaked
2 green onions, sliced (including tops)
3 beaten eggs
1 cup light cream
½ teaspoon salt
½ teaspoon grated lemon peel
¼ teaspoon dry mustard
dash mace
¼ cup sliced almonds

Sprinkle cheese evenly in pie shell. Top with crab meat. Sprinkle with green onions. Combine eggs with cream and seasonings. Pour over crab meat. Top with almonds. Bake in slow oven 325° F. about 45 minutes, or till set. Remove from oven. Let set 10 minutes. Makes 6 servings.

MRS. EARL (JEAN) HAMILTON
Mount Clemens, Michigan

Lobster Casserole

3 tablespoons butter
1 pound cooked lobster (shrimp may be used)
3 tablespoons flour
3 slices of bread (crusts removed)
3 cups rich milk
salt and pepper

Cut lobster into bite-sized pieces and cook slowly in butter. Combine flour with seasonings and sprinkle over lobster. Add milk slowly, stirring to blend. Cook until thickened. Add bread that has been torn into small bits. Pour into greased baking dish. Top with buttered crumbs. Bake at 350° F. for 30 minutes.

"Certainly delicious and would cost a fortune in a restaurant!"

Mrs. Wilmer (Evaleen) Lambert
Syracuse, New York

It is impossible to do justice to a study of the ministry of Jesus to human need without giving consideration to divine healing (Mendell Taylor).

Maine Lobster Casserole

3 tablespoons butter
1 pound cooked lobster meat
3 tablespoons flour
¾ teaspoon dry mustard
3 slices white bread (crusts removed)
2 cups rich milk (part cream)
salt and pepper to taste

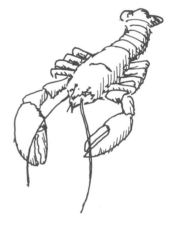

And Abraham hastened into the tent unto Sarah, and said, Make ready quickly three measures of fine meal, knead it, and make cakes upon the hearth (Gen. 18:6).

Cut lobster into bite-size pieces and cook slowly in butter to start pink color. Do not cook too long or too fast or it will toughen. Combine flour with seasonings and sprinkle over lobster; add milk slowly, stirring to blend. Cook, stirring gently, until thickened. Add bread torn into small pieces. Pour into greased casserole; top with buttered crumbs and bake about 30 minutes at 350° F. or until bubbly and brown.

"Make this once and it will be your favorite lobster recipe. It can be made a day ahead and baked just before serving. Better yet, it can be frozen and used months later! Allow extra baking time when frozen. Delicious!"

Mrs. Jack (Joyce) Shankel
Augusta, Maine

Tuna Cantonese

½ cup sandwich spread
1½ cups hot medium cream sauce
2 cans tuna (regular size)
1 tablespoon minced onion
1 container chow mein noodles

Gradually add the sandwich spread to the cream sauce over very low heat. Add tuna, tearing apart with fork. Heat thoroughly. Warm noodles in slow oven, 300° F. Place serving portion on individual plate and spoon tuna mixture over top. Makes 4 servings.

"This is a lovely lunch, with green salad, hard rolls or crackers, and fresh fruit compote for dessert."

Mrs. Neil (Ruth) Hightower
Winnipeg, Manitoba, Canada

Tuna Corn Casserole

1 can tuna
1 can whole kernel corn, drained
potato chips
1 cup medium white sauce

Prepare white sauce (butter, flour, milk). Make layers of the other ingredients. Corn, tuna, broken chips, corn, tuna, chips, etc. Pour white sauce over the top. Bake at 325° F. for 35 to 45 minutes. Double recipe for 2 families.

Mrs. Charles (Barbara) Jones
Nacogdoches, Texas

Cheesy Zucchini Bake

1 pound lean ground beef
½ yellow onion, chopped
½ teaspoon garlic powder
1 pound fresh zucchini
6 ounces (generous) longhorn cheese, grated
1 10¾-ounce can mushroom soup, undiluted

Brown meat with onion and garlic salt. Wash zucchini and cut off tips (do not peel). Cut in ¼ inch slices. Cook for no more than 5 minutes in a small amount of water. Drain. Grease a 1½ quart baking dish and put in half of the meat, then half of the zucchini, then half the cheese. Repeat layers. Mix soup with ¼ cup water and pour over the top. Bake at 350° F. for 40 minutes uncovered. May be refrigerated until ready to bake.

MRS. LARRY (ARLIE) HULL
Centralia, Washington

Italian Broccoli Casserole

2 10-ounce packages frozen cut broccoli
2 beaten eggs
1 can cheddar cheese soup
½ teaspoon crushed oregano
1 8-ounce can stewed tomatoes, cut up
3 tablespoons grated Parmesan cheese

Cook broccoli 5-7 minutes, drain well; combine eggs, soup, and oregano. Stir in tomatoes and broccoli. Turn the vegetable cheese mixture into a 6 x 10 x 2" baking dish. Sprinkle with Parmesan cheese. Bake uncovered in 350° F. oven for about 30 minutes or until heated thoroughly. Serves 6-8.

MRS. BOB (MARY LEE) HUFF
Alexandria, Indiana

Summer Squash Casserole

2 pounds (6 cups) yellow summer squash, sliced
¼ cup chopped onion
1 can condensed cream of chicken soup
1 cup sour cream
1 cup shredded carrot
1 8-ounce package herb-seasoned stuffing mix
½ cup butter or margarine, melted

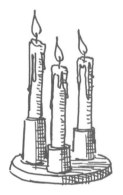

Tell me what you eat, and I will tell you what you are (Anthelme Brillat-Savarin).

In saucepan, cook sliced squash and chopped onion in boiling salted water for 5 minutes, drain. Combine cream of chicken soup and sour cream. Stir in shredded carrot. Fold in drained squash and onion. Combine stuffing mix and butter or margarine. Spread half of stuffing mixture in bottom of 7½ x 12 x 2-inch baking dish. Spoon vegetable mixture atop. Sprinkle remaining stuffing over vegetables. Bake in 350° F. oven for 25 to 30 minutes or till heated through. Makes 6 servings.

"Zucchini squash may be used in place of summer squash."

MRS. B. G. (LOU) WIGGS
Bedford, Indiana

Squash Casserole

2 pounds squash, sliced
½ onion, chopped
½ teaspoon salt
2 eggs, beaten
½ cup crushed crackers
¼ pound grated American cheese
¼ cup margarine
pepper
paprika

Combine squash, onion, and salt; boil with a little water until tender. Cook; drain. Mix in eggs lightly. Layer in buttered casserole with crackers and cheese. Dot with margarine. Sprinkle with pepper and paprika. Bake at 350° F. for 20 minutes until brown.

MRS. JAMES C. (EVELYN) HESTER
Carthage, Missouri

Beef Broccoli Pie

1 pound ground beef
2 tablespoons all-purpose flour
¼ cup chopped onion
¾ teaspoon salt
½ teaspoon garlic salt
1 ½ cups milk
1 3-ounce package cream cheese
1 beaten egg
1 10-ounce package chopped broccoli, cooked and drained
2 packages crescent rolls
1 4-ounce Jack cheese
milk to brush on crust

Brown meat and onion and drain off fat. Stir in flour, salt, and garlic salt. Add milk and cream cheese, stir and cook until mixture is thickened and smooth. Add beaten egg, stirring for one or two minutes. Stir in broccoli. Line oblong baking dish with one package of crescent rolls, forming a crust. Pour in cooked mixture and top with sliced Jack cheese. Roll out second package of rolls to form crust to cover top. Brush with milk and cut steam slits. Place in 475° F. oven for 10 minutes then reduce heat to 375° F. until golden brown on top.

"I borrowed this recipe from my sister, Mrs. Harold Webster, who lives in Barstow, California."

MRS. ROBERT (MARJORIE) GOSLAW
Santa Ana, California

Broccoli Cheese Casserole

2 packages chopped broccoli (or 1 large 20-ounce frozen)
1 cup dry Minute Rice
1 cup mushroom soup (if you are serving with chicken use
    creamy chicken or mushroom soup)
1 cup (8-ounce) Cheese Whiz
2 tablespoons butter

Mix altogether and put in a casserole dish. Fits nicely in 1½-quart Corning Ware dish. Bake at 350° F. for 45 minutes, or until rice is thoroughly done.

"I have substituted cheddar cheese soup for Cheese Whiz; it is less expensive and I couldn't tell the difference. This is almost a meal in itself and can be substituted for meat if served with a salad."

MRS. PAUL (JUANITA) FORGRAVE
Columbus, Ohio

Serve is the key word—for this week, for this day, for all time. To offer assistance, to minister, to care—that is the Christian's calling; that is the glory of Christian living; that is what makes a Christian different. And if a Christian isn't different, what point is there in what he professes? (M. Lunn).

Good Ole Spaghetti

1½ tablespoons oil
1 large onion, cut up fine
1 pound lean hamburger
½ can tomato sauce
1 quart jar tomatoes
¼ teaspoon each:
    cinnamon
    cloves
    ginger
    paprika
    garlic salt
1 tablespoon sugar (may want to add more)
2 bay leaves
¼ pound soaked dry mushrooms (optional)
1 pound spaghetti

Saute onions in oil in a large kettle. Add meat and brown. Add rest of ingredients and salt and pepper to taste. Simmer 3-4 hours. Add water if sauce gets too thick. Serve with the cooked spaghetti.

MRS. PERRY (MARY) WINKLE
Lewiston, Idaho

Sabbath Bean Dish

1 small can baby limas, drained
1 can butter beans (regular size)
1 can kidney beans (regular size, drained)
1 large can pork and beans
¼ pound bacon, diced
1 cup brown sugar
½ cup vinegar
1 teaspoon garlic salt
2 medium chopped onions

Mix together and bake at 350° F. for 3 hours. Excellent with ham or beef.

"The above recipe comes from the Gettysburg National Park area in Pennsylvania."

MRS. LEE (JOAN) MCCLEERY
Upper Marlboro, Maryland

Deluxe Potato Casserole

1 stick margarine
1 cup chopped onion
1 can cream of chicken soup
1 pint sour cream
1 2-pound bag of frozen hash brown potatoes
    (thaw 30 minutes at least)
2 cups grated cheese
salt and pepper to taste

Combine ingredients. Put in large 9 x 13" casserole. Top with crushed potato chips and paprika. Bake at 375° F. for 1 hour. This can be prepared and frozen then baked later.

"This is not an orginal recipe, but one my daughter gave me and is very good to prepare and have on hand for a special occasion."

MRS. VERL (NAOMI) BALLMER
Mishawaka, Indiana

Vegetables

Company Vegetable Casserole

1 package each of frozen:
baby lima beans
cut green beans
corn

Cook each separately according to directions, then drain all in a colander.

Add:

'Tis an ill cook that cannot lick his own fingers (Shakespeare).

¼ cup cut-up pimento
¼ cup cut-up onion tops (this is the essential ingredient)

Prepare a white sauce of:
¼ cup flour
¼ cup butter
1 teaspoon salt
½ teaspoon white pepper
2 cups milk

After white sauce thickens, add ¼ cup Parmesan cheese and let it melt. Mix together with other ingredients and pour in greased casserole. Top with buttered bread crumbs. (I use about 1½ cups crumbs mixed with ¼ cup melted butter). Bake at 300° F. until bread crumbs brown, or about 45 minutes. If casserole is frozen, allow at least 1½ hours for baking.

"This never fails to bring compliments. May be fixed ahead of time and frozen."

MRS. DAN (ELEANOR) ROAT
Havana, Illinois

Vegetable Casserole

2 large packages mixed vegetables (broccoli, cauliflower,
    and carrots)
1 pound Velveeta cheese, cubed
1 tube Ritz crackers, crushed
1 stick butter

Cook vegetables. Melt butter (being careful not to get too brown),
stir in crackers. Grease a 3-quart casserole, put vegetables in, add
the cubed cheese on top and then the cracker mixture on top of
this. Bake in 350° F. oven for 20 minutes, or until cheese melts.

MRS. WILLIAM (MARGARET) GRIFFIN
Indianapolis, Indiana

Vegetables Supreme

If we profess to love God
and our country, nothing
short of absolute honesty
and integrity is required
when we make out the tax
check or the tithe (George J.
Reed).

2 18-ounce packages mixed frozen vegetables
1 pound package Velveeta cheese
1 stack Ritz crackers, crushed
1 stick (¼ pound) margarine, melted

Cook frozen vegetables as directed on package. Drain thoroughly.
Put in 3-quart casserole. Cut up Velveeta cheese over top of
vegetables. Mix crushed Ritz crackers in melted margarine and
put on top of vegetables and cheese. Bake at 350° F. until cheese
melts.

MRS. DON (JEAN) SMALL
Bloomington, Indiana

Corn Pudding

1 can whole kernel corn, drained
1 can cream-style corn
3 eggs, beaten
½ cup sugar
3 tablespoons melted butter
2-3 tablespoons flour
¾ cup milk

Mix above together except flour and milk. Mix flour and milk together until smooth, then mix altogether and pour into greased
baking dish. Bake at 375° F. approximately 1¼ hours or until
firm and slightly browned. Do not cover with a lid.

MRS. LEE (JOAN) McCLEERY
Upper Marlboro, Maryland

Almond Vegetables Mandarin

1 cup thinly sliced carrots
1 cup green beans, cut about 1 inch
2 tablespoons salad oil
1 cup thinly sliced cauliflower
½ cup sliced green onion
1 cup water
2 teaspoons chicken stock base
2 teaspoons cornstarch
pinch garlic powder
½ cup unblanched whole almonds

Cook and stir carrots and beans with oil in skillet (or electric skillet) over medium high heat, 2 minutes. Add cauliflower and onion; cook 1 minute longer. Add mix of water, chicken stock base, cornstarch, and garlic. Cook and stir until thickened. Vegetables should be crisp-tender. If they need further cooking, reduce heat, cover and steam to desired doneness. Add almonds. Recipe may be doubled only; do not make large quantity at one time. Makes 4-6 servings.

MRS. CHARLES (CHRISTIANA) PICKENS
Dodge City, Kansas

Onion Shortcake

1 small onion
¼ cup butter
1½ cups corn muffin or bread mix
1 egg
⅓ cup milk
1 cup cream-style corn
¼ teaspoon salt
¼ teaspoon dill weed
1 cup grated sharp cheddar
2 drops Tabasco

Slice onion and saute in butter. Combine muffin mix, egg, milk, corn, Tabasco. Pour into buttered 8-inch square pan. Mix in small bowl: sour cream, salt, dill, onions, and half the cheese. Spread over batter. Sprinkle with remaining cheese. Bake at 425° F. for 25 to 30 minutes. Serve warm.

"Excellent with ham or as the one hot dish with a cold buffet (or Sunday dinner with leftovers). This dish is more like a corn pudding than a bread."

MRS. DICK (JODY) GROSS
Wenham, Massachusetts

Onion Casserole

5 medium onions
4 ounces potato chips
½ pound mild cheese
1 can cream of mushroom soup
1 soup can milk

In a buttered casserole, place alternate layers of thinly sliced onions, crushed potato chips, and grated cheese. Pour soup and milk over the top. Bake for 1 hour at 350° F.

"One of our favorites and brings raves from guests."

MRS. OVID (LAURA) YOUNG
Bourbonnais, Illinois

Copper Carrot Pennies

2 pound carrots
1 small green pepper
1 medium onion
¾ cup vinegar
salt and pepper to taste
1 can tomato soup
½ cup salad oil
1 cup sugar
1 teaspoon prepared mustard
1 teaspoon Worcestershire

Slice and boil carrots in salted water until fork-tender. Remove from hot water; rinse in ice water: then alternate layers of carrots, onion rings cut thin, and pepper rings. Make marinade of remaining ingredients, heating until sugar dissolves. Refrigerate until cold, then pour mixture over vegetables and refrigerate. May be prepared in advance, keeps for weeks.

"The secret to crisp carrots is to keep them cold after rinsing with ice water."

MRS. CARL (BARBARA) SUMMER
Bethany, Oklahoma

Carrot Casserole

2 bunches of carrots
½ pound cheese (American or Velveeta)
1½ sticks margarine
1 cup cracker crumbs, Ritz or soda crackers

Clean and slice (not too thinly) two bunches of carrots. Melt the cheese and ½ stick of margarine. Place carrots in a casserole and pour cheese mixture over all. Melt the stick of margarine, add crumbs, lightly brown, and sprinkle over the casserole dish. Bake at 350° F. for 15 minutes or until bubbly.

MRS. FLOYD H. (CAROL) POUNDS
Peoria, Illinois

Carrot Pudding

3 cups cooked and mashed carrots (do not salt)
2 eggs, beaten
1 tablespoon flour
½ teaspoon nutmeg
½ cup sugar
½ teaspoon salt
2 cups milk

Combine above ingredients (after mixing dry ingredients together). Bake uncovered in a buttered casserole. Dot with butter. Bake in a 350° F. oven for 1 to 1½ hours.

MRS. KENNETH (RUBY) PEARSALL
Nampa, Idaho

When he came to himself, he said, How many hired servants of my father's have bread enough and to spare, and I perish with hunger! (Luke 15:17).

Marinated Carrots

5 cups sliced carrots
1 medium onion
1 small green pepper
1 can tomato soup
½ cup salad oil
1 cup sugar
¾ cup vinegar
1 teaspoon prepared mustard
1 teaspoon Worcestershire sauce
1 teaspoon salt
½ teaspoon pepper

Cook carrots until tender, but firm. Drain. Cool. Mince green pepper and slice onion. Mix with cooled carrots. Cover with remaining ingredients and marinate about 12 hours. Keeps 2 weeks in refrigerator.

MRS. ARNOLD (ADELAIDE) WOODCOOK
Nampa, Idaho

Carrot-Cheese Casserole

2 pounds carrots
4 tablespoons chopped onion
14 soda crackers, crushed
cheese sauce
buttered cracker crumbs

Cook carrots in boiling salted water till tender. Mash carrots; add onion and crackers. Blend in cheese sauce. Pour mixture into casserole and top with buttered cracker crumbs. Bake 30-40 minutes in a 350° F. oven.

Cheese sauce
2 tablespoons butter
2 tablespoons flour
½ teaspoon salt
¼ teaspoon pepper
1½ cups milk
1 cup diced processed cheese spread

Melt butter, add seasoning and flour. Stir in milk gradually. Blend in diced cheese.

MRS. FRANKLIN (MAY LOU) COOK
Nashville, Tennessee

Cabbage Casserole

1 head cabbage, shredded
1 onion
1 stalk celery
1 stick butter
2 cups bread crumbs
1 teaspoon pepper
1 teaspoon salt
2 eggs

Boil cabbage, onion, celery, briefly. Let steam, put butter, salt, and pepper with it. Cool, then put bread and eggs (beaten lightly), mix thoroughly, pour in buttered casserole dish. Bake at 350° F. for 20 minutes.

"This dish has caused many "Please-give-me-the-recipe" remarks. I have made it several times for Dr. and Mrs. Strickland and they love it."

MRS. L. H. (LUCILLE) ROEBUCK
Georgetown, Kentucky

Sweet-Sour Cabbage

1 medium head of cabbage
¼ pound bacon, diced
1 onion, diced
½ cup sugar
3 tablespoons flour
water
vinegar

Cook chopped cabbage in 2 cups water. Drain and save water. Dice onion and bacon; saute till bacon is crisp. Mix sugar and flour together in 1-cup measure. Add enough vinegar to make 1 cup. Stir until smooth. Add the water saved from the cabbage to bacon and onion. Thicken this with the flour, vinegar, and sugar mixture. Pour over cabbage and mix. Reheat and serve.

"This is great to take to covered dinners. People seem to really enjoy it. I take it in my crock pot so I can keep it warm for serving."

MRS. CALVIN (MARJORIE) JANTZ
Olathe, Kansas

Summer Squash Casserole

2 pounds yellow summer squash
1 medium onion
3 tablespoons butter or margarine
1 cup milk
2 eggs, beaten
1¼ cups grated cheddar cheese
1 cup cracker crumbs
salt and pepper to taste

Combine sliced squash and chopped onion. Cook until tender. Drain and then mash with potato masher. Add remaining ingredients, reserving ½ cup of cheese to sprinkle on top. Pour into buttered casserole. Bake at 375° F. until firm and cheese is melted, about 45 minutes.

"This casserole can be prepared on Saturday evening and baked on Sunday while you complete the remainder of your Sunday dinner. I have prepared this casserole many times and always get compliments from my dinner guests."

MRS. DAVID (GENEVA) BARTON
Riverside, California

Sunday Squash

1½ pounds yellow squash
1 onion, chopped
1 egg
2 tablespoons butter or margarine
2 tablespoons flour
1 cup milk
1 cup grated cheese
1 cup salt-rising bread crumbs, buttered

Let everyone sweep in front of his own door, and the whole world will be clean (Goethe).

Cook squash and onion until tender. Salt to taste. Drain and mash in blender. Add 1 beaten egg. Make medium white sauce with butter, flour, and milk. Add grated cheese to sauce. Combine sauce and squash. Place in baking dish. Top with buttered salt-rising bread crumbs. Bake 30 minutes at 350° F.

MRS. JOHN A. (JUSTINE) KNIGHT
Bethany, Oklahoma

Squash Deluxe

2 pounds squash, drained
1 tablespoon sugar
½ cup mayonnaise
½ cup chopped onion
¼ cup chopped green pepper
1 egg
½ cup grated cheddar cheese
½ cup pimento
salt and pepper to taste
½ stick margarine

Cook squash and drain. Add all ingredients. Top with cracker crumbs. Bake 45 minutes at 350° F.

"This freezes well."

MRS. ROBERT (HESTER) WILSON
Nashville, Tennessee

Woe unto you, scribes and Pharisees, hypocrites! for ye make clean the outside of the cup and of the platter, but within they are full of extortion and excess (Matt. 23:25).

Summer Squash Supreme

2 pounds summer squash (6 cups sliced)
½ cup onion, chopped
1 can condensed cream of chicken soup
1 cup sour cream
1 cup shredded carrots
1 8-ounce package herb-seasoned stuffing mix
½ cup melted margarine or butter

In saucepan cook squash and onions in boiling salted water for 10 minutes. Drain. Combine soup and sour cream. Stir in carrots. Fold in drained squash. Combine stuffing mix with butter. Put about half of stuffing in bottom of 12 x 7" pan or dish. Spoon vegetable mix on top. Sprinkle remaining stuffing mix over vegetables. Bake at 350° F. for 30 minutes.

MRS. PHIL (MILDRED) SMITH
Falls Church, Virginia

An ugly construction cannot glorify its architect. An impure life cannot praise its Creator. A holy life consistently glorifies God (Eunice Bryant).

Squash Casserole

    2 pounds of squash
    1 tablespoon sugar
    ½ cup mayonnaise
    ½ cup chopped onion
    ¼ cup chopped green peppers (optional)
    1 egg, beaten
    ½ cup grated cheddar cheese
    ½ cup pimentos (optional)
    ½ stick margarine
    salt and pepper to taste

For the law of the Spirit of life in Christ Jesus hath made me free from the law of sin and death (Rom. 8:2).

Cook squash, and drain. Mix other ingredients together and gently fold in squash. Pour into greased casserole dish. Top with cracker crumbs which have been buttered with cooking oil. Bake 45 minutes at 350° F.

MRS. EUGENE (FAYE) STOWE
Englewood, Colorado

Spanish-Style Pinto Beans
(Frijoles)

    2 pounds dry pinto beans
    2 large onions, quartered
    4 cloves garlic
    2 teaspoons salt
    ½ teaspoon black pepper
    ½ teaspoon comino seed
    1 can roasted green chilies, diced
    1 large can tomatoes, chop into large pieces

Put beans in large pan and cover with water. Cook until almost tender. Add the above ingredients the last 1½ hours of cooking.

MRS. STANLEY (PATTY) McELRATH
Tempe, Arizona

Zucchini Casserole

Whatever makes men good Christians, makes them good citizens (Daniel Webster).

4 or 5 medium squash
1 green pepper, cut fine
½-¼ pound medium Tillamook cheese, diced
2 tablespoons butter
salt and pepper
1 egg, beaten
¾ cup milk
bread crumbs

Scrub, dice, and parboil squash in 2-3 tablespoons water until barely cooked. Drain. In medium casserole, make alternate layers of squash, green pepper, cheese, butter, salt and pepper. Pour over egg mixed with the milk. Sprinkle with bread crumbs. Bake at 350° F. for 1 hour or until set and bubbly. Makes 6-8 servings.

MRS. NEAL (EVA) DIRKSE
Corvallis, Oregon

Baked Zucchini

A merry heart doeth good like a medicine (Prov. 17:22).

5 large tomatoes
1 or 2 Bermuda onions
6 zucchini squash, sliced unpeeled
bread crumbs or cereal
shredded sharp cheese
season salt
butter or margarine

Place sliced tomatoes on bottom of casserole dish. Cover tomatoes with sliced Bermuda onions. Add sliced, unpeeled zucchini over both. Sprinkle bread crumbs or cereal crumbs generously over all. Dot with butter—season with seasoned salt and dash of pepper. Sprinkle small bag shredded sharp cheese over all. Bake 1 hour at 350° F. in 9 x 13" casserole.

MRS. PAUL (JOANNE) BASHAM
Livermore Falls, Maine

Zucchini Casserole Imperial

4 cups sliced zucchini
2 cups boiling water
2 eggs

1 cup mayonnaise
1 onion, chopped
¼ cup chopped green pepper
1 cup grated Parmesan cheese
salt and pepper to taste
1 tablespoon butter or margarine
2 tablespoons buttered bread crumbs (optional)

Cook zucchini in water until just tender; drain. In large bowl beat eggs. Stir in mayonnaise, onion, green pepper, cheese, salt, and pepper. Add zucchini. Turn into greased 1½-quart baking dish. Dot with butter and sprinkle with bread crumbs. Bake in 350° F. oven for 30 minutes or until bubbly. Makes 6 servings.

MRS. TED (HELEN) MARTIN
Kansas City, Missouri

These things have I spoken unto you, that my joy might remain in you, and that your joy might be full (John 15:11).

Green Bean Casserole

2 cans drained green beans (whole or other)
1 small can mushrooms
1 can cream of mushroom soup
1 cup grated cheese
1 can French fried onion rings (not frozen)

Add liquid from mushrooms to mushroom soup. Then into casserole dish put 2 layers in this order; green beans, ½ of mushrooms, ½ of cheese, a little mushroom soup, a few French fried onion rings. Repeat. Reserve most French fried onion rings for top. Bake 350° F. for 30 minutes.

"Easy! Good to take for a church supper."

MRS. JARRELL (BERNIECE) GARSEE
Boise, Idaho

Any God-ordered assignment brings a responsibility that the sincere, true follower of Christ cannot treat lightly (D. I. Vanderpool).

Green Beans with Crunchy Onions

2 16-ounce cans French-style green beans, drained
1 10½-ounce can condensed cream of mushroom soup
1 3½-ounce can French fried onion rings

In ungreased 1-quart casserole, mix beans and cream of mushroom soup. Bake uncovered 35 minutes. Sprinkle French fried onions on top. Bake 5 to 10 minutes longer.

MRS. GENE (ONALINE) FRYE
Youngstown, Ohio

Piquant Green Beans
(In an Electric Skillet)

2 packages frozen whole green beans
½ cup water
½ teaspoon salt
4 strips bacon
2 tablespoons pimentos
2 tablespoons red wine vinegar
¼ teaspoon sugar
1 tablespoon Worcestershire sauce
¼ teaspoon dry mustard
2 drops Tabasco sauce

Place green beans in saucepan with water and salt. Cook on high until steaming; turn to low or simmer and cook 10 minutes or until tender. Cut bacon into ½ inch strips; saute on medium until crisp; drain and add to beans. Add remaining ingredients to bacon fat in skillet. Heat and pour over beans; mix well. Makes 6 servings.

MRS. WILLIAM (EVELYN) PRINCE
Butler, Pennsylvania

Swiss Beans

2 tablespoons butter
2 tablespoons flour
1 teaspoon salt
¼ teaspoon pepper
1 teaspoon sugar
2 teaspoons grated onion
1 cup sour cream
4 cups drained green beans
½ pound processed Swiss cheese
½ cup cereal crumbs
2 tablespoons melted butter

Combine first six ingredients, add sour cream gradually, place over heat and stir constantly until thick. Fold in beans, pour into 1½-quart casserole. Grate cheese and sprinkle over bean mixture. Combine cereal crumbs with melted butter and sprinkle over top. Bake in 400° F. oven for 20 minutes. Makes six servings.

"This is delicious with a salad for lunch. Acquired from my friend Muriel Ranum, Columbus, Ohio."

MRS. DONALD (EVELYN) GIBSON
Olathe, Kansas

Schnitzel Green Beans

4 slice bacon or
¼ pound chopped leftover ham
3 onions, sliced thin
1 quart fresh cut string beans
2 cups tomatoes
1 teaspoon salt
¼ teaspoon pepper
¼ cup boiling water

Dice bacon and fry crisp. Add onion slices and saute until tender. Put in saucepan with rest of ingredients and cook until very tender.

MRS. KENNETH (CARRIE) DODD
Newport, Oregon

Exotic Celery Casserole

4 heaping cups diced celery
1 can cream of mushroom soup
1 small can chopped pimentos, undrained
1 6-ounce can water chestnuts sliced
1 cup slivered almonds

Cook celery in salted water. Drain. Dice pimentos; combine with liquid. Saute almonds in butter. Combine all ingredients. Put into greased casserole dish. Bake at 350° F. for 30-40 minutes.

MRS. C. WILLIAM (TWYLA) ELLWANGER
Bourbonnais, Illinois

And now I beseech thee, lady, . . . that we love one another (2 John 5).

Celery Casserole

4 cups celery, cut up
1 5-ounce can of water chestnuts, sliced
1 can cream of chicken soup, undiluted
3 tablespoons butter
1 cup bread crumbs
½ small package slivered almonds

Boil celery 5-10 minutes or until done in salted water. Add chestnuts and soup and put in buttered casserole. Melt butter, mix with bread crumbs. Mix in slivered almonds. Spread buttered crumbs and almond mixture over celery mixture. Place in oven. Bake 35 minutes at 375° F.

MRS. ELVIN (LOIS) HICKS
Edmonds, Washington

Broccoli Supreme

2 packages frozen chopped broccoli
2 tablespoons chopped onion
½ cup margarine
4 ounces Pepperidge Farm bread cubes
1 can cream of mushroom soup
1 can cream of chicken soup

Cook broccoli according to directions on package, and drain. Combine broccoli, onions, and stuffing. Dribble melted margarine over top after placing other ingredients in casserole dish. Then spoon soups over top. Do not mix. Bake 350° F., covered for 30 minutes, then uncovered for 15 minutes.

MRS. FLOYD O. (BARBARA) FLEMMING
Louisville, Ohio

Broccoli-Bean Casserole

2 packages frozen chopped broccoli
2 packages frozen lima beans
1 can chopped water chestnuts, sliced thin
1 packet Lipton's onion soup
1 can mushroom soup
1 pound sour cream
1 stick butter or margarine
4 cups Rice Krispies

Cook broccoli and lima beans for 7 minutes. Drain and add: water chestnuts, onion soup, sour cream, mushroom soup. Mix and put in large casserole. Melt butter, add 4 cups Rice Krispies, put on top of casserole. Bake 30-40 minutes at 350° F.

"Can be made the day ahead and put in oven when ready to use."

MRS. DAVID L. (ESTHER) GRANGER
Celina, Ohio

Broccoli and Corn Scallop

2 tablespoons chopped onion
2 tablespoons butter
1 tablespoon flour
1¼ cups milk
8 ounces shredded natural Monterey Jack cheese
1 12-ounce can whole kernel corn, drained
½ cup cracker crumbs
2 packages frozen broccoli spears cooked and drained
*   or 1 bunch of fresh broccoli cooked and drained*

Saute onion in 1 tablespoon butter, blend in flour. Gradually add milk. Cook, stirring constantly until thickened. Add cheese, stir until melted. Stir in corn and ¼ cup crumbs. Arrange broccoli in 7 x 11" baking dish with the stems pointing toward the center (the heads will be touching the sides of the dish). Pour cheese sauce over the broccoli (covering the stems only). Toss crumbs and remaining butter and sprinkle over casserole. Bake uncovered at 350° F. about 45 minutes.

"This dish is especially colorful. It can be made ahead and covered and refrigerated overnight."

Mrs. John (Charlotte) Maxwell
Lancaster, Ohio

Eiffel Tower Spinach

2 10-ounce packages chopped spinach
3 tablespoons butter or margarine
1 tablespoon finely chopped onion
2 tablespoons flour
¼ cup canned milk
⅛ teaspoon ground nutmeg
⅛ teaspoon black pepper
½ teaspoon salt

Topping
1 can undiluted mushroom soup
1 cup grated cheddar cheese

Although the change wrought by regeneration is mysterious, it is visible (L. E. Humrich).

Thaw and drain spinach in a colander. In a saucepan, over medium heat, melt butter, slowly saute onion till limp but not brown, add flour and mix. Stir in spinach, milk, nutmeg, salt, and pepper, until blended. Simmer 2 minutes. Correct seasonings if needed. Pour spinach mixture into a 9-inch square buttered pyrex dish. Top with undiluted mushroom soup and spread with grated cheese. Bake till bubbly and cheese is melted, about 30 minutes. Serves 8. Oven 375° F.

"While in Paris we had dinner with dear friends in the Eiffel Tower Restaurant. I was intrigued with the spinach and have tried to imitate the recipe as closely as possible. It is a family favorite and can be made ahead of time and refrigerated ready to pop into the oven after church."

Mrs. Jerald D. (Alice) Johnson
Overland Park, Kansas

Spinach Souffle

4 packages chopped spinach, defrosted
1 large (1-pint size) carton sour cream
1 package dry Lipton onion soup mix
medium sharp cheddar cheese

Cook spinach in a very little water for 3-5 minutes. Drain well and mix in sour cream and soup mix. Put into a greased casserole and top with grated cheese. Bake 30 minutes at 350° F.

"Sometimes I add 2 or 3 slices of crisp bacon, chopped. This casserole takes such little preparation time, but is so delicious. Even if you do not like spinach, you will like it!"

MRS. CLIFF (BILLIE) BARROWS
Greenville, South Carolina

Eggplant Deluxe

And as they were eating, Jesus took bread, and blessed it, and brake it, and gave it to the disciples, and said, Take, eat; this is my body (Matt. 26:26).

Eggplant
tomatoes
sliced cheese
spice, if desired
Morton Season salt, or similar

Wash, slice eggplant in one-half-inch width (a bit thicker if desired), place slice of fresh tomato on that. Can use canned whole tomatoes if others not available. Place cheese on top of tomato, using season salt if desired. In 350° F. oven, bake one half hour. Leave eggplant skin on to preserve shape.

"My husband would never touch eggplant until I devised this recipe. It is now his favorite vegetable."

MRS. SHERWOOD ELIOT (WINOLA) WIRT
Poway, California

Scalloped Eggplant

1 large eggplant, peeled and diced
⅓ cup milk
½ can condensed cream of mushroom soup
½ can condensed cream of celery soup
1 egg slightly beaten
½ cup chopped onions
1 small jar pimentos, drained and chopped
¾ cup Pepperidge Farm herb-seasoned bread stuffing

Cook the eggplant in slightly salted, boiling water until tender (6 or 7 minutes), then drain. Stir the milk into the celery and mushroom soups and blend in the egg. Add the drained eggplant, onion, pimento, and the bread stuffing; toss lightly to mix. Turn into a buttered baking dish.

For topping; lap American cheese strips over the top (or grated cheese). Bake in a moderate oven (350° F.) for 20 minutes or until hot.

"When we ordered this at a well-known cafeteria, we liked it so much I obtained the recipe and fix it at home now."

MRS. HAROLD (NELLA) HARCOURT
Kilgore, Texas

Deluxe Potato Dish

1 2-pound bag frozen hash brown potatoes (thaw 30 minutes)
1 cup chopped onion
1 can cream of chicken soup
1 pint sour cream
1 stick margarine, melted
2 cups grated or cubed colby cheese
salt and pepper to taste (careful of too much salt)

Mix ingredients together. Top with crushed potato chips and paprika. Bake in 375° F. oven for 1 hour. Makes one 9 x 13" or two 8-inch pans. Freeze one and bake the other.

MRS. ORVILLE (JOY) MAISH, JR.
Mason, Michigan

Number yourself unashamedly and vividly with the Christians. Be known as one by the way of your habits, actions, and speech. This must be your everyday, week-in-and-week-out method of operation (Chuck Millhuff).

Potato Casserole

6 medium potatoes, cooked with salt and drained
¼ cup butter
1 pint sour cream
1 can condensed cream of chicken soup
⅓ cup chopped onion
1½ cups grated sharp cheese

Blend the first 5 ingredients, then put the grated sharp cheese over the top and bake at 350° F. for 45 minutes. Sprinkle parsley over the top.

MRS. MELVIN (GENEVA) McCULLOUGH
Colorado Springs, Colorado

Creamy Potato Bake

1 can cream of celery soup
½ cup milk
1 3-ounce package cream cheese
½ cup onion liquid

Mix above in saucepan and heat.

1 large sack tater tots
1 16-ounce can small whole onions

Place these two items in 9 x 13" pan, add salt and pepper, then pour soup mixture over.

Cover with foil and bake at 350° F. for 1¼ hours. Remove foil and top with shredded cheddar cheese and return to oven to melt cheese.

MRS. L. A. (DIXIE) SUITER
Roseburg, Oregon

Potatoes Supreme

6 large potatoes
¼ cup margarine
1 can cream chicken soup
¼ can milk
⅓ cup chopped green onion
1½ cups grated cheddar cheese
1 pint sour cream
1 cup crushed cornflakes
2 tablespoons melted butter

Boil potatoes with skins, cool, peel, grate. Warm togather: margarine, soup, milk; Add: onions, cheese, sour cream. Mix with potatoes and sprinkle with topping of cornflakes and butter. Bake about 45 minutes at 350° F.

"This dish can be made up ahead and cooked when needed. Can even be frozen (before cooking). Thaw before baking."

MRS. PAUL (PEARLE) BENEFIEL
Glendora, California

Scalloped Potatoes

7½ pounds potatoes
1½ cups butter or margarine
½ cup flour
4 teaspoons salt
1 teaspoon white pepper
2 quarts milk

Pare and cut potatoes into thin slices. Cover with boiling water and simmer 10 minutes. Drain and spread in shallow greased baking pans. Blend together melted butter, flour, and seasonings. Add milk slowly and cook until thickened and smooth; stir constantly. Pour sauce over potatoes. Sprinkle with paprika, cover, and bake in 350° F. oven for 1½ hours. Remove cover and brown. Makes 25 servings.

Mrs. Melvin (Evelyn) Abney
Irvine, Kentucky

Party Mashed Potatoes

8 to 10 cooked potatoes
1 cup sour cream
3 ounces of cream cheese
¼ teaspoon onion flakes
dash of garlic salt
add milk if necessary for right consistency

Mash potatoes and add remaining ingredients. Beat until light and fluffy. Add milk if necessary. Put in buttered casserole dish. Dot with butter. Sprinkle with paprika. Refrigerate until needed. Bake for 30-45 minutes at 350° F.

Mrs. James (Beverly) Smith
Olathe, Kansas

Some people strengthen the society just by being the kind of people they are (John W. Gardner).

Rice Pilaff

2¼ cups uncooked rice
2½ coils fideo (vermicelli)
1 cube butter
3 or 4 garlic cloves or 1 teaspoon garlic puree
1 can mushrooms
2 cups chicken broth
1 can consomme soup

Therefore take heed to your spirit, that ye deal not treacherously (Mal. 2:16).

Melt butter over high heat till it bubbles. Add crushed fideo and lightly brown. Add remaining ingredients. Stir lightly, bring to boil. Stir once, cover, reduce heat to very low. Cook 20-25 minutes without lifting cover. (Do not use aluminum or granite pans).

Mrs. Wayne (Alice) Quinn
Vancouver, Washington

Onion Rice

1⅓ cups rice (not instant)
1 can consomme soup
1 can onion soup
1 4-ounce can mushrooms
⅓ cup butter melted

Combine all these ingredients in 1½-quart casserole. Cover. Bake at 375° F. for 1 hour and 10 minutes. At 35 minutes, stir, cover tightly again and finish baking. It is just as tasty if reheated.

"After serving this dish many times over a period of years, no one yet has shown any indication they did not like it. Seconds are the norm. I got it from Muriel Ranum, Columbus, Ohio."

MRS. DONALD (EVELYN) GIBSON
Olathe, Kansas

Apple Stuffed with Sweet Potato

apples or sliced pineapple
yams
butter
brown sugar
salt and pepper
juice of pineapple
little nutmeg

Core large red apples and cut crosswise into two circles. Allow one half for each person. Place in shallow baking pan with cut side of circle up. Fill core and cover cut side of apple with brown sugar and bake slowly until tender. Have ready well seasoned and smoothly mashed sweet potato. Pile on top of apple, swirling potatoes in attractive peaks. Cover with melted butter and place in hot oven long enough to reheat and brown lightly.

You may use pineapple rings and flavor the sweet potato with the pineapple juice. Much quicker and less work; and you have the same effect.

"I serve this with chicken pie, peas, gelatin salad, and strawberry parfaits for dessert. This is my favorite luncheon."

MRS. JAMES E. (FLORA) HUNTON
Springfield, Illinois

Candied Yams

4 medium-size sweet potatoes
2 cups granulated sugar
1 cup brown sugar
2 cups water
½ cups orange juice
1 dozen marshmallows
1 cup pecans
2 tablespoons red hots
1 teaspoon vanilla
½ stick margarine

Peel potatoes and boil in clear water until they are about half done. In the meantime, boil water, both kinds of sugar, orange juice, and margarine until this begins to thicken. Then drain the water from the potatoes and put them into the liquid and add pecans and vanilla and cook until they are candied. Then place in a pyrex dish and put marshmallows on top and place in oven until marshmallows are a golden brown. Makes at least 12 servings.

MRS. RUBY HOLLAND
North Little Rock, Arkansas

To get maximum attention, it's hard to beat a good, big mistake (Gazette).

Sweet Potato Casserole

3 cups canned sweet potatoes, drained
½ cup milk
2 eggs
1 stick margarine softened
½ cup sugar
1 teaspoon vanilla

Topping
1 cup brown sugar
⅓ cup flour
⅓ cup margarine, softened
1 cup pecans, chopped

Mix potato mixture together with electric mixer. Spread in buttered 9 x 13-inch casserole dish. Bake at 350° F. for 35 minutes after crumbling over top the topping mixture, made by combining the topping ingredients. Makes 6-8 servings.

MRS. RUSSELL (PATRICIA) LONG, SR.
Barberton, Ohio

Breads & Muffins

Thou shalt be his witness
unto all men of what thou
hast seen and heard (Acts
22:15).

Pineapple Nut Bread

3½ cups flour
  4 tablespoons baking powder
 ½ teaspoon soda
  1 teaspoon salt
1½ cups coarsely chopped nuts
  6 tablespoons soft butter
1½ cups light brown sugar, packed
  2 eggs
  2 cups crushed pineapple

Set oven for 350° F. Butter two 1-pound loaf pans. Sift together the measured flour, baking powder, soda, and salt. Stir in
1½ cups nuts. In mixing bowl cream: 6 tablespoons soft butter,
brown sugar, beat in eggs, and continue to beat until mixture is
smooth. Stir in half the flour and nut mixture. Stir 2 cups crushed
pineapple, including juice. Stir in remaining flour mixture until
well blended. Divide batter between the 2 pans. Combine 4 tablespoons sugar and 1 teaspoon cinnamon; sprinkle half over batter
in each pan. Bake 50 to 60 minutes. Cool 5 minutes and turn
out on rack to cool.

"Very good and freezes well."

MRS. BUD (MARION) JONES
South Portland, Maine

Pumpkin Bread

5 cups flour
4 cups sugar
3 cups pumpkin
2 cups raisins, nuts, and dates (raisins optional, cut up dates, finely cut nuts)
1 cup salad oil
1 teaspoon (each) salt, cinnamon
½ teaspoon cloves
4 teaspoons soda

Mix in large bowl in order given. Grease and flour small bread pans. Make 4 loaves. Bake 60 to 70 minutes at 350° F.

MRS. JO KINCAID
Nampa, Idaho

Everywhere Jesus went, changes took place; the laws of nature were suspended: waves stilled, devils subdued, diseases healed, sins forgiven, death conquered. Even so now, the coming of Christ into a human heart and life means change: old things passed away, new affections, habits, purposes, disciplines, fellowship (M. A. [Bud] Lunn).

Orange Bread

4 cups flour
4 eggs
½ pound margarine
2 cups sugar
½ cup buttermilk
1 teaspoon soda
1 cup candy orange slices
1 cup nuts
1 cup chopped dates
salt

Chop candy orange slices into 1 cup flour, add dates and nuts. Cream margarine and sugar, add eggs, mix well. Sift soda, salt, and rest of flour. Add to creamed mixture with buttermilk. Add orange slices, dates and nuts last. Use bread pans or 1-pound tin cans for small round loaves.
Optional: Ice lightly with a mixture of concentrated orange juice and powdered sugar.

"Small round loaves of bread make good Christmas gifts."

MRS. STAN (PAT) MEEK
Waco, Texas

Banana Surprise Loaf

2 cups sifted all-purpose flour
3 teaspoons baking powder
½ teaspoon salt
¼ teaspoon nutmeg
1 cup dates (optional)
½ cup butter or margarine
1 cup sugar
2 eggs
1 tablespoon lemon juice
1½ cups mashed bananas (about 3 medium bananas, fully ripe)

Sift together flour, baking powder, salt, and nutmeg; add dates and toss lightly. Cream together butter and sugar; beat in eggs and lemon juice. Add dry ingredients to creamed mixture alternately with mashed bananas; after each addition, beat until smooth. Turn into greased 9 x 5 x 3-inch loaf pan. Bake in moderate oven (350° F.) for 40 minutes or until cake tester inserted in center comes out clean. Cool 10 minutes before removing from pan.

MRS. GEORGE (EVELYN) HUFF
Nashville, Tennessee

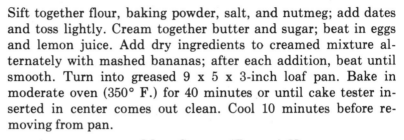

Date Bread

2 teaspoons soda
1½ cups boiling water
1 package chopped dates
1¾ cups sugar
1 tablespoon butter
1 egg
2¾ cups flour
1 cups chopped nuts
1 teaspoon vanilla

Add soda to boiling water and pour this over dates which have been chopped into small pieces. Let this mixture stand while you cream sugar, butter, and egg. Drain water from date mixture into creamed mixture. Add flour and beat with dates. Add nuts and vanilla. Pour into greased loaf pan. Bake at 350° F. Will fill two average loaf pans. Bake around 45 minutes.

"Will fill two average loaf pans or angel food pan or Bundt pan. Very delicious at holiday seasons or for fancy sandwiches with cream cheese filling."

MRS. LEON (ELIZABETH) WYSS
San Diego, California

Oatmeal Applesauce Bread

1½ cups rolled oats
½ cup all-purpose flour
½ cup whole wheat flour
½ cup packed brown sugar
¼ cup bran
1 teaspoon baking soda
1 teaspoon baking powder
1 teaspoon cinnamon
½ teaspoon salt
1 cup applesauce
⅓ cup oil
2 eggs
1 cup raisins
½ cup chopped walnuts

After deep conviction of sin, I found sweet, personal reconciliation with Christ. No longer an alien, no longer a stranger, I found myself one with the family of God. One with God— one with His people! (Arch Edwards)

In large bowl, mix well, oats, flour, sugar, bran, soda, baking powder, cinnamon, and salt. Stir in applesauce, oil, and eggs until blended. Stir in raisins and nuts until well mixed. Turn into lightly greased and floured or nonstick 9 x 5 x 3-inch loaf pan. Bake in preheated 350° F. oven for 50 to 60 minutes or until pick inserted in center comes out clean. Cool in pan 10 minutes. Turn out on rack. Cool completely. Wrap and store. Best eaten next day.

"Delicious health bread. Good for breakfast or snack."

MRS. JAMES F. (THELMA) CULLUMBER
Tucson, Arizona

Date-Nut Bread

Combine

2 cups chopped dates
1½ cups boiling water
2 teaspoons soda

Mix together
1 cup sugar
2 cups flour
1 egg
2 tablespoons butter or shortening

Add
½ to ¾ cups nutmeats

Combine date mixture with second mix. Pour in greased and floured pan. Bake one hour at 350° F.

MRS. RONALD (VIOLA) WESLEY
Sumter, South Carolina

Date Orange Whole Wheat Bread

3 cups level whole wheat flour
3 teaspoons baking powder
½ teaspoon salt
1 cup of milk
1 cup honey
1 egg slightly beaten
⅓ cup salad oil
1 full cup cut-up dates
½ cup sunflower seeds or walnuts
1 large orange

Place first three ingredients in large mixing bowl with dates and nuts. Wash orange and place by quarters in blender with milk. Add egg, honey, oil to milk-orange mixture and stir enough to dampen. Grease loaf pan and bake in 350° F. for about 1 hour. Test for doneness.

Mrs. Thomas (Kay) Hermon
Little Rock, Arkansas

Let your speech be alway with grace, seasoned with salt, that ye may know how ye ought to answer every man (Col. 4:6).

Tiny Herbed Biscuits

1 can (10) refrigerated biscuits
¼ cup butter or margarine
1½ teaspoons celery flakes
1½ teaspoons parsley flakes
½ teaspoon dill weed or seed
1 teaspoon instant minced onion
1½ tablespoon grated Parmesan cheese

Melt butter in an 8- or 9-inch round cake pan. Stir in all the seasonings (except cheese). Quarter each biscuit and roll in butter mixture; leave in pan—just keep adding more pieces until all have been turned around and covered with mixture. Sprinkle with cheese. Bake in 425° F. oven for 12 to 15 minutes. Place plate over top of cake pan and turn over; they come out of pan easily.

"You can melt butter, and add other ingredients on Saturday night. While the oven heats, you can melt this mixture which was refrigerated overnight, and Sunday dinner is not delayed."

Mrs. Bud (Maxine) Goble
Winamac, Indiana

Cheese Biscuits

8 or 10 ounces sharp cheddar cheese, grated
1 pound sausage
3 cups Bisquick

Mix ingredients and form into small (approximately 1 inch) balls. Place on cookie sheet not touching each other. Bake 15 minutes at 375° F. You may freeze and pop in the oven anytime. Be sure to thaw some and allow a little longer to bake. If you make the balls too large they will not cook done before browning.

"These are *great* for Sunday morning breakfast with juice and coffee. Takes no time to prepare when you have them available in freezer. You can bake them while working on your Sunday dinner preparation, even with company for breakfast. As a hors-d'oeuvre, make very small marble size, and cook for less time."

Mrs. B. (Leota) Downing
Evansville, Indiana

Jesus began to preach, and to say, Repent: for the kingdom of heaven is at hand (Matt. 4:17).

Fool-proof Biscuits

2 cups regular flour
4 teaspoons baking powder
½ teaspoon salt
½ cup shortening
1 large egg
sweet milk

Sift first 3 ingredients together. Work shortening in by hand. Place egg in measuring cup. Add milk to make one cupful. Add milk and egg to dry ingredients, and stir in with spoon. Shape into soft lump and put out on floured board. Cut and shape into size desired, and bake to golden. Bake in 450° F. oven.

"To make good shortcake buns, add 2 tablespoons sugar and one teaspoon vanilla. Pat biscuits a little flatter, and use larger cutter. Split when done and cover with strawberries."

Mrs. Bill (Gloria) Gaither
Alexandria, Indiana

Pressing more closely to
Him who is leading,
When we are tempted to
turn from the way;
Trusting the arm that is
strong to defend us,
Happy, how happy, our
praises each day!
Eliza E. Hewitt

Zucchini Bread

2 eggs
1 cup oil
2 cups sugar
2 teaspoons vanilla
2 cups grated zucchini
2 cups plain flour
1 teaspoon salt
1 teaspoon baking soda
1 teaspoon cinnamon
½ teaspoon baking powder
½ cup walnuts, chopped
½ cup raisins

Mix first 5 ingredients in order given. Sift together dry ingredients: flour, salt, baking soda, cinnamon, baking powder. Add dry ingredients to egg mixture. Add walnuts and raisins. Pour in greased and floured loaf pans. Bake at 350° F. for 1 hour.

"Very good and something different!"

MRS. GLEN (CHARLOTTE) JONES
Chattanooga, Tennessee

Zucchini Bread

3 eggs
2 cups grated zucchini squash
1 cup oil
2 teaspoons vanilla
2 cups sugar
3 cups flour
3 teaspoons cinnamon
1 teaspoon salt
1 teaspoon soda
¼ teaspoon baking powder
½ cup nuts (optional)

Note: Wash zucchini, grate with peeling and seeds, unless it is large—then scoop out the soft center and use the more solid part.

Beat eggs until foamy. Add oil, vanilla, and squash to egg mixture. Stir well; add dry ingredients. Bake at 325° F. until done. While still warm, sprinkle with sugar. This recipe makes two loaves.

"This bread freezes well. It can be used right from the freezer. It can also be used as a dessert with ice cream and nut sauce."

MRS. JOHN (CHARLOTTE) MAXWELL
Lancaster, Ohio

Fabulous Fruit Kuchen

1 cup granulated sugar
½ cup shortening
2 eggs
½ cup milk
½ teaspoon salt
3 teaspoons baking powder
2 cups flour
1 teaspoon vanilla
1 can pie filling (we like cherry)

Topping
½ cup margarine
½ cup granulated sugar
1 cup flour

Confectioners' sugar and water for glaze

Preheat oven to 350° F. Cream sugar with shortening. Add eggs. Combine dry ingredients and add to first mixture alternately with milk. Add vanilla. Pour batter into greased jelly roll pan (10½-inch by 15¼-inch). Drop fruit on batter in about 18 "plops." Do not spread fruit. Combine topping mixture until crumbly and sprinkle over batter and fruit. Bake at 350° F. for 50 to 60 minutes or until brown and crispy on edges. While warm drizzle with confectioners' sugar and water glaze. Serve warm or cold.

"Can be made in a 9-inch square pan also. Great while warm with a scoop of ice cream. If using ice cream, it might be preferable to omit the glaze. Good as a coffee cake, too."

Mrs. Roy E. (Doris) Carnahan
Ellicott City, Maryland

Southern Spoon Bread

3 cups milk
1 cup water-ground cornmeal
1 teaspoon salt
3 eggs
3 level teaspoons baking powder
butter, size of a walnut

Stir meal into 2 cups milk. Let come to a boil, making a mush. Add remainder of milk, well-beaten eggs, salt, baking powder, and melted butter. Bake in moderate oven for 30 minutes or until brown. Serve in dish in which it has been baked.

Mrs. John W. (Celia) May
Mount Sterling, Kentucky

A charge to keep I have,
A God to glorify;
A never-dying soul to save,
And fit it for the sky.
Charles Wesley

Corn Spoon Bread

2 eggs
1 Jiffy corn muffin mix
1 8-ounce can cream-style corn
1 8-ounce can whole kernel corn
1 cup sour cream
½ cup melted butter
1 cup shredded Swiss cheese or other preferred cheese

Set oven temperature at 350° F. Bake in Corning Ware dish or any 1½-quart casserole. Combine ingredients except for cheese. Bake 35 minutes. Put cheese on top, bake 10 minutes more.

MRS. MARVIN (GARNET) BEAM
Xenia, Ohio

My son, despise not thou the chastening of the Lord, nor faint when thou art rebuked of him: For whom the Lord loveth he chasteneth, and scourgeth every son whom he receiveth (Heb. 12:5-6).

Onion Kuchen

1 large (about 1 pound) sweet Spanish onion
6 tablespoons butter or margarine
4 eggs
1¼ cups commercial sour cream
½ teaspoon salt
1 teaspoon caraway seed
½ cup milk
1¾ cups buttermilk baking mix

Peel and quarter onion. Slice into thin strips; there should be about 3½ cups not packed down. In a 10-inch skillet containing 4 tablespoons of the butter, gently cook the onion, stirring often, until wilted and yellowed. In a medium mixing bowl beat 3 eggs; gradually stir in the sour cream, keeping smooth. Stir in the salt, caraway seed, and cooked onion; set aside. Melt the remaining 2 tablespoons butter; set aside. In a medium mixing bowl beat remaining egg with milk to combine; add the melted butter and the baking mix; stir just until dry ingredients are moistened—dough will not be smooth. Turn into a buttered glass baking dish (11¾ by 7½ by 1¾ inches) or similar utensil, and spread evenly. Spread onion mixture over dough. Bake in preheated 375° F. oven until dough is browned and topping is set—30 minutes. Cut in squares and serve at once. Makes 8 servings.

"If serving for Sunday dinner, prepare topping and refrigerate. Measure other ingredients and set aside, ready to mix and assemble before baking. This is a quicker version than the yeast dough onion kuchen made in Germany. Serve instead of potatoes or rolls."

MRS. JERALD D. (ALICE) JOHNSON
Overland Park, Kansas

Coffee Cake

1¼ cups flour
1 cup brown sugar
¼ teaspoon salt
⅓ cup shortening
1 teaspoon baking powder
¼ teaspoon soda
¼ teaspoon cinnamon
¼ teaspoon nutmeg
½ cup sour milk
1 egg, beaten

Sift flour, measure. Combine with sugar, salt, and shortening. Blend until crumbly. Reserve ¼ cup for topping. To remainder, add baking powder, soda, spices, milk and egg. Blend. Pour into greased 8-inch square pan. Sprinkle with reserved crumbs. Bake at 375° F. for 25 to 30 minutes.

"For fancy topping, add chopped nuts and extra cinnamon."

Mrs. Bert (Lola) Daniels
Oklahoma City, Oklahoma

Sour Cream Coffee Cake

2 sticks butter
1½ cups sugar
3 eggs
1 cup sour cream
1 teaspoon almond or vanilla flavoring
½ teaspoon salt
1 teaspoon soda
1 teaspoon baking powder
2½ cups flour

Topping
1 cup brown sugar
1 tablespoons cinnamon
½ cup pecans
3 tablespoons butter, melted

Grease and flour three 9-inch aluminum coffee cake pans or small loaf pans. Cream butter and sugar: add eggs, and vanilla (or other flavoring). Sift dry ingredients, flour, salt, baking powder, and soda. Add alternately with sour cream. Pour batter into 3 pans. Sprinkle with half of topping mixture, brown sugar, cinnamon, pecans, and butter. Cut into batter with knife. Sprinkle remaining mixture on the tops. Bake at 350° F. about 25 minutes.

Mrs. Glen (Charlotte) Jones
Chattanooga, Tennessee

Raspberry-Cream Cheese Coffee Cake

1 3-ounce package cream cheese
4 tablespoons margarine
2 cups packaged biscuit mix
⅓ cup milk
½ cup raspberry preserves
1 cup sifted confectioners' sugar
1 to 2 tablespoons milk
½ teaspoon vanilla

Cut cream cheese and margarine into biscuit mix until crumbly. Blend in milk. Turn onto floured surface; knead 8-10 strokes. On waxed paper, roll dough to a 8 x 12-inch rectangle. Turn onto greased baking pan (cookie sheet or jelly roll pan); remove waxed paper. Make 2½ inch cuts at 1 inch intervals on long sides. Pour on filling made from preserves and fold strips over filling. Bake in 425° F. oven for 12 to 15 minutes. Combine sugar, remaining milk, and vanilla; drizzle over the top and serve warm. Delicious!

Mrs. B. G. (Lou) Wiggs
Bedford, Indiana

Cinnamon Rolls

2 cups flour
3 teaspoons baking powder
1 teaspoon salt
½ cup sugar
⅓ cup shortening or margarine
1 egg plus milk to make ¾ cup

Cut shortening into dry ingredients. Add milk and egg, stir briskly with fork. Knead lightly on floured surface. Roll out to desired thickness. Butter. Sprinkle with brown sugar and cinnamon. Roll up and cut into 1-inch widths. Bake at 450° F. for 10-15 minutes.

"Teenagers love these!!"

Mrs. Melvin (Lorna) Tucker
Victoria, British Columbia, Canada

Cinnamon Biscuits

2 cups sifted flour
3 tablespoons sugar
4 teaspoons baking powder
½ teaspoon cream of tartar
½ teaspoon salt
½ cup oil
⅔ cup milk
2 tablespoons melted margarine
⅓ cup sugar
2 teaspoons cinnamon
½ cup raisins

Sift dry ingredients; add oil and milk all at once; stir until mixed. Turn out on lightly floured surface; knead gently ½ minute. Roll or pat into rectangle 12 x 16 inches, ¼ inch thick; brush with melted margarine. Combine ⅓ cup sugar and cinnamon; sprinkle over surface. Sprinkle raisins over top. Roll as jelly roll. Cut in 12 equal pieces and bake in muffin tins lined with paper bake cups. Bake in hot oven (425° F.) 10 to 12 minutes or till done. Makes one dozen.

MRS. T. P. (JOAN) ESSELSTYN
Republic of South Africa

In Christ there is no East or
West,
In Him no South or North;
But one great fellowship of
love
Thro'out the whole wide
earth.
John Oxenham

Jalapeño Corn Bread

2 eggs, slightly beaten
1 cup self-rising cornmeal
1 large can yellow cream-style corn
1 cup milk
½ cup cooking oil
1 pound hamburger meat
1 large onion
1½ to 3 jalapeño peppers (depending on size) finely
    chopped
8 ounces sharp cheddar cheese, grated

Saute 1 pound hamburger meat and drain. Mix in a separate dish, eggs, cornmeal, corn, milk, oil. Pour ½ of the cornmeal mixture in a greased casserole dish or iron skillet. Spread the hamburger meat over this, then add onions, peppers, and cheese, and pour remaining ½ of cornmeal mixture on top. Bake in 425° F. oven as you would cornbread.

MRS. SOLON (RUBY) DAVIS
Jackson, Mississippi

Corn Light Bread

2½ cups cornmeal
1 cup flour
1 cup sugar
¾ teaspoon soda
¾ teaspoon salt
2 cups buttermilk
½ cups sweet milk

Mix the cornmeal, flour, and sugar together. Add the soda and salt to the buttermilk and sweet milk. Combine the liquid ingredients with the dry ingredients. Bake at 450° F. for 10 minutes and 350° F. for 25 minutes, in a 10-inch black iron skillet to which 2 tablespoons of shortening has been added. Melt shortening in oven while preheating.

"Delicious and easy."

MRS. NEIL B. (BONNIE) WISEMAN
Olathe, Kansas

Quick Buttermilk Bread Sticks

4 packages Fleishman's dry yeast
1½ cups warm water
2 cups buttermilk
1 cup cream cottage cheese
3 eggs
½ cup safflower oil
5 tablespoons molasses (I use blackstrap)
4 teaspoons baking powder
4 teaspoons salt
1 cup white flour (Gold Medal)
2 cups rye flour
1 cup soy flour
4 cups whole wheat flour
¾ cup unhulled sesame seeds
2 cups unsalted sunflower seeds
½ cup pumpkin seeds
½ cup all-purpose bran
½ cup wheat germ

In large mixer bowl, dissolve yeast in warm water with molasses. Add buttermilk, eggs, cottage cheese, white flour, baking powder, salt, and oil. Blend with mixer ½ minute, scraping sides constantly. Beat 2 minutes at medium speed. (If you have a mixer with only one beater or a bread hook, you can do it all with the mixer). Stir in nuts and seeds, then add rest of flours.

Turn dough out on well-floured (whole wheat flour) board or cabinet top. Knead 5 minutes. Place dough in greased bowl, cover with wet, warm cloth. Set on a warm, wet turkish towel (hastens first rising) till double. Turn out on floured board or counter, cut off pieces about the size of large eggs. Roll in whole wheat flour or sesame seeds and roll between hands (Until it is about the size of your first finger in diameter). Place on greased cookie sheets. Bake immediately for 20 minutes at 375° F. If you desire browner outside, bake 5 minutes longer. Place on double thickness of grocery sacks and let cool. They freeze beautifully (if any left). You may add dried onion or garlic flakes, or any other seasonings you like.

"I hope you really enjoy these, they are a little extra work but well worth it."

MRS. FRANK (VEVA) HARRIS
Denver, Colorado

Bubble Bread

    1 cup milk
    2 packages dry yeast
    ½ cup warm water
    ½ cup butter
    ½ cup sugar
    1 teaspoon salt
    2 eggs
    5½ cups flour
    ½ cup melted butter
    1 cup sugar
    2 tablespoons cinnamon
    chopped nuts (optional)

What therefore God hath joined together, let not man put asunder (Mark 10:9).

Scald milk and allow to cool. Dissolve yeast in warm water. Beat with mixer the butter, sugar, salt, and eggs. Add cooled milk and dissolved yeast and mix. Add flour and knead 5 to 10 minutes. Let rise until double. Shape into balls the size of walnuts. Dip in melted butter, then into the sugar and cinnamon mixture. Place in greased angel food cake pan. Sprinkle nuts over each layer. Let rise to the top of the pan. Bake at 375° F. for 15 minutes, then at 325° F. for 30 to 40 minutes.

"This is good served with any meal. It is especially pretty to use on a buffet table. A candle can be placed in the center. Guests may easily pull off the desired pieces of bread."

MRS. CLARENCE (SUE) KINZLER
Nampa, Idaho

Honey Wheat Bread

1 package dry yeast
1 cup warm water
½ cup honey
1 tablespoon salt
2 tablespoons shortening
1 cup scalded milk
3 cups whole wheat flour
3 cups white flour

He will take your daughters to be confectionaries, and to be cooks, and to be bakers (1 Sam. 8:13).

Dissolve yeast in warm water. Combine honey, salt, shortening, and hot milk; stir until shortening melts. Cool to lukewarm. Add yeast mixture. Gradually add flours. Knead until satiny, 8-10 minutes. Place in greased bowl; cover. Let rise in warm place for 2 to 2½ hours. Punch down; let rise again. Shape into 2 loaves. Put in greased pans, 9 x 5 inches. Let rise until tops of loaves are above pan edges. Bake at 350° F. for 50 to 60 minutes.

"For freezer: prepare same as the above. After shaping the loaves, place loaves in freezer loaf pans. Put in plastic bags and place in freezer. Then when you want to use them, take from freezer 6 hours before baking time, let rise and bake at 350° F. for 50-60 minutes."

MRS. VIRGIL (VIRGINIA) APPLEGATE
Cincinnati, Ohio

Swedish Rye Bread

2 cups sweet whole milk
2 teaspoons caraway seed
2 teaspoons aniseed
½ teaspoon salt
2 heaping tablespoons shortening
1 cup brown sugar
2 Fleishman's yeast cakes
2½ cups white flour
2 cups rye flour
¾ cup white flour for kneading process

Boil together for 5 minutes: milk, caraway seed, aniseed, salt, shortening, and brown sugar. Let cool. When cool, add 2 yeast cakes that have been dissolved in a little warm water. Then make a soft sponge by adding 2 cups white flour. Add rye flour and knead 10 minutes. Using part of the ¾ cup of extra flour, let rise until double in size. Then knead again for 10 minutes. Put into loaf pans, let rise until double. Bake for about 35 minutes at 350° F. according to size of loaves. Makes 2 loaves.

MRS. H. T. (VERA MAY) STANLEY
Grand Rapids, Michigan

Doughnuts

2 cups warm water
3 envelopes yeast
3 eggs
1½ tablespoons baking powder
⅓ cup sugar
¾ cup shortening or cooking oil
6 cups flour (approximate)
1½ teaspoons salt
1½ teaspoons vanilla

Dissolve yeast in ½ cup of the warm water. Add melted shortening or oil and sugar to rest of water. When cool, add eggs, baking powder, salt, vanilla, and yeast mixture. Add enough flour to form soft dough. Let rise 20 minutes. Roll out ½-inch thick on floured board. Cut with doughnut cutter. Deep fry until golden brown. Glaze: when cool, glaze with a mixture of icing sugar, hot water, and vanilla flavoring.

"These doughnuts are light and delicious. A real favorite with my family and the youth of our church."

Mrs. Glenn (Hertha) Follis
Edmonton, Alberta, Canada

Angel Rolls

1 package dry yeast
¼ cup warm water
1 cup scalded milk (if powdered milk is used, do not scald)
2 eggs
½ cup sugar
1 teaspoon salt
½ cup cooking oil
4 cups unsifted flour

Combine on Saturday night: dry yeast in warm water. Beat 2 eggs in large mixing bowl. Add sugar, salt, and milk. Stir into mixture the dissolved yeast and oil. Add flour and stir. Let set covered overnight. You may hurry recipe by using 2 packages of yeast. Make in early morning and serve at noon.) Next morning, put dough on floured board, turn over several times and divide into 2 parts. Do not work flour into dough. Roll each part round like a pie. Cut each into 16 wedges and roll up into roll (wide edge first). Place on greased pans or cookie sheets about 1½ inches apart. Let rise until after church. Bake 12 minutes at 375° F.

"There is no roll recipe to compare to this recipe."

Mrs. Jo Kincaid
Nampa, Idaho

One loaf of bread, and one cake of oiled bread, and one wafer out of the basket of the unleavened bread that is before the Lord (Exod. 29:23).

Perhaps we should not ask another question until we learn to listen and act upon answers He has already given (Debbie Salter).

The ravens brought him bread and flesh in the morning, and bread and flesh in the evening; and he drank of the brook (1 Kings 17:6).

Pecan Rolls

Basic Dough
> 2 packages active dry or 2 cakes compressed yeast
> 1 cup water
> 1 teaspoon sugar
> 2 cups milk, scalded
> ⅔ cup melted butter or margarine
> ¾ cup sugar
> 4 teaspoons salt
> 2 beaten eggs
> 10 to 11 cups sifted enriched flour

Soften active dry yeast in warm water (110° F.) or compressed yeast in lukewarm water (85° F.); add 1 teaspoon sugar to yeast mixture. Add milk, cooled to lukewarm; margarine or butter melted; sugar; and salt. Add eggs; beat well. Add flour to make soft dough, let stand 10 minutes covered; knead on lightly floured surface till smooth and elastic. Place in greased bowl, turning once to grease surface, and cover; store in refrigerator. Dough will keep for 5 or 6 days.

The upward trail leads, aided by the Shepherd, beside still waters, through death valley, in green pastures, by the enemy, but forever into the house of the Lord (Neil Wiseman).

Pecan rolls
> 1½ cups brown sugar
> 2 tablespoons light corn syrup
> ½ cup and 4 tablespoons butter or margarine
> chopped or halved pecans
> 1 teaspoon cinnamon

Combine 1 cup brown sugar, light corn syrup, 4 tablespoons butter or margarine, heat slowly till mixture has a glazed look. Prepare deep muffin tins by greasing well and placing chopped or pecan halves in bottom of each tin. Add 2 or 3 teaspoons of above sugar glaze to each tin also. Now pinch off enough dough to roll rectangle 16 x 8 inches and roll ¼ inch thick on lightly floured board. Melt ½ cup butter or margarine. Brush onto rectangle. Sprinkle with ½ cup brown sugar and cinnamon. Roll as for jelly roll, seal edge, cut in 1-inch slices, place in prepared muffin tins, cover, let rise till double in bulk. Bake (350°-375° F.) for 20-25 minutes. Remove from pan immediately, cool, bottom side up. Serve warm.

MRS. BLAINE (JULIA) PROFFITT
Lincoln, Nebraska

Hot Rolls

> 1 cup shortening
> ¾ cup sugar
> 1 cup boiling water

Cream shortening, sugar, then pour boiling water over it. Let cool.

Dissolve:
2 packages yeast in 1 cup warm water

Add to first mixture
2 eggs, well beaten
2 teaspoons salt
6 cups flour sifted

Form 2 or 3 balls of dough to fill greased muffin pans half full. Or form in rolls using 1 large ball of dough. Let rise till double in bulk, about 2 hours. Bake in hot oven at 425° F. for 15 minutes. Dough will keep for 10 days in the refrigerator. Punch down daily.

MRS. JACOB W. (HELEN) BLANKENSHIP
Houston, Texas

Gramma Reed's Cinnamon Rolls

Soften

2 packages yeast
1 cup warm water
1 tablespoon sugar

Let this set for at least 15 minutes.

Add

1½ cups water
3 cups flour
½ cup sugar
2 teaspoons salt (let rise 1 hour)

Add

⅔ cup chicken fat
2 cups flour or more until dough can be easily handled

I won't quarrel with my bread and butter (Jonathan Swift).

Let rise 1 hour. Roll out dough, liberally spread with butter, sugar, brown sugar and cinnamon. Roll up and slice into rolls and put in buttered 9 x 13" pan. Let rise 1 hour and bake for 30 minutes at 350° F.

"Chicken fat is what makes this recipe unique. Sometimes you can buy chicken fat in the store. Or when you purchase chicken, notice chunks of fat usually in the cavity of the chicken. Put the fat with ½ cup of water and simmer for 30 minutes. Refrigerate and the golden fat will surface. This is what you use in the rolls. These rolls must not be hurried!"

MRS. GEORGE (MARTHA REED) GARVIN, JR.
River Forest, Illinois

Feather Bed Rolls

1 cup shortening or margarine
¾ cup white sugar
1 teaspoon salt
1 cup boiling water
2 eggs
2 small cakes yeast
1 cup ice water
7 cups flour

Cream together shortening, sugar, and salt. Add boiling water and let cool a few minutes. Dissolve yeast in the cup of very cold water (let stand a few minutes and it will dissolve). Add eggs and blend into first mixture. Blend in yeast water. Add and blend in the flour. Let rise to double in bulk. Roll on floured surface to make rolls. Place on greased sheet. Let rise again. Bake approximately 15 minutes in 400° F. oven. Makes about 48 good size crescent rolls. One-half of this recipe is plenty for family of six.

"This was Mrs. S. T. Ludwig's recipe. A great favorite."

MRS. GORDON (ALICE JEAN) WETMORE
Kansas City, Missouri

Perfect Sunday Dinner Rolls

1 package dry yeast, dissolved in ¼ cup of warm water
½ cup sugar
2 eggs
1 cup warm water
½ cup oil
1 teaspoon salt
4 cups flour

Add sugar to yeast and water. Beat eggs in warm water and add oil and salt. Add to the yeast and sugar mixture. Gradually add flour. This dough is rather sticky and will raise at least twice its size, so use large bowl (it is not necessary to knead the dough). Let stand overnight and make out in morning by dividing the dough into about 4 parts. Be sure to use flour on the board or wax paper. Cut like a pizza and roll large end to small end and place on greased pans. Let stand until you get home from church then pop into the oven for 8 minutes at 375° F.

"They will melt in your mouth and you just cannot fail."

MRS. JAMES (ELIZABETH) SOUTHWORTH
Austin, Texas

Sunday Dinner Rolls

2 eggs
⅔ cup sugar
1 package yeast
1 cup warm water
½ cup cooking oil
¼ cup powdered milk
4 cups of flour (approximately)
1 teaspoon salt

Combine all ingredients except flour in large bowl and beat well with electric mixer. Add flour and salt and beat by hand until well mixed, this will be a sticky dough. Let stand overnight. Sunday morning before church, roll out in 2 large circles, using flour as needed. Cut pie shaped and roll. Place on greased cookie sheet. Let rise until after church. Bake 375° F. oven for 12 to 15 minutes.

"Easy, excellent homemade rolls that even a beginner can excel in making."

MRS. KENNETH (CARRIE) DODD
Newport, Oregon

When we talk about the God who made all things, we are using the language of faith (T. E. Martin).

No-Fail Yeast Rolls

1 cup milk
½ cup shortening
1 cake compressed yeast
½ cup sugar
3 eggs, beaten slightly
2 teaspoons salt
5 cups flour

Scald cup of milk and shortening. Dissolve yeast in ½ cup lukewarm water. When milk and shortening are cooled to lukewarm, add to dissolved yeast. Add sugar and salt and stir thoroughly. Add beaten eggs. Then add sifted flour to above mixture and thoroughly beat. Grease bowl to let yeast raise. Pat down yeast mixture and rub top with shortening. Cover and let raise until double. Press down yeast and divide into 3 balls. Roll each ball into pie shape and cut into 12 wedges. Roll into crescent shape. Let rise. Bake at 375° F. for 12 minutes.

"These rolls are delicious for Sunday dinner. The yeast can be made up Saturday evening and left to rise. Sunday morning before church they can be cut into rolls."

MRS. JOHN (DORIS) DICKEY
Birmingham, Michigan

Dilly Bread

    2 packages yeast
    ½ cup warm water
    2 cups lukewarm cottage cheese
    4 tablespoons sugar
    2 tablespoons minced onion
    2 tablespoons butter
    4 teaspoons dill seed
    2 unbeaten eggs
    2 teaspoons salt
    ½ teaspoon soda

Soften yeast in warm water. Mix all ingredients together with yeast. Add 4½ to 5 cups flour. Cover and let rise till double (1 hour). Stir down and place in two pans. Let rise 30-40 minutes. Bake at 350° F. for 30 minutes.

MRS. DENNIS (ELSIE) KINLAW
Wilmore, Kentucky

Dilly Casserole Bread

    1 package dry yeast
    1 cup creamed cottage cheese, heated to lukewarm
    2 tablespoons sugar
    1 tablespoon butter
    1 teaspoon salt
    1 unbeaten egg
    ¼ cup warm water
    1 tablespoon instant minced onion
    2 teaspoons dill seed
    2¼ to 2½ cups flour
    ¼ teaspoon soda

Soften yeast in water. Combine in mixing bowl: warm cottage cheese, sugar, onion, butter, dill seed, salt, soda, egg, and softened yeast. Add flour to form stiff dough, beating well after each addition. Cover; let rise in warm place (85-90° F.) until light and doubled in size (50-60 minutes). Stir down dough. Turn into well-greased 8" round (1½ to 2 quart) casserole. Let rise 30-40 minutes. Bake in 350° F. oven for 40-50 minutes. Brush hot bread with soft butter and sprinkle with salt. Makes a round loaf.

MRS. HERB (MIRIAM) HALL
Olathe, Kansas

Oleo Rolls

2 sticks oleo
½ teaspoon salt
¼ cup sugar (approximate)
2 eggs, beaten
1 package dry yeast
1 cup heated milk
4 cups flour

Melt oleo in small pan. In bowl beat eggs, add salt, sugar, milk, oleo, and yeast dissolved in warm water (about ¼ cup). Add flour 1 cup at a time until you can handle it with your hand. Store in the same bowl. Cover with Handi-Wrap and towel. Keep in refrigerator overnight before using. Cut 4 sections in bowl. Take out one section and roll out thin (pizza size) on floured board. Cut eight ways. Roll up pie wedges for crescent rolls. Let rolls rise on cookie sheet 4 hours. The bottom will brown first. Heat oven 400° F., cook 10-12 minutes.

MRS. JAMES (LOUISE) COOK
Seymour, Indiana

We belong to God by the
"branding" of the Spirit
(H. T. Reza).

Spoon Rolls

1 package dry yeast
2 cups lukewarm water
4 cups self-rising flour
¼ cup sugar
1 egg
¾ cup melted shortening (or oil)

Dissolve yeast in water, mix together in a large bowl with all other ingredients. Store covered in refrigerator and use as desired, keeps several days. To cook, spoon batter into well greased muffin tins and bake immediately at 425° F. for 20 minutes; you do not have to wait for mix to rise, it can be used at once.

MRS. JAMES R. (MARY) STAGGS
Allardt, Tennessee

Cranberry Muffins

¾ cup cranberries
¾ cup powdered sugar
2 cups flour
3 teaspoons baking powder
1 teaspoon salt
¼ cup sugar
1 egg, well beaten
1 cup milk
4 tablespoons shortening, melted

Mix cranberries with powdered sugar and let stand while preparing the muffin mixture. Sift dry ingredients. Add egg, milk, and melted shortening all at once. Mix only until dry ingredients are moistened. Fold in sugared cranberries. Fill greased muffin tins to ⅔ full. Bake in moderate oven, 350° F. for 20 minutes. Makes 12 muffins.

"My family enjoys these for a holiday or Sunday morning breakfast."

MRS. ROBERT (EVA) SHEPPARD
Anchorage, Alaska

We have redemption through his blood, even the forgiveness of sins (Col. 1:14).

Bran Muffins

½ cup white sugar
1 cup shortening
5 teaspoons soda
1 teaspoon salt
4 cups Kellogg's All-Bran
2 cups Nabisco 100% Bran
2 cups boiling water
4 eggs, beaten
5 cups flour, sifted
1 quart buttermilk

There is no solution to the world's ills through military power or political strategy. May we never let up in proclaiming Jesus Christ, God's Gift to a troubled, sinful, warring world! (M. A. [Bud] Lunn).

Pour boiling water over 100% bran. Let stand. Cream shortening and sugar. Add beaten eggs and buttermulk. Add All-Bran. Let stand while you sift flour, soda, and salt and add to All-bran mixture. Fold in cooled 100% bran. Bake at 375° F. for 15 to 18 minutes. The dough will keep in the refrigerator for 6 weeks. When you want to make muffins take out just the amount needed and do not stir mixture, but spoon into muffin tins and bake.

"Very moist and delicious!"

MRS. ROSS E. (IRENE) PRICE
Colorado Springs, Colorado

Bran Flakes Muffins

1½ cups Kellogg's 40 Percent Bran Flakes
⅔ cup milk
1 egg
¼ cup soft shortening
1 cup sifted flour
2½ teaspoons baking powder
½ teaspoon salt
¼ cup sugar

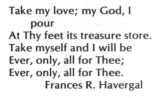

Combine bran flakes, milk, egg, and shortening; beat well. Sift together flour, baking powder, salt, and sugar. Add to first mixture, stirring only until combined. Fill greased muffin pans ⅔ full. Bake in moderately hot oven (400° F.) about 30 minutes. Makes 10 muffins, about 2½ inches in diameter.

"May add fresh blueberries to mixture. Very easy . . . very mmmmmmm!"

MRS. JAMES C. (EVELYN) HESTER
Carthage, Missouri

Six Weeks Bran Muffins

1 heaping cup soft shortening
3 cups sugar
4 eggs
5 cups flour
5 teaspoons soda
1 teaspoon salt
4 cups Kellogg's All-Bran
1 quart buttermilk
2 cups Nabisco 100% Bran
2 cups boiling water

Add 100% Bran to boiling water; let stand. Mix shortening, sugar, eggs, flour, soda, and buttermilk. Add 100% Bran mixture. Fold in All-Bran and salt. Bake muffins 15 minutes at 400° F. This batter is much better to let stand in refrigerator a few days before using. It will keep for several weeks—just dip out and use what you want.

If desired, add frozen blueberries, seedless raisins, white raisins, in the batter at the time of baking. Will keep 6 weeks in refrigerator.

MRS. LEWIS (ERMA) CURTISS
West Chester, Ohio

Carrot Muffins

4 eggs
2 cups sugar (brown or white)
1¼ cups cooking oil
2 cups grated carrot
1 cup raisins
½ cup chopped nuts
2½ cups flour
1 teaspoon soda
3 teaspoons baking powder
½ teaspoon salt

Mix in order given. Cook in muffin tins at 375°-400° F., for 15 minutes, or longer if needed.

MRS. BOB (ELMYRA) RIMINGTON
Calgary, Alberta, Canada

Maine Blueberry Muffins

⅓ cup shortening
1 cup sugar
1 egg
¼ teaspoon salt
⅔ cup milk
1⅔ cups flour
1¾ teaspoons baking powder
1 teaspoon vanilla
1 cup blueberries (fresh or frozen)

Cream shortening and sugar. Add beaten egg, salt, and milk. Add dry ingredients and vanilla. Fold in blueberries. Bake at 350° F. for 18-20 minutes. Makes 12 large muffins.

"Have served these many times!"

MRS. JACK (JOYCE) SHANKEL
Augusta, Maine

Special Desserts

The joy that the Lord gives is marvelous. It springs up in sorrow and in trouble like a palm tree springing up in a desert (Selected).

Butterscotch Torte

First layer
1 cup flour
1 stick margarine, softened
1 cup chopped pecans

Mix together and press in bottom of 11 x 13" pan. Bake for 15 minutes at 325° F. Cool.

Second layer
1 cup powdered sugar
1 8-ounce package cream cheese, softened
1 4½ ounce Cool Whip

Mix well and spread on cooled first layer.

Third layer
2 small packages instant butterscotch pudding
3 cups milk

Mix together and spread on second layer.

Fourth layer
1 large Cool Whip

Put Cool Whip on third layer. Also, sprinkle chopped pecans on top of Cool Whip (usually 1 cup, more or less, as desired). Chill for several hours or overnight.

Mrs. James W. (Jean) Daniel
Henryetta, Oklahoma

Chocolate Torte

1 cup flour
1 stick margarine
¾ cup walnuts
1 cup Cool Whip
1 cup confectioners' sugar
1 8-ounce package cream cheese
3 small packages instant chocolate pudding
4½ cups milk

Mix flour, margarine, and walnuts and press in 9 x 13" pan. Bake at 350° F. for 12-15 minutes. Cool. Mix: 1 cup Cool Whip, confectioners' sugar, and cream cheese. Spread over crust. Mix pudding with 4½ cups milk. Pour over cream cheese layer. Top with Cool Whip, sprinkle with chocolate or nuts.

MRS. MALCOLM (MARY) DELBRIDGE
Lansing, Michigan

In the cross of Christ I glory,
Tow'ring o'er the wrecks
of time.
All the light of sacred story
Gathers round its head
sublime.
John Bowring

Caramel Dumpling

1 cup flour
2 teaspoons baking powder
1 tablespoon sugar
¼ teaspoon salt
½ cup milk
1 teaspoon vanilla
½ cup nuts

Mix ingredients until well blended. Drop by teaspoon into boiling sauce. Sauce: ¾ cup white sugar, ¾ cup brown sugar, 1½ cups of water. Put in pan with lid, turn on low flame for 15 or 20 minutes depending on size of dumplings. Don't lift lid until first 15 minutes has elapsed. Serve with whipped topping.

MRS. DARREL L. (OLETHA) SLACK
Billings, Montana

When the fulness of the time was come, God sent forth his Son, made of a woman (Gal. 4:4).

Cherry Dream Delight

6 egg whites
¾ teaspoon cream of tartar
2 cups sugar
¾ cup finely chopped nuts
2 cups crushed Hi-Ho crackers
Dream Whip
can of cherry pie filling

Beat 6 egg whites with ¾ teaspoon cream of tartar until foamy. Continue beating, gradually adding sugar. Beat until stiff and glossy. Add nuts and crackers. Bake in 9 x 13" pan for 25 minutes at 350° F. When cool, top with Dream Whip (mixed according to directions on package). Top this with a can of cherry pie filling. Makes 16 servings.

Mrs. Perry (Mary) Winkle
Lewiston, Idaho

Strawberry Blitz Torte

1 cup sifted cake flour
1 teaspoon baking powder
¼ teaspoon salt
½ cup shortening
½ cup sugar
4 egg yolks
3 tablespoons milk
1 teaspoon pure vanilla extract

Meringue
4 egg whites
½ teaspoon salt
¼ teaspoon cream of tartar
1 cup sugar
½ teaspoon pure vanilla

Filling and topping
1 cup cream, whipped
4 tablespoons confectioners' sugar
2 cups sliced strawberries
8 strawberries for garnish

With electric mixer, cream shortening and sugar until creamy. Add beaten egg yolks and stir in milk and vanilla. Add sifted dry ingredients at low speed and beat until smooth. Pour into 2 greased 8-inch pans. Lightly pile half of the meringue mixture over batter in each pan, spread evenly. Bake until meringue is pale gold, about 35 minutes at 350° F. Remove from pans, keeping meringue side up. Add filling and topping.

Meringue: Beat egg whites, salt, and cream of tartar until they stand in soft peaks. Add sugar, 2 tablespoons at a time, beating thoroughly. Add vanilla. Filling: Combine whipped cream and confectioners' sugar. Fold in sliced strawberries. Spread half between layers (meringue side up) and use remaining as topping. Decorate with whole berries. Refrigerate.

Mrs. Don (Jean) Small
Bloomington, Indiana

Chocolate Cream Cheese Torte

1 stick butter or margarine
1 cup flour
½ cup chopped nuts
1 cup Cool Whip
1 8-ounce package cream cheese
1 cup powdered sugar
2 packages instant chocolate pudding mix
3 cups cold milk
1 tablespoon vanilla
1 cup Cool Whip

Blend butter, flour, and chopped nuts. Press into 9 x 13" pan. Bake 15 minutes at 350° F. Cool thoroughly. Mix together the Cool Whip, cream cheese, and powdered sugar. Whip until thoroughly blended. Spread on crust and chill. Mix together the 2 packages instant pudding mix and the cold milk and vanilla. Whip until thick. Spread on cream cheese layer. Chill. Cover chocolate layer with Cool Whip and sprinkle additional chopped nuts. Keep refrigerated until eaten.

"This is so good! Butterscotch pudding is great and lemon is refreshing as substitutes for the chocolate."

Mrs. B. J. (Berl) Garber
Carthage, Missouri

Chocolate Special

1 cup flour
1 cube margarine, melted (let cool)
1 cup chopped nuts

First layer
1 cup powdered sugar
1 teaspoon vanilla
1 cup Cool Whip (purchase medium size and use balance for frosting)
1 large package cream cheese

Second layer
2 small packages instant chocolate pudding
3 cups milk
1 teaspoon vanilla

Third layer
Frost with remaining Cool Whip, grate Hershey bar and sprinkle on top

First 3 ingredients mix like crust. Pat in pan. Bake at 350° F. for 25 minutes. First layer, mix and pour over crust, second layer mix and pour over first layer, third layer, see above.

MRS. REESE (ELLEN) VERNER
Scottsdale, Arizona

Instant Dessert

Crust
½ cup margarine
½ cup nuts, chopped
1 cup flour

Mix and put in a 9 x 13" pan, bake at 350° F. for 15 minutes.

Cream
1 8-ounce package cream cheese
1 cup powdered sugar
⅔ carton Cool Whip (13-ounce size)

Spread cream on cool crust. Prepare one large package instant chocolate pudding and spread over above. Spread remaining Cool Whip on top and sprinkle with chopped nuts.

MRS. L. A. (DIXIE) SUITER
Roseburg, Oregon

Oh, to be like Thee! blessed
    Redeemer,
  This is my constant
      longing and prayer.
Gladly I'll forfeit all of
      earth's treasures,
  Jesus, Thy perfect likeness
      to wear.
    Thomas O. Chisholm

Lemon Dessert

½ cup chopped nuts
1 cup flour
1 cube butter or margarine
1 cup and 2 tablespoons powdered sugar
1 8-ounce package cream cheese
1 9-ounce container Cool Whip
2 small packages instant lemon pudding
3 cups cold milk

Cream all together chopped nuts, flour, butter, 2 tablespoons powdered sugar; press into a 9 x 13-inch pan. Bake at 373° F. for 15 minutes. Cream together: cream cheese, 1 cup powdered sugar, and 1 cup Cool Whip. Spread this over cooled crust. Mix instant pudding and milk. Beat until it begins to thicken, then spread over cheese mixture. Spread remaining Cool Whip over pudding mixture and sprinkle with chopped nuts.

MRS. GENE (PATRICIA) ANSPACH
Coos Bay, Oregon

Pistachio Pudding Cake

Crust
1⅓ cups flour
  1 stick margarine
⅓ cup chopped pecans or walnuts

Filling
  2 packages instant pistachio pudding
  3 cups milk
  2 cups confectioners' sugar
  1 8-ounce package cream cheese, softened
  large size Cool Whip

Crust: work margarine into flour well, add pecans, and pat into a 9 x 13" cake pan or glass Pyrex pan. Bake at 350° F. for 15-20 minutes. Set aside to cool 15-20 minutes. Filling: mix instant pudding with milk. Mix cream cheese and confectioners' sugar with electric mixer. Blend in very large bowl, Cool Whip and instant pudding (not with electric mixer unless very low speed). Pour filling on crust. Chill. May sprinkle finely chopped nuts on top.

"For more crust and larger pan, you may increase the crust recipe to: 2 cups flour, 1½ stick margarine and 1 cup pecans. Filling will still be enough. Delicious!"

MRS. WILLIAM G. (KATHRYN) HILL
Circleville, Ohio

Pistachio Dessert

  1 small box (one layer size) yellow cake mix
½ cup ground nuts
  1 3-ounce package instant pistachio pudding mix
  8 ounces cream cheese
  2 cups milk
  1 large can crushed pineapple, drained
  9 ounces Cool Whip
½ cup nuts
½ cup coconut

Make boxed cake mix according to directions, add ground nuts to batter. Bake in 9 x 13" pan at 350° F. for 10 minutes. Cool. Beat cream cheese until soft; add milk gradually; then add pudding mix. Spread mixture on top of cooled cake. Cover top of pudding with drained crushed pineapple. Spread Cool Whip over top and garnish with nuts and coconut.

MRS. L. THOMAS (LOIS) SKIDMORE
Medina, Ohio

Pineapple Ice Box Cake

½ pound butter
1½ cups sugar
4 eggs
1 package lemon gelatin
1 No. 2 can crushed pineapple
1 cup chopped nuts
1 pound vanilla wafers
whipped cream

Drain pineapple. Heat ½ cup pineapple juice and pour over gelatin and let dissolve. Cream butter and sugar. Add beaten egg yolks; beat well; add cooled pineapple-gelatin mixture, nuts, and pineapple. Fold in egg whites. Line oblong pan with butter. Put ½ pound of crushed wafers on bottom of pan. Pour mixture on top. Top with remaining wafers. Refrigerate. Serve with whipped cream and top each serving with a cherry. Makes 8 servings.

"Easy as pie!"

MRS. CHARLES (MARJORIE) BLAKE
Wyckoff, New Jersey

Choco-Cherry Pecan Dessert

1½ cups vanilla wafer crumbs
¾ cup butter or margarine, softened
1¾ cups sifted confectioners' sugar
2 eggs
½ teaspoon favorite flavoring
2 tablespoons cocoa
1 cup heavy cream
1 cup chopped pecans
¼ cup sliced maraschino cherries

Each one of us is a part of His kingdom. Wherever we are, whatever our task, whatever our burden, we are not in competition. We are workers together with Him. What joy! (Carolyn Lunn).

Combine crumbs with ¼ cup butter; mix well. Reserve 2 tablespoons; press remainder onto bottom of a 9-inch square baking dish. Chill. Cream remaining ½ cup butter with 1½ cups confectioners' sugar. Add eggs one at a time, beating two minutes after each addition. Add flavoring. Spread mixture over crumb base. Combine remaining ¼ cup confectioners' sugar, cocoa, heavy cream. Whip until stiff. Fold in pecans and cherries. Spread over filling mixture. Sprinkle with reserved crumbs. Chill 24 hours, or may be frozen.

"This was printed on the vanilla wafer box several years ago."

MRS. RALPH E. (DELORES) FOX
Indianapolis, Indiana

Cherry Pretzel Delight

1 bag small pretzels
1¼ sticks of butter or margarine
3 tablespoons sugar
1 12-ounce package cream cheese
1 cup 10-x sugar
1 can cherry filling
1 small container Cool Whip

Cream sugar and cream cheese together and add 1 small container of Cool Whip. Crush pretzels, add melted butter and sugar. Spread in buttered 9 x 15" pan. Bake 7 minutes at 375° F. Remove from oven, cool a few minutes, and spread second mixture over crust. When this is cool, spread 1 jar of cheery pie filling on top. Cut in squares. A dollop of whipped cream is nice on it. Can be prepared early and frozen, or the day before and kept covered in refrigerator.

"This is a not-too-sweet dessert. The pretzel crust tastes a bit like crushed nuts."

MRS. ROBERT (MIRIAM) WILFONG
Kennett Square, Pennsylvania

Peppermint Freeze

1½ pints whipping cream, whipped
5 teaspoons sugar
½ teaspoon vanilla (or to taste)
2 cups miniature marshmallows, white
1 cup crushed hard peppermint candy, powder fine

Prepare and mix in order given. Put in 9 x 13" Tupperware container or Pyrex, cover and freeze overnight. Remove from freezer ½ to 1 hour before serving. Serve in squares.

"Use as a light dessert or ladies' tea. Optional: You may make a graham cracker base for variation."

MRS. THAREN (MAXINE) EVANS
Crawfordsville, Indiana

Ice Cream Macaroon Loaf

1 dozen coconut macaroons
1 cup chopped nuts, pecans
little less than ¾ pint whipping cream
1 quart orange or lime sherbet

Toast the macaroons and nuts slightly. Whip cream, crumble macaroons and soak in whipped cream a few minutes. Add nuts, Stir. Place a layer of cream mixture in pan, a layer of sherbet, then layer of cream mixture. I like the lime sherbet best. Place in freezer section of refrigerator. Can be made the day before serving.

"Easy to make, and a refreshing dessert."

MRS. A. LEWIS (BERTHA) SHINGLER
Pasadena, California

Mint Ice Cream with Hot Fudge Sauce

Ice Cream
1½ pounds peppermint candy, crushed (Boston mint pillows)

Dissolve in
1 quart cold half-and-half
2 eggs, beaten
1 pint cream, whipped

O Thou who art the Author of every good and perfect gift to come to us, we pray for the blessing of one thing more: a grateful heart (George Herbert).

Fold together, eggs and cream. Combine mixtures, fill freezer to about ⅔ level with whole milk. Freeze. (Manual freezers are more fun.) Makes 1 gallon.

Hot Fudge Sauce:
¼ cup butter
1½ squares unsweetened chocolate

Melt together.
¼ cup dry cocoa
¾ cup granulated sugar
dash salt

Mix and blend with above.

Slowly add to chocolate mixture.

½ cup heavy cream

Bring to a boil stirring constantly. Remove from heat immediately.

Add
1 teaspoon vanilla

Serve hot

"Homemade ice cream is a popular summer pastime here in Idaho."

MRS. KENNETH (RUBY) PEARSALL
Nampa, Idaho

Those who live in the Lord never see each other for the last time (German saying).

Choco-Mint Freeze

1¼ cups (28) finely crushed vanilla wafers
4 tablespoons butter, melted
1 quart peppermint stick ice cream, softened
2 squares (2 oz.) unsweetened chocolate
3 well-beaten egg yolks
1½ cups sifted confectioners' sugar
½ cup chopped pecans
1 teaspoon vanilla
3 egg whites
¼ cup butter

Toss together crumbs and melted butter. Reserve ¼ cup crumb mixture; press into 9 x 9 x 2" baking pan. Spread with softened ice cream; freeze. Melt ¼ cup butter and chocolate over low heat; gradually stir into egg yolks with the confectioners' sugar, nuts, and vanilla. Cool. Beat egg whites till stiff and fold into chocolate mixture. Spread over ice cream; top with reserved crumb mixture; freeze. Makes 12 servings.

MRS. WALTER M. (PAULINE) HUBBARD
Sacramento, California

Neiman-Marcus Fresh Flower pots

small red clay flower pots
round of sponge cake
ice cream
meringue
drinking straws
fresh flowers

Line the bottom of individual size clay flower pots with rounds of sponge cake. Top cake with several kinds of ice cream, then pile high with meringue. Brown in a very hot oven. Poke two straws in each flower pot. Insert fresh flower stem in each straw. These look so pretty and are delicious too.

MRS. RALPH E. (DELORES) FOX
Indianapolis, Indiana

Homemade Vanilla Ice Cream

6 eggs, separated
2 cups whipping cream
1 can Eagle Brand milk
2½ cups sugar
2 tablespoons vanilla
whole milk

Beat egg yolks with mixer for at least 5 minutes. Add sugar and Eagle Brand milk and continue beating until well blended. In a separate bowl, beat egg whites until they stand in peaks. In a separate bowl, whip cream. Add the whipped cream and the egg whites to the sugar mixture. Add vanilla and enough whole milk to fill a 6-quart freezer.

"Because I am a working housewife and because we love to entertain, we make homemade ice cream as a special treat for our guests—there's not much fussing on my part!"

Mrs. Jack (Lee) Eigsti
Lincoln, Nebraska

Fruit Ice Cream

juice of 3 oranges
juice of 3 lemons
3 bananas
1 small (flat) can of crushed pineapple
3 cups sugar
½ pint whipping cream
milk

Mix orange and lemon juice with bananas in blender. Add pineapple, sugar, and whipped cream. Put in 4-quart ice-cream freezer. Fill with milk to freezing level.

Mrs. Curtis (Marge) Smith
Olathe, Kansas

They that trust in their wealth . . . none of them can by any means redeem his brother (Ps. 49:6-7).

Lime Ice Cream

2 3-ounce packages lime gelatin
3 cups sugar
2 lemons
3 quarts milk

Dissolve the gelatin in 2 cups boiling water. Add sugar, lemon juice, and grated lemon rinds. Add 2 quarts of milk and chill. When ready to freeze, pour into ice-cream freezer can and fill up with rest of milk. Makes one gallon.

"This is one of our family's favorite homemade ice cream recipes. It has a real smooth taste and is delicious looking."

Mrs. B. J. (Berl) Garber
Carthage, Missouri

It may be possible to be a Christian without any overt acts of love (what a meager existence!), but if we are to wear the mark of a Christian, we must give evidence of it by our love to all men— friends, neighbors, enemies, but especially those "who are of the household of faith" (Galen D. Wilcox).

Ice Cream Balls

vanilla ice cream
1 cup graham cracker crumbs
2 tablespoons white sugar
½ teaspoon cinnamon
¼ cup crunchy peanut butter

Sauce
2 cups brown sugar
⅓ cup white Karo syrup
½ cup evaporated milk
⅓ cup margarine

Shape ice cream into balls and place in freezer. Mix together other ingredients. Roll balls into mixture and freeze. Boil sauce ingredients together for 20 minutes. Serve over ice cream (can use Hershey's chocolate sauce also).

MRS. JAMES (SHARON) MONCK
Racine, Wisconsin

Ice Cream Balls

1 cup graham cracker crumbs
¼ cup chunky peanut butter
2 tablespoons sugar
1 quart vanilla ice cream
chocolate flavored syrup (or maple)
whipped cream
maraschino cherries

Blend graham cracker crumbs, peanut butter, and sugar. Scoop ice cream into large balls (or desired serving size). Roll in crumb mixture until well coated. Freeze until serving time. Top with syrup, whipped cream, and cherries.

MRS. DONALD (JOYCE) ESTEP
Paden City, West Virginia

Fresh Peach Ice Cream

5 large eggs, well beaten
2½ cups sugar
½ pint whipping cream
1 small can evaporated milk
6-8 fresh ripe peaches (sweeten to taste)
homogenized milk

Prepare peaches in a blender until very smooth. Sweeten to taste and set aside. Beat whole eggs in an electric mixer. Add sugar and continue to beat. Add whipping cream and evaporated milk. Blend peaches with the above mixture and pour into a gallon ice-cream freezer. Pour in enough homogenized milk to fill container. Use plenty of ice and ice cream salt to freeze.

MRS. WILLIAM (BETTY) SLONECKER
Nashville, Tennessee

Fabrin's Peach Ice Cream

5 cups mashed fresh peaches (substitute mashed berries,
*   or 2 cups peanut butter)*
1 lemon
2 cups sugar
4 eggs, separated
pinch of salt
1 quart milk
1 pint whipping cream
2 teaspoons vanilla

Prepare the fresh peaches, cover with lemon juice and 1 cup of the sugar. Mash and then set aside. Beat egg whites with a pinch of salt until stiff. Add ½ cup sugar and continue to beat until mixture resembles a meringue. Set aside. Beat the egg yolks well, add ½ cup sugar and continue to beat until lighter in color. Now add the milk, cream, and peach mixture to the egg yolks. Then fold in egg whites, add vanilla. Taste, flavor, and color until it suits you. Freeze in a 1-gallon freezer, being sure to use plenty of rock salt. Pack and let sit 1 to 2 hours before serving.

Action, not speech, proves the man (Selected).

The best use of life is to use it for something that outlasts it (Selected).

MRS. JOHN (JOYCE) FABRIN
Selma, California

Orange-Pineapple Sherbet

2 cans Eagle Brand condensed milk
1 1-pound can crushed pineapple, in own juice
2 quarts Orange Crush soda (or 6 regular size bottles)

Combine milk and pineapple and pour into freezer can. Finish filling can with soda. Freeze as usual. Makes 4 quarts. For larger quantity, add more soda.

MRS. ED (KITTY) BAKER
Pittsburgh, Pennsylvania

Ice Cream Dessert

2 cups crushed Ritz crackers (2 stacks)
1 stick margarine
2 boxes instant pudding (any flavor)
4 cups ice cream (vanilla or other flavor to compliment pudding)
2 cups milk
1 medium container Cool Whip

Mix crushed crackers with melted margarine. Press into 9 x 13" pan to make a crust. Mix instant pudding with milk. Beat on low speed until stiff. Add ice cream to pudding. Mix smooth. Pour over crust. Cover with Cool Whip. Garnish with cherries or nuts. Refrigerate overnight.

MRS. JACK (DARYL) CHRISTNER
Bradford, Pennsylvania

Peach-a-Berry Cobbler

Filling
1 tablespoon cornstarch
¼ cup brown sugar
½ cup peach juice
2 cups sliced peaches (large tin)
1 cup fresh mulberries (blueberries or other may be used)
1 tablespoon margarine
1 tablespoon lemon juice

Cobbler crust
1 cup sifted flour
½ cup granulated sugar
1½ teaspoons baking powder
½ teaspoon salt
½ cup milk
¼ cup soft butter or margarine
1 recipe Nutmeg Topper

Mix first three ingredients; add fruits. Cook and stir until mixture thickens. Add margarine and lemon juice. Pour into 8¼ x 1¾-inch round baking dish. Cobbler crust: Sift together dry ingredients. Add milk and butter all at once; beat smooth. Spread over fruit. Sprinkle with Nutmeg Topping:

Nutmeg Topping
Mix 2 tablespoons sugar with ¼ teaspoon nutmeg. Bake cobbler in moderate oven (350° F.) 30 minutes or till done. Makes 6 servings.

MRS. T. P. (JOAN) ESSELSTYN
Republic of South Africa

Quick Peach Cobbler

1 cup plain flour
1½ cups sugar
1½ teaspoons baking powder
½ teaspoon salt
1 cup milk
1 stick margarine or butter
1 large can peaches

Mix as you add ingredients. Blend with fork. Melt stick of margarine and pour on top of mixture. Add sliced peaches and juice to mixture. Sprinkle brown sugar and cinnamon on top. Bake 35-45 minutes at 350° F.

"This is a Sunday favorite! I mix this together as we sit down for dinner. By dessert time it is ready to take from oven and top with ice cream or whipped topping."

MRS. BILL (BARBARA) TATE
Charlotte, North Carolina

Pavlova

6 egg whites
1 teaspoon white vinegar
¾ cup sugar
1 teaspoon vanilla
½ pint whipped cream
crushed pineapple
strawberry ice cream, slightly softened

Beat egg whites and vinegar until frothy. Gradually beat in sugar until glossy and stiff. Add vanilla. Cut a 9-inch round of brown or waxed paper and dampen with water. Place on cookie sheet. Put egg mixture on paper and pull it up slightly at the edges, giving it a "pie plate" effect. Bake 1 hour at 250° F. Meringue should be a nice, rich cream color and firm, but not hard. When cool remove paper carefully and place meringue on a large plate. Cover with whipped cream, then a layer of crushed pineapple, and finally a layer of the ice cream. Slice like a pie. It is pretty and delicious.

"I was taught to make this dessert by a dear friend in Australia when we lived there. It is perfect for company, and my children begged me to make it often. I used the leftover egg yolks in custard. A ½ teaspoon of cream of tartar or cornstarch is also used by some cooks to keep the meringue in shape. This is added to the sugar."

MRS. WALTER H. (ETHEL) SMYTH
Boynton Beach, Florida

Peach Cobbler

½ cup butter
1 cup all-purpose flour
2 teaspoons baking powder
1½ cups sugar
¾ cup milk
2-3 cups frozen peaches
½ cup water

Melt butter in baking dish. Mix flour, baking powder, 1 cup of sugar, and milk; pour into baking dish. Arrange peaches over batter. Sprinkle remaining ½ cup sugar over peaches and pour water over peaches. Bake in preheated oven for 50 minutes.

"This is a quick- and easy-to-prepare dessert. Also easy to use with other fruits. Especially delicious served hot."

MRS. BOB (MARY JO) KETCHUM
Shawnee, Oklahoma

Apple Kuchen

Dough
¼ teaspoon nutmeg
¼ cup shortening
2 eggs, beaten
½ cup milk
¾ teaspoon salt
1½ cups sifted flour
½ cup cornmeal
1½ teaspoons baking powder
¾ cup sugar

Topping
16 to 20 raw apple slices, peeled
2 to 3 tablespoons melted butter
½ cup sugar
½ teaspoon cinnamon

For dough, sift together dry ingredients. Cut in shortening until mixture resembles coarse crumbs. Add eggs and milk; stir until dry ingredients are moistened. Pour into greased 8-inch square baking pan. (For thinner cake use slightly larger pan.) For topping, dip apple slices in melted butter. Combine sugar and cinnamon. Dip apple slices in some of this mixture. Arrange apples in rows over dough, sprinkle remaining sugar mixture on top. Bake at 400° F. for 35 to 40 minutes. Top with homemade ice cream or Cool Whip. Best when served warm.

MRS. W. E. (DOROTHY) RHODES
San Antonio, Texas

Apple Walnut Cobbler

  5 medium-size tart apples
½ teaspoon cinnamon
  1 cup sifted flour
  1 cup sugar
¼ teaspoon salt
½ cup evaporated milk
½ cup sugar
½ cup black walnuts, chopped
  1 teaspoon baking powder
  1 egg, beaten
⅓ cup melted butter or margarine

Peel apples and slice thinly into greased baking dish. Combine ½ cup sugar with cinnamon and sprinkle over apples. Sift together flour, 1 cup sugar, baking powder, and salt, and set aside. Combine egg, milk, and butter. Add sifted dry ingredients all at once and beat until smooth. Pour batter over apples, sprinkle nuts over the top. Bake 50 minutes at 325° F. Serve warm with ice cream or cream.

MRS. JOHN W. (CELIA) MAY
Mount Sterling, Kentucky

Fruit Pizza

  1 package (1 pound, 2 ounce) refrigerated sugar cookie
      dough
  1 8-ounce package cream cheese
⅓ cup sugar
½ teaspoon vanilla
banana slices
orange sections
green grape halves
strawberry halves
blueberries
¼ cup orange marmalade
peach or apricot preserves
  1 tablespoon water

Cut dough into ⅛-inch slices. Line 14-inch pizza pan with slices, overlapping slightly. Bake at 375° F., 12 minutes. Cool. Blend softened cream cheese, sugar, and vanilla. Spread over cookie crust. Arrange fruit over cream cheese layer (use any combination of fresh or drained canned fruit). Glaze with marmalade or preserves mixed with water. Chill.

MRS. DUANE (EVELYN) LANDRETH
Indianapolis, Indiana

One of my favorite bumper stickers is "Christians are not perfect—just forgiven." It lacks a little in theology but it carries a powerful message. Our primary uniqueness is the redemptive grace of God—for which we "offer to God a sacrifice of praise" and become committed to "share with others" (Chester O. Galloway).

Fruit Pizza

    1 package sugar cookie dough
    1 8-ounce package cream cheese
    ⅓ cup sugar
    ½ teaspoon vanilla
    ¼ cup fruit preserves (orange, peach, or apricot)
    2 tablespoons water
    strawberries, mandarin oranges, or pineapple

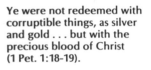

Oil 12-inch pizza pan. Cut dough in ⅛ inch slices. Place overlapping for the crust. Bake at 375° F. for 12 minutes. Cool. Blend cheese, vanilla, and sugar, and pour over the crust. Add fruit of your choice in a circular pattern. Make a glaze out of preserves and water and put over fruit. Dip banana slices in lemon to garnish. Serve chilled.

MRS. CURTIS (MARGE) SMITH
Olathe, Kansas

Ye were not redeemed with corruptible things, as silver and gold . . . but with the precious blood of Christ (1 Pet. 1:18-19).

Apple Pizza

    2½ cups flour
    1 teaspoon sugar
    1 teaspoon salt
    1 cup shortening
    ⅔ cup water, mixed with
    1 egg yolk
    2 or 3 handfuls corn flakes
    8 or 10 pie apples, sliced
    1¼ cups white sugar, with
    1½ teaspoons cinnamon

Cut shortening into flour, sugar, salt. Add water and egg yolk mixed together. Put half of dough into cooky sheet with sides. Sprinkle corn flakes on dough. Add apples, sugar. Roll out rest of dough, cover top. Beat egg white slightly, spread on top. Bake at 350° F. for 40-50 minutes. After baking, sprinkle with powdered sugar frosting: 1 teaspoon butter or margarine, 2 tablespoons milk. Heat until butter melts. Add powdered sugar until consistency is right to spread easily, also add 1 teaspoon vanilla. Makes 16 or so servings.

MRS. GRADY (DOROTHY) CANTRELL
Walnut Creek, California

Best Cottage Pudding

Cake
- 1 egg
- ½ cup sugar
- ½ cup milk
- 1 cup flour
- 2 teaspoons baking powder
- 3 tablespoons butter (melt in pan)

Topping
- 1 cup sugar
- 2 tablespoons flour
- 1 cup boiling water
- 2 tablespoons butter
- 1 teaspoon vanilla

Cake: beat egg with sugar with rotary egg beater. Add milk and flour which has been sifted with the baking powder. Beat well. Add the butter and 1 teaspoon of vanilla. Bake at 350° F. until cake springs back at touch.

Topping: combine flour and sugar, add water; boil till clear; add butter and vanilla.

MRS. G. H. (HAZEL) SAFFELL
Sheridan, Wyoming

Date Pudding

(Upside Down Cake Style)

First Step
- 1 tablespoon margarine or butter
- ¾ cup brown sugar
- ¾ cup very hot water (this dissolves other ingredients)

Second step
- ½ cup sugar
- ¾ cup flour
- 1 teaspoon baking powder (omit if using self-rising flour)
- ½ cup milk
- ½ cup chopped nuts
- ½ cup chopped dates (approximately 12)
- 1 teaspoon vanilla

Generously grease 8 x 11" baking dish. Put first mixture in and dissolve. Mix second mixture (batter) and pour in first mixture. Spread around but do not stir and mix. (Batter comes together while baking). Bake 30 minutes at 350° F. Serve warm or cold with dip of ice cream or Cool Whip.

MRS. B. (LEOTA) DOWNING
Evansville, Indiana

God blessed them, and God said unto them, Be fruitful, and multiply, and replenish the earth, and subdue it: and have dominion over the fish of the sea, and over the fowl of the air, and over every living thing that moveth upon the earth (Gen. 1: 28).

More love to Thee, O Christ,
More love to Thee!
Hear Thou the prayer I make
On bended knee.
Elizabeth Prentiss

Ah! when shall all men's good be each man's rule, and universal peace lie like a shaft of light across the land? (Tennyson).

Rhubarb Crisp

1½ pounds (5 cups) rhubarb, sliced
1 3-ounce package strawberry gelatin
⅔ cup sugar
¾ cup flour
1 stick (½ cup) margarine
¾ cup brown sugar
¾ cup rolled oats
½ teaspoon cinnamon

Combine rhubarb, gelatin, sugar, and ½ cup flour; mix well.
Turn into an 8-inch square pan. Melt margarine; mix with ½ cup
flour, brown sugar, rolled oats, cinnamon. Sprinkle over rhubarb
in pan. Bake at 375° F. for 45 minutes or till rhubarb is tender.
Serve warm, topped with a dip of ice cream. Makes 6 to 8
servings.

"I usually double the recipe and put one in the freezer."

DON CORNWELL
Mission, Kansas

Baked Peach Pudding

2 cups sliced raw peaches

Batter
¾ cup sugar
½ cup milk
4 tablespoons margarine
½ teaspoon baking powder
1 cup flour

Topping
1 cup sugar
1 tablespoon cornstarch
¼ teaspoon salt
1 cup boiling water

Batter: combine sugar and margarine. Add dry ingredients and
milk. Spread over peaches.

Topping: mix sugar, cornstarch, and salt. Sift this mixture over
batter. Pour boiling water over all and bake at 325° F. for 50 minutes in 9 x 13" pan. Serve warm with cream.

"This is a cross between cobbler and pudding. You can use
rhubarb and apples. It is so good, I double the recipe."

MRS. MELVIN (EVELYN) ABNEY
Irvine, Kentucky

Apple Pudding

    1 cup granulated sugar
    ¼ cup cooking oil
    pinch of salt
    1 egg
    1½ cups flour
    1 teaspoon soda
    1 teaspoon cinnamon
    ½ cup water
    2 cups diced apples
    nuts (optional)

Combine sugar, oil, salt, and egg. Add soda and cinnamon to the flour and add to the creamed sugar alternately with the water. Add the peeled diced apples. Bake in a greased and floured 8-inch square baking dish at 350° F. for 35 to 40 minutes.

"May be served plain or with a powdered sugar glaze icing."

MRS. ROBERT F. (DOROTHY) STYERS
Chillicothe, Ohio

Dufloppy

    1 pound vanilla wafers
    ½ cup shortening
    2 cups powdered sugar
    6 eggs
    ½ cup cocoa
    4 tablespoons boiling water
    ½ cup nutmeats
    1 teaspoon vanilla

Grind one pound of vanilla wafers and separate into three parts. Put one part in a pan and add the following mixture: shortening and 1 cup powdered sugar; cream together and add three well-beaten egg yolks, nutmeats, vanilla, and three egg whites beaten stiff. Mix well. Then add another third of the vanilla wafers in a layer.

On top of this add the following mixture: 1 cup powdered sugar, cocoa; blend the two and add boiling water, 3 beaten egg yolks, and 3 egg whites beaten stiff. Mix well. Finish with a layer of the remaining ground vanilla wafers, and put in refrigerator for 12 hours. Serve with whipped cream. No portion of this is cooked.

MRS. DARREL L. (OLETHA) SLACK
Billings, Montana

Vegetable Pudding

½ cup grated raw potato
½ cup grated raw carrots
½ cup chopped dates
½ cup sugar
¼ cup margarine
½ teaspoon soda (bicarb)
pinch salt
1 egg
little milk
2 heaping tablespoons flour

Add all ingredients in basin, mix with beaten egg and milk (not too stiff). Steam in basin for 2 hours. Serve with whipped cream.

MRS. GIDEON (JEANETTE) TREDOUX
Republic of South Africa

Creamy Rice Pudding

1½ cups cooked rice
1 cup milk
2 slightly beaten eggs
⅓ cup sugar
1 tablespoon butter or margarine
1 teaspoon vanilla

Combine first four ingredients and cook in double boiler, stirring constantly till mixture coats metal spoon. Remove from heat and add butter and vanilla. Pour into a serving bowl and let stand for 30 minutes. Serve with condiments, such as raisins, crushed pineapple, chopped dates, cream, shredded chocolate, coconut, etc.

MRS. MELVIN (LORNA) TUCKER
Victoria, British Columbia, Canada

Fruit Supreme with Ginger Ale

1 pint strawberries or 2 16-ounce packages frozen whole
    strawberries
4 large navel oranges
2 grapefruit
1 8-ounce package pitted dates, halved
2 pints lemon sherbet
ginger ale (as desired)

Peel and section grapefruit and oranges. Wash berries, drain, cut in half. (Chill fruit about 2 hours.) Pack sherbet into 1-quart mold and freeze until firm, at least 3½ hours. Select decorative bowl, unmold sherbet (loosen edges with sharp knife, dip bottom quickly in hot water, and invert in center of dish) and surround with fruit; pour ginger ale over fruit and serve.

MRS. CHARLES (FANNY) STRICKLAND
Olathe, Kansas

Blueberry Dessert

20 graham cracker squares, crushed
¼ pound butter or margarine
½ cup chopped pecans
30 large marshmallows
½ cup milk
1 large carton Cool Whip
1 can blueberry pie filling
1 tablespoon lemon juice

Mix graham cracker crumbs, melted butter, and pecans. Spread ½ of mixture in a buttered 8 x 8" or 6 x 10" dish. Melt marshmallows with milk in top of double boiler. Set aside to cool to room temperature. Do not let set. When cool, add Cool Whip to marshmallow mix. Spread ½ of this over graham crackers. Add lemon juice to blueberry pie filling. Spread over marshmallow mix. Then add remaining marshmallow mix and spread remaining graham cracker mix over top. Refrigerate overnight.

MRS. LLOYD GLENN (PHYLLIS) MCARTHUR
Ardmore, Oklahoma

I don't want to fall, but I also know that with the little time left in this world, God could be crowded out if I don't take time to see the drawings and only look at the tape. Forgive me, Son (Walt Moore).

Strawberry Special

1 angel food cake
1 large package strawberry gelatin
2 packages frozen strawberries
1 small container Cool Whip

Slice angel food cake and line large rectangular pan—1 inch thick. Mix gelatin as directed, but use juice from strawberries with cold water addition. Spread strawberries evenly over cake. Pour gelatin over strawberries. Let set in refrigerator. At serving time, spread with Cool Whip.

"Easy and delicious."

MRS. JOHN F. (JANET) HAY
Camby, Indiana

Cracked Ice

1 box red gelatin
1 box green gelatin
1½ cups water
1 cup vanilla wafers, crushed
⅓ cup sugar
⅓ cup margarine, melted
⅓ teaspoon cinnamon
½ pint whipping cream
¼ cup sugar
1 package unflavored gelatin
¼ cup cold water
1 cup hot pineapple juice

Prepare one box each of red and green gelatin, using 1½ cups water per box. Chill in cake pan. Mix wafers, ⅓ cup sugar, melted margarine, and cinnamon. Sprinkle in bottom of 9 x 13" dish; leave some for top. Whip cream and ¼ cup sugar. Dissolve one package unflavored gelatin in ¼ cup cold water; add hot pineapple juice. Chill till syrupy and fold in whipped cream mixture. Cut gelatin in small squares and mix in cream mixture. Pour in dish and sprinkle with remaining topping. Chill overnight.

MRS. EUGENE S. (ORETHA) JUSTICE
Mount Sterling, Kentucky

French Pastry

Graham cracker crust

Filling
2 eggs, beaten
1 cup powdered sugar
½ cup butter or margarine
Cool Whip topping

Line bottom of 8-inch square pan or pie plate with graham cracker crumbs (mixed with butter and sugar) to form crust. Slowly cook ingredients for filling, stirring constantly until thick. Cool. Spread Cool Whip over crumbs. Put all of filling over Cool Whip and then put good amount of Cool Whip over filling. Sprinkle more crumbs over top. (Cream may be tinted with food coloring if desired.) Place in freezer until ready to serve.

"This recipe came from a gourmet restaurant in Missouri. Delicious, and so easy!"

MRS. FLOYD O. (BARBARA) FLEMMING
Louisville, Ohio

Grape-Nut Dessert

    2 egg whites
    2 tablespoons sugar
    ⅓ cup Grape-Nuts
    ¼ cup nuts
    ¼ cup maraschino cherries
    1 tablespoon maraschino cherry juice
    ¼ teaspoon almond
    ¼ teaspoon vanilla
    1 cup whipped cream or Dream Whip
    ¼ cup powdered sugar

Beat egg whites quite stiff, but not dry. Add sugar gradually. Add other ingredients. Add whipped cream to which powdered sugar has been added. Put in gem pans or paper cup molds and then into the freezer. Can be made the day before serving. This recipe can be doubled.

"Tastes somewhat like ice cream with nuts. Can be served for any occasion."

MRS. O. E. (NEOLA) BEESON
Council Bluffs, Iowa

Pumpkin Squares

    1 1-pound can (2 cups) pumpkin
    1 cup sugar
    1 teaspoon salt
    ½ teaspoon ginger
    1 teaspoon ground cinnamon
    ½ teaspoon ground nutmeg
    1 cup chopped pecans
    ½ gallon vanilla ice cream, softened
    36 gingersnaps or ginger wafers

Combine pumpkin, sugar, salt, and spices. In a chilled bowl, fold pumpkin mixture into ice cream; add chopped pecans. Line the bottom of 9 x 13 x 2-inch pan with half of gingersnaps; top with half ice cream mixture. Cover with another layer of gingersnaps; add remaining ice cream mixture. Freeze, cut in squares; top with whipped cream and pecan halves. Makes 18 generous servings.

MRS. WALTER M. (PAULINE) HUBBARD
Sacramento, California

Chocolate Toffee Meringue

6 egg whites
1¾ cups sugar
1 teaspoon vanilla
12 Heath chocolate toffee bars
2 cups whipping cream (sweetened with 2 tablespoons
*   powdered sugar)*
1 teaspoon vanilla

Meringue: Beat egg whites and add sugar slowly. Add vanilla.
Mix thoroughly. Spread mixture evenly on two 9 x 12" cookie
sheets that have been lined with waxed paper. Bake in 300° F.
oven 30-35 minutes or until mixture seems dry. Remove from
oven and remove waxed paper immediately. Cool. Crush or grind
Heath bars. Put a layer of meringue in a 9 x 12" container.
Spread a layer of whipped cream, then a layer of crushed candy.
Repeat. Swirl the top layer. Store in the refrigerator several hours
or overnight before serving.

"This won first prize in a local newspaper contest in one of the
cities where we lived. It is delicious."

                    MRS. R. DALE (BETTY) FRUEHLING
                    Bucyrus, Ohio

Lemon-Frozen Yogurt Parfait

1 4-ounce package lemon pie filling
½ cup sugar
1¾ cups water
2 eggs
1 tablespoon butter
frozen vanilla yogurt

Mix lemon pie filling with sugar and ¼ cup water. Add egg yolks,
slightly beaten. Blend well. Add 1½ cups water, and cook and
stir over low heat until mixture is thickened. Remove from heat
and add butter. Cool. Beat egg whites until firm and fold into
cooled lemon mixture.

To serve: Fill parfait glasses with alternate layers of lemon mixture and frozen vanilla yogurt. Top with buttered cracker
crumbs. You might add maraschino cherries. This dessert can be
stored in refrigerator several hours.

                    MRS. NEIL (RUTH) HIGHTOWER
                    Winnipeg, Manitoba, Canada

Minted Creme Dessert

1 7-ounce jar Kraft marshmallow creme
¼ cup milk
few drops of peppermint extract and green food coloring
2 cups heavy cream, whipped

Combine marshmallow creme, milk, extract, and food coloring, mixing until well blended. Fold into whipped cream and freeze. Serve in sherbet or parfait glasses.

MRS. TALMADGE (GENELL) JOHNSON
Jackson, Mississippi

Whipped Delight

1 can Wilderness pie filling (any flavor)
1 can Eagle Brand milk
1 can crushed pineapple, undrained
1 large container Cool Whip

Mix all ingredients and freeze until stiff.

MRS. JOHN (VENITA) HANCOCK
Bradley, Illinois

4-Layer Delight Dessert

1 cup flour
½ cup chopped nuts
½ cup margarine

Mix well and pat into 9 x 13" dish. Bake 25 minutes at 375° F. Cool.

1 cup Cool Whip
1 cup powdered sugar
1 8-ounce package cream cheese

Mix until fluffy. Spread on crust.

2 packages instant pudding (vanilla, chocolate or coconut)
3 cups cold milk

Mix 2 minutes and spread on cheese layer. Spread more Cool Whip on top. Toasted pecans, almonds, or coconut may be sprinkled as a topping. Refrigerate. Will keep in refrigerator for several days.

MRS. MARSHALL (EDWINA) STEWART
Hamlin, Texas

Cherry Delight

1 section graham cracker crumbs
1 stick melted margarine
1 8-ounce package cream cheese
1 cup powdered sugar
½ pint whipping cream
1 tablespoon sugar
¾ cup nuts, chopped
2 cans prepared cherry mixture

Put graham cracker crumbs and margarine in Pyrex dish and bake for 10 minutes at 400° F. Cool. Combine cream cheese and powdered sugar together and spread over crust. Whip cream, add 1 tablespoon sugar, spread over cheese mixture. Spread nuts over cream mixture. Spread 2 cans cherry mixture over nuts. Sprinkle nuts on top and refrigerate overnight.

MRS. J. V. (PAT) MORSCH
Orlando, Florida

Layered Dessert

Mix together:
1 cup flour
½ cup chopped nuts
½ cup margarine

Press into bottom of 9 x 11" pan. Bake in moderate oven until brown.

Mix:
1 8-ounce package cream cheese
1 cup powdered sugar

Add to mixture:
1 large container Cool Whip.

Pour on cooled crust.

Mix and pour over cream cheese mixture:
2 packages instant butterscotch pudding
2½ cups cold milk

Pour over pudding
1 small container Cool Whip

Sprinkle with crushed nuts and toasted coconut. Set in refrigerator overnight.

MRS. JOHN (RUTH) STOCKTON
Olathe, Kansas

Two-Toned Dessert

1 cup flour
½ cup butter or margarine
½ cup pecans, chopped
2 tablespoons sugar
1 8-ounce cream cheese
1 cup powdered sugar
1 9-ounce Cool Whip
1 3-ounce package chocolate instant pudding
1 3-ounce package vanilla instant pudding
2½ cups milk
6-9 ounces Cool Whip
toasted coconut (optional)

Mix flour, butter, nuts, and sugar like pastry, and press into 9 x 13" pan. Bake 10-15 minutes at 350° F. Cool. Beat cream cheese and powdered sugar until fluffy; fold in Cool Whip; spread on top of crust. Mix puddings and milk well; spread on second layer. Spread 6-9 ounces Cool Whip on top and sprinkle with toasted coconut if desired. Refrigerate 12 hours.

MRS. AARON (MARY) KNAPP
Omaha, Nebraska

Strawberry Gelatin Dessert

2 3-ounce boxes strawberry gelatin
2 cups boiling water
2 boxes frozen strawberries, partially thawed
1 can crushed pineapple, drained

Combine above ingredients and chill until set.

Topping
1 cup sugar
1 cup pineapple juice, from above fruit (if not enough, add water to equal a cup)
2 tablespoons cornstarch
1 egg yolk
2 tablespoons butter

Mix topping ingredients and bring to a boil. Cool. Mix 1 package Dream Whip or use 2 cups Cool Whip. Fold pineapple mixture into Cool Whip. Spread over gelatin. Sprinkle nuts on top if desired.

"This lucious dessert may be served as a salad. It is especially nice for holiday meals."

MRS. GEORGE (KAY) SCUTT
Valparaiso, Indiana

The only obstacle to man's reconciliation to God is the barrier erected by man's willful disobedience (Selected).

Fresh Fruit Trifle

½ large pound cake sliced (or 1 small pound cake)
1 recipe custard sauce
2 cups whipped cream, slightly sweetened
3 cups fresh strawberries or peaches (or bananas in winter)

Custard sauce
In heavy saucepan blend:
1 egg
½ cup sugar
2 tablespoons cornstarch
dash salt

Slowly add:
2 cups milk

Cook until thickened. Stir in vanilla and cover. Stir occasionally. When cool, add:
½ cup coffee cream.

Blend till smooth.

Line your prettiest crystal or silver bowl with slices of pound cake with edges overlapping. Pour custard sauce over cake and smooth evenly. Cover completely with sliced berries or peaches. Spread whipped cream over all and decorate with more fresh whole berries or sliced peaches. Refrigerate for several hours. Makes 10 servings.

MRS. DOUGLAS (ELAINE) FARMER
Salem, Oregon

Every consideration of the majesty of God brings us to a hushed tongue, a humbled heart, and a blessed tomorrow (Neil B. Wiseman).

Lemon Dessert Delight

Crust
1 cup flour
½ cup margarine
½ cup chopped nuts

Mix together all the crust ingredients and pat into an ungreased 9 x 13" pan. Bake 15 minutes at 350° F. Cool.

Filling
1 8-ounce package cream cheese
1 cup powdered sugar
9 ounces prepared whipped topping
3 cups milk
2 3¾-ounce packages instant lemon pudding

Cream together softened cream cheese and powdered sugar. Fold in 1½ cups dessert topping and spread over cooled crust. Beat milk and instant pudding mix together with mixer until thick. Spread over cheese mixture. Spread remaining dessert topping over all. Sprinkle with chopped nuts, if desired, and chill at least 2 hours before serving.

"You may wish to substitute chocolate instant pudding for lemon instant pudding. Your guests will clamor for the recipe."

MRS. BOB (DODIE) SMEE
Visalia, California

Angel Delight

1 angel food cake
2 packages unflavored gelatin
1 cup sugar
1 No. 2 can crushed pineapple, undrained
1 cup chopped nuts
1 cup coconut
1 cup maraschino cherries
3 packages Dream Whip

In a large bowl, put the unflavored gelatin and ¼ cup cold water, stir just enough to soften gelatin. Add 1 cup boiling water and 1 cup sugar. Stir until dissolved. To this, add crushed pineapple not drained, nuts, coconut, and maraschino cherries. Put this in the freezer section of refrigerator for 15 minutes.

While this is in freezer, prepare 3 packages Dream Whip according to directions on package. Pull angel food cake apart (1" size) and place in shallow oblong pan. Mix ⅔ of the Dream Whip with refrigerated mixture and pour over pieces of angel food cake. Spread remaining Dream Whip on top. Refrigerate overnight.

MRS. PATRICIA (GENE) ANSPACH
Coos Bay, Oregon

Marshmallow Squares

30 (or more) graham wafers rolled fine
24 marshmallows cut in quarters
¼ pound walnuts, chopped fine
1 8-ounce package candied cherries
1 can sweetened condensed milk

Crush 7 graham wafers and spread in bottom of buttered 9 x 13" pan. Combine the above ingredients (add graham wafers until mixture is not sticky) and spoon into the wafer crumbs. Sprinkle crushed wafers on top. Chill then cut into squares.

MRS. BERT (LOLA) DANIELS
Oklahoma City, Oklahoma

Frozen Dessert

1 can frozen orange juice
1 can mandarin oranges
1 large can fruit cocktail
4-5 bananas
1 cup sugar

Combine juices from the fruit cocktail and the mandarin oranges
with the frozen orange juice and sugar. Bring to a boil. Cool
until cold. Mix remaining ingredients and freeze. Pour 7-Up
over frozen servings.

MRS. ARNOLD (ADELAIDE) WOODCOOK
Nampa, Idaho

Frozen Delight

1 can cherry pie filling
1 can Eagle Brand milk
1 large can drained crushed pineapple
2 bananas, mashed
1 cup chopped pecans
2 cups miniature marshmallows
1 large container Cool Whip

Mix all ingredients together, freeze, and serve.

MRS. DALE (ANNA JEAN) YATES
Temple, Texas

Vicki's Raspberry Delight

3 boxes frozen raspberries, mashed
3 cartons whipping cream
1 11-ounce box vanilla wafers
4 tablespoons cornstarch

Heat raspberries with cornstarch to thicken. Cool. Crumb vanilla
wafers. Whip cream. In 9 x 13" dish layer ⅔ of the crumbs,
½ the whipping cream, all the raspberries, ½ the whipped cream,
and ⅓ the crumbs. Chill several hours or overnight. Makes 12-15
servings.

"This recipe always receives compliments. It is light and yet
rich."

MRS. ROBERT (CAROLYN) SCOTT
Orange, California

Frosty Strawberry Freeze

1 cup unsifted flour
½ cup melted butter or margarine
¼ cup brown sugar, firmly packed
½ cup chopped walnuts
2 egg whites
1 cup granulated sugar
1 package frozen strawberries, almost thawed or 2 cups
    sliced fresh strawberries
2 tablespoons lemon juice
1 cup heavy cream, whipped
extra strawberries for garnish

Preheat oven to 375° F. Mix flour, brown sugar, nuts, and butter till well blended. Spread on large cookie sheet or jelly roll pan. Bake about 15 minutes, stirring often to keep it separate, till golden brown toasted. Cool. In large mixer bowl, combine egg whites, sugar, berries, and lemon juice. Beat at high speed about 15 minutes, until thick and creamy. (You should cover top of bowl with waxed paper so it won't spatter.) Fold in whipped cream. Crumble nut crust and sprinkle ½ of crumbs on bottom of 9 x 13-inch baking dish. Spread creamy mixture over crumbs and top with remaining crumbs. Cover and freeze 6 hours or longer. Remove from freezer about 15 minutes before serving. Cut in squares and garnish with berries. Makes 10-12 servings.

MRS. JOHN (EUNICE) KING
Turlock, California

French Silk

¾ cup sugar
½ cup butter or margarine
1 square unsweetened chocolate
1 teaspoon vanilla
2 eggs
8-10 crushed graham crackers
1 package Dream Whip or small carton of prepared
    whipped topping
¼ cup maraschino cherry juice
crushed nuts (optional)

First layer: Cream sugar and butter until light and fluffy. Add the chocolate (melted and cooled). Add vanilla. Add 1 egg and beat 5 minutes. Add the other egg and beat 5 minutes more. Pour this over the crushed graham crackers.

Second layer: Add the cherry juice to the whipped topping and put on first layer. Top with crushed nuts.

MRS. FORREST (MARGARET) WHITLATCH
Des Moines, Iowa

The story of God's will and workings, through Him, is most exciting. When we cut the hold of self-mastery and come to sense the movements of God, there is always excitement (Hilda Lee Cox)

Sunday Delight

6 eggs
2 cups sugar
½ cup crushed Zwieback (5 pieces)
½ teaspoon salt
¾ cup Farina (Cream of Wheat)
2 teaspoons baking powder
1 teaspoon vanilla
1 cup chopped nuts

Cream sugar and egg yolks, add dry ingredients, nuts, and vanilla; beat egg whites until stiff and fold into mixture. Pour into greased square pans and bake at 350° F. for 20 to 30 minutes. It will look rather flat and crusty. When cool, break or cut in 1-inch squares. Whip one pint of cream. Line a mixing bowl with wax paper. Arrange one layer of cake squares in bottom of bowl and then one layer of whipped cream, repeat until bowl is full, ending with cake on top. Let stand in refrigerator overnight.

To serve, invert mixture from bowl to a large plate or cake stand. Whip enough cream to cover, garnish with nuts and cherries.

"This is a pretty, elegant-looking dessert that brings many comments from guests."

MRS. HARRY (MARION) RICH
Kansas City, Kansas

Blueberry Dream Dessert

1 cup flour
1 stick margarine
¾ cup chopped pecans
1 8-ounce package cream cheese
2 cups Cool Whip
1 cup sugar
1 21-ounce can blueberry pie filling

Make crust of flour, margarine, pecans. Bake at 350° F. until light brown (crust in bottom of 9 x 13" pan only). Whip softened cream cheese and sugar until light and fluffy. Fold in 2 cups Cool Whip. Spread over crust. Top with can of blueberry pie filling. Refrigerate for several hours before serving.

To serve: cut in squares and top with a little Cool Whip.

MRS. T. W. WILSON
Montreat, North Carolina

Butterscotch Brickle Layer Dessert

1 cup flour
1 cup chopped pecans
1 stick margarine, melted
1 8-ounce cream cheese, softened
1 cup Cool Whip (or other whipped topping)
1 cup confectioners' sugar
2 packages butterscotch pudding (instant may be used)
1 large container Cool Whip (or other whipped topping)
1 cup Heath Brickle Chips

Mix flour, pecans, and margarine. Spread in 9 x 13 pan. Bake for 20 minutes at 350° F. Cool. Mix cream cheese, Cool Whip, and confectioners' sugar until creamy. Spread over baked layer. Prepare pudding, using only 3 cups milk. Cool and spread over second layer. Top with Cool Whip and sprinkle with Heath Brickle Chips. Refrigerate several hours or overnight.

Variations: Use chocolate pudding and sprinkle chocolate shavings on top. Use lemon or vanilla pudding and sprinkle toasted coconut on top.

MRS. JOEL E. (DALEY) LOVE
Lakeland, Florida

Raspberry Delight

½ cup margarine
2 egg yolks
1 cup white sugar
1 teaspoon vanilla
2 tablespoons cornstarch
1 pint frozen raspberries
1¼ cups flour
¼ teaspoon soda
¼ teaspoon salt
4 tablespoons chopped walnuts
2 egg whites

He breaks the pow'r of
canceled sin;
He sets the pris'ner free.
His blood can make the
foulest clean;
His blood availed for me.
Charles Wesley

Beat margarine and egg yolks with ⅓ cup sugar until light and fluffy. Add vanilla and sifted flour, soda, and salt. Spread in ungreased pan. Combine ¼ cup sugar, cornstarch, and raspberries. Cook until thick. Spread this over uncooked mixture. Sprinkle 2 tablespoons nuts over this. Beat egg whites, gradually add 1 tablespoon sugar and spread over above mixture. Sprinkle with nuts. Stand in pan of water and bake at 350° F. for 30 minutes.

"A delicious dessert that never fails to rate compliments. I like to serve it with a scoop of vanilla ice cream."

MRS. DANIEL J. (JOYCE) DERKSEN
Burnaby, British Columbia, Canada

Ye have received the Spirit of adoption, whereby we cry, Abba, Father. The Spirit itself beareth witness with our spirit, that we are the children of God (Rom. 8:15-16).

Butterfinger Dessert

¼ *cup butter*
4 *egg yolks*
2 *tablespoons sugar*
2 *cups powdered sugar*
1 *pint whipping cream*
1 *angel food cake*
6 *Butterfinger candy bars*

Slice cake to cover bottom rectangular Tupperware dish (9 x 13"). Beat together first 4 ingredients. Whip cream, fold into mixture. Pour over angel food cake. Crush candy bars and sprinkle over top. Refrigerate overnight.

Mrs. James (Sharon) Monck
Racine, Wisconsin

"Let every thing that hath breath praise the Lord" (Ps. 150:6).

Bettie's Hot Fudge Dessert

Sift together 3 times:
2½ *cups sifted flour*
4 *tablespoons cocoa*
2 *teaspoons baking soda*
¼ *teaspoon salt*

Cream: ⅔ cup shortening with 2 cups sugar, 1 teaspoon vanilla; add 1 egg and cream until light and fluffy; add 1 more egg and beat again. Add 1 cup buttermilk alternately with flour mixture. After all flour and milk is well mixed, add 1 cup boiling water and mix well. Bake at 325° or 350° F. Bake in floured loaf pan. This makes a big cake, 13½ x 8¾ x 1¾" pan for fudge cake, or 2 layers, or cupcakes. For Hot Fudge Cake, bake in large pan; when ready to serve, cut the cake into squares. Cut the squares into the middle, cut a piece of ice cream and put in the middle, so you would have cake, ice cream and cake. Pour Hot Fudge over the top, add Cool Whip and cherries.

Hot Fudge Sauce
1 *stick butter (melted)*
1 *6-ounce package chocolate chips*

The Lord executeth righteousness and judgment for all that are oppressed (Ps. 103:6).

Melt butter, add chocolate chips to melted butter, add one large can evaporated milk, 1 pound box powdered sugar (sifted), and one teaspoon vanilla. Let cook on low heat until thickens.

Mrs. Harold (Bettie) Graves
San Antonio, Texas

Mincemeat Cottage Pudding

2 cups sifted flour
3 teaspoons baking powder
½ teaspoon salt
½ cup brown sugar
⅔ cup milk
2 eggs, well-beaten
1 tablespoon grated lemon rind
¼ cup shortening, melted

Boil down:
1 9-ounce package mincemeat
½ cup water

Sift dry ingredients. Add brown sugar to eggs, stirring until dissolved; add milk. Combine lemon rind, cooled melted shortening and cooled mincemeat, add to milk mixture. Add liquid ingredients to dry ingredients and stir just enough to blend. Turn into prepared 8 x 8 x 2" pan; bake at 350° F. for 40-45 minutes. Pecans and/or dates may be added.

"Serve with 1 cup whipped cream combined with ½ can whole cranberry sauce."

MRS. WILLIS (WANONAH) SNOWBARGER
Bourbonnais, Illinois

Pistachio Pudding Dessert

Step I
1 cup flour
⅓ cup sugar
1 stick margarine

Mix together and press into bottom of 9 x 13" pan. Bake at 350° F. for 12-15 minutes.

Step II
1 8-ounce package cream cheese
½ of a 9-ounce container Cool Whip
⅔ cup powdered sugar

Beat together. Spread on crust from step I when it is cool.

Step III
3 packages pistachio instant pudding
4 cups milk

Beat until thick and pour over step II. Spread remaining Cool Whip on top. Sprinkle nuts on top.

MRS. EDWARD (SHIRLEY) RICHEY
Gahanna, Ohio

Hollandse Applegebak

2¼ cups self-rising flour
½ teaspoon cinnamon
½ pound butter
¾ cup sugar
6 medium tart apples (about 2 pounds)
¼ pound raisins (4 ounces)
4 ounces cashews (unsalted)

Grease springform pan. Grate apples, add raisins, rinse with cold water. Add cinnamon, sprinkle 1 tablespoon sugar. Let set. Measure flour then sift with sugar, cube butter, knead by hand. Add 3 shakes salt. Form ball; bounce in hands to remove cracks. Take two-thirds of dough; spread in bottom and up sides of springform pan. Put in pan, layer of apple mix, sprinkle layer of cashews, sprinkle with cinnamon. Repeat three times. Use remaining dough and cover with lattice strips. Brush top with: 1 egg, beaten and mixed with 4 drops water.

"Not necessary, but it is delicious, to cover top with apricot preserves when baked. Store in refrigerator overnight before serving."

MRS. MERRITT (LINDA) NIELSON
Rotterdam, The Netherlands

Lemon Dream Pie

1 can Eagle Brand milk
1 can lemon pudding
1 can fruit cocktail, drained
1 bowl Cool Whip
3 tablespoons pure lemon juice
2 graham cracker crusts (I use the prepared ones)
chopped nuts

Fold all ingredients together in a large bowl until smooth and creamy. Divide equally in crusts. Sprinkle with chopped nuts, and chill for at least 45 minutes.

MRS. BILL (GLORIA) GAITHER
Alexandria, Indiana

Cakes & Pies

White Coconut Pie

  1 tablespoon gelatin
  ¼ cup cold water
  ½ cup sugar
  4 tablespoons flour
  ½ teaspoon salt
1½ cups milk
  ¾ teaspoon vanilla
  ¼ teaspoon almond extract
  ½ cup whipping cream, whipped until stiff

Meringue
  3 egg whites
  ¼ teaspoon cream of tartar
  ½ cup sugar
  1 cup moist coconut

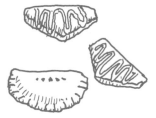

Have you a heart that "listens" to the Spirit's voice? (Selected).

Soften gelatin in cold water. Mix together in saucepan: sugar, flour, salt; and stir milk in gradually. Cook over low heat, stirring until it boils. Boil 1 minute. Remove from heat. Stir in softened gelatin. Cool. When partially set, beat with rotary beater until smooth. Blend in vanilla, almond extract, and gently fold in whipping cream. Carefully fold into a meringue of egg whites, cream of tartar, and sugar. Fold in 1 cup of coconut. Pile into cooled, baked pie shell. Sprinkle with moist shredded coconut. Chill until set (about 2 hours). Serve cold. Take chilled pie out of refrigerator 20 minutes before serving.

"This is an absolutely beautiful and delicious pie especially for the holidays."

MRS. VERNON (CAROLYN) LUNN
Farmington Hills, Michigan

Millionaire Pie

1 stick margarine
2 cups powdered sugar
1 egg
1 medium size can crushed pineapple
½ cup chopped pecans
½ pint whipping cream

Cream together butter, powdered sugar, and the egg. Place in your favorite pie shell which has been prebaked. Place in ice box while you are whipping the cream. Whip cream until it forms peaks. Fold in drained crushed pineapple and nuts. Put this mixture on top of the butter mixture.

"This is one of the favorites of our church board."

MRS. JAMES (ELIZABETH) SOUTHWORTH
Austin, Texas

Milk Pie

2 cups milk
¼ cup sugar
3 tablespoons flour
1 tablespoon corn flour
¼ teaspoon salt
2 tablespoons butter
3 eggs
1 stick cinnamon
pie shell

Boil milk with cinnamon. Mix flour, corn flour, salt, and sugar. Pour hot milk over flour mixture and stir with wooden spoon until smooth. Cook slowly and stir until done and thick. Remove from heat and stir in butter (or margarine). Let cool slightly. Beat eggs well and add to mixture. Roll out pastry and put into pie dish. Then add milk mixture. Bake in warm oven for 20 minutes (425° F.). Decrease heat after 10 minutes (375° F.). Let it cool off and sprinkle cinnamon sugar over top.

"This is a traditional South African pie."

MRS. GIDEON (JEANETTE) TREDOUX
Republic of South Africa

Buttermilk Pie

2 cups sugar
3 tablespoons flour
2 whole eggs, beaten
½ cup melted butter or margarine
1 cup buttermilk
2 teaspoons lemon extract

Mix sugar and flour together and add to the rest of the ingredients. Bake in unbaked pie shell for 10 minutes at 450° F. Reduce heat to low and bake until firm (may be tested by inserting knife into center to see that it comes out clean).

MRS. I. L. (RUTH) STIVERS
Lonsdale, Arkansas

The Spirit of Christ bids us to receive others with dignity and respect regardless of their station in life (Wanda King).

Coconut Buttermilk Pie

3 8- or 9-inch uncooked pie crusts
3¾ cups sugar
½ cup flour
½ teaspoon salt
6 eggs
1 cup buttermilk
1 teaspoon vanilla
2 sticks margarine, melted
1 teaspoon butter extract
1¾ to 2 cups coconut

Blend sugar, flour, eggs, and salt. Add buttermilk, vanilla, butter extract, and melted margarine. Mix and pour into 3 uncooked pie shells. Sprinkle about ½ to ¾ cup of coconut on top of each pie and bake about 40 minutes. Test for firmness. Bake at 350° F.

"The good part about this recipe is that it makes 3 pies at once. You will really get the raves when this is served. It is delicious. Also, it is very easy to make. I use Pet Ritz pie crust, if I don't have time to make my own."

MRS. ERWIN (RUTH ELIZABETH) DAVIS
Austin, Texas

Date Pie

2 eggs, beaten until fluffy
1 cup sugar
1 stick margarine, melted
3 teaspoons milk
½ cup pecans, chopped
5 squares graham crackers, rolled fine
¼ teaspoon salt
1 cup dates, cut in small pieces
1 teaspoon vanilla

Mix all ingredients together. Place in well greased 9-inch pan. Bake 30 minutes at 325° F. Serve with whipped cream. No crust required.

MRS. T. R. (EVANGELINE) PARTEE
Whittier, California

Strawberry Pie

1 3-ounce package strawberry gelatin
1¾ cups water
¾ cup sugar
2 tablespoons cornstarch

Bake and cool one 10-inch pie shell. Wash and stem 1 quart strawberries; they may be whole or sliced. Place berries in pie shell. Cook the above mixture until clear. When cool, pour over the berries. Chill for at least 2 hours. Top with whipped cream or similar topping.

MRS. WAYNE (MARION) ACTON
Coraopolis, Pennsylvania

Perhaps today your burden is greater than your capacity. Tell the Lord, for He will either lighten the load or, by His power, increase your capacity to bear the burden. "For I the Lord thy God will hold thy right hand, saying unto thee, Fear not; I will help thee" (Isaiah 41:13). We're going to make it, for our God is able (Nona Kelley).

Cookie Creme Pie

1 package Oreo cookies (or similar)
½ gallon vanilla ice cream
2 tablespoons creme de menthe syrup
*   (or 2 tablespoons peppermint flavoring)*
few drops of green food coloring

Let ice cream soften. Stir in mint flavoring. Add coloring, if desired. Crush Oreos. Spread on bottom and sides of greased pie pans, two 8-inch pans, or long cake pan. Spread ice cream over the crust. Freeze. Whipped topping may be added, with crumbs sprinkled on top.

"Substitute maraschino syrup for a red dessert with cherry flavor. Or try 4 tablespoons crunchy peanut butter in the ice cream with graham cracker crusts."

MRS. LORNE (JOYCE) MACMILLAN
Toronto, Canada

Pennsylvania Dutch Shoofly Pie

First: mix together
 1 cup flour
 ⅔ cup light brown sugar
 1 tablespoon of margarine or butter

Take out ½ cup of the above mixture

Second: *add 1 cup Karo syrup*
 1 beaten egg
 ¾ cup cold water

Blend together with first step.

Third: *then add 1 teaspoon baking soda and ¼ cup hot water*

Pour into unbaked pie shell (9 inch) and sprinkle the ½ cup of crumb mixture on top. Bake 400° F. for 10 minutes, 325° F. for 35 minutes. Pie is finished when knife inserted in center comes out clean. Served best warm with whipped cream.

MRS. LLOYD (HARRIET) GORDON
Pennsville, New Jersey

Easy Lime Pie

1 large can frozen limeade
1 9-ounce carton of whipped topping
1 large can Eagle Brand milk (sweetened condensed)
1 prepared graham cracker crust

Thaw limeade, mix all ingredients in mixer. Pour into a graham cracker crust and chill for one hour. Top with more whipped topping. Refrigerate overnight. Makes 8 servings.

MRS. JACK (RACHEL) ARCHER
Mount Vernon, Ohio

Mile-high Strawberry Pie

Crust and topping
½ cup margarine
¼ cup brown sugar
1 cup flour
½ cup finely chopped nuts

Filling
1 10-ounce package frozen strawberries, slightly thawed
2 egg whites, unbeaten
¾ cup sugar
1 teaspoon vanilla
1 teaspoon lemon juice
1 cup whipped cream, or Dream Whip

Mix ingredients for crust. Press into 9 x 13" pan. Bake 350° F. for 15 minutes. Cool and crumble. Put half back into the bottom of the pan, press down. Combine first five ingredients for filling, beat at high speed for 20 minutes. Do not underbeat. Fold in whipped cream. Pour into crumb crust. Sprinkle remaining crumbs on top. Freeze until serving time. Makes 18-20 servings.

MRS. WILLIAM (MAE) BAHAN
Moncton, New Brunswick, Canada

Fresh Strawberry Pie

1 package vanilla flavor pudding/pie filling
1 package strawberry gelatin
2 cups water
1 teaspoon lemon juice
1½ cups prepared whipped topping
1 cup sliced strawberries
1 baked 9-inch pie shell, cooled

Combine pudding mix, gelatin, water, lemon juice in saucepan. Cook and stir over medium heat until mixture comes to a boil. Pour into bowl and chill until thickened. (To speed chilling, place bowl in larger bowl of ice water and stir until thick.) Fold in whipped topping, blend well; stir in strawberries. Pour into pie shell. Chill until set, 1-2 hours. Garnish with whipped topping and strawberries.

MRS. CECIL (SHARON) CARROLL, JR.
Pittsfield, Illinois

Pecan Pie

3 eggs slightly beaten
¾ cups sugar
1 cup white Karo syrup
1 or 1½ cups chopped pecans
¼ cup melted butter or margarine
2 tablespoons lemon juice
1 teaspoon vanilla flavoring

Combine ingredients and pour into unbaked pie shell. Bake for 10 minutes in 450° F. oven; then turn to 300° F. and bake for 45 minutes to 1 hour.

"After I turn the oven temperature down to 300° F., I open the door for a minute or so to let the oven cool down rapidly."

MRS. SOLON (RUBY) DAVIS
Jackson, Mississippi

Into thine hand I commit my spirit (Ps. 31:5).

Lemon Pecan Pie

3 whole eggs
⅓ stick margarine, melted (do not use whipped margarine)
1½ cups white sugar
¾ cup pecan halves or pieces
1 teaspoon lemon extract
juice of ½ lemon

Mix ingredients in order given, but do not use a mixer or beat until frothy. Pour into 8-inch unbaked pie shell. Put in preheated oven (350° F.) and bake about 10 minutes, then cut oven temperature to about 300° F. (slow oven) and bake until crust is browned and pie filling is set. Too rapid cooking will cause pecans to scorch and crust to brown before center of pie has finished cooking. For variety, try Orange Pecan Pie: substitute juice of ½ fresh orange for the lemon juice, and 1 teaspoon orange extract in lieu of lemon extract.

MRS. WENDELL (BONNIE) PARIS
Henryetta, Oklahoma

These things have I spoken unto you, that my joy might remain in you, and that your joy might be full (John 15: 11).

Jesus increased in wisdom and stature, and in favour with God and man (Luke 2: 52).

Kentucky Pecan Pie

1 cup white corn syrup
1 cup dark brown sugar
⅓ teaspoon salt
⅓ cup melted butter
1 teaspoon vanilla
3 whole eggs, slightly beaten
1 heaping cup shelled pecans

Combine syrup, sugar, salt, butter, vanilla, and mix well. Add slightly beaten eggs. Pour into a 9-inch unbaked pie shell. Bake in preheated 350° F. oven for approximately 45 minutes. When cool, you may top with whipped cream or ice cream.

MRS. JAMES C. (WILMA) SHAW
Concord, California

Likewise, our circumstances, no matter how banal, should never permit us to enter into God's presence casually, flippantly, or untidily (Howard H. Hamlin).

Pecan Pie

1 package vanilla pudding
1 cup white corn syrup
¾ cup evaporated milk
1 egg, slightly beaten
1 cup chopped pecans
1 unbaked pie shell

Blend the pudding and syrup together. Gradually add the milk and egg. Stir in the pecans. Pour this mixture into the pie shell and bake at 375° F. for about 40 minutes, until the top is firm and begins to crack. Cool at least 3 hours before serving.

MRS. ROSS (HARRIETTE) HAYSLIP
Tucson, Arizona

No matter what conditions
Dyspeptic come to feaze,
The best of all physicians
Is apple pie and cheese.
Eugene Field

Apple Pecan Pie

1 9-inch pie shell
¼ cup chopped pecans
6 cups sliced peeled apples
1 cup sugar
2 teaspoons flour
½ teaspoon cinnamon
¼ teaspoon nutmeg
Spicy Pecan topping

Sprinkle chopped pecans in bottom of shell. Combine apples, sugar, flour, cinnamon, and nutmeg. Turn into pie shell and spread topping over apples. Bake 40-45 minutes at 425° F.

Topping
¼ cup butter
½ cup flour
½ teaspoon cinnamon

Blend and stir in ¼ cup chopped pecans.

"This is a delicious variation of two old favorites. Especially good at Thanksgiving and Christmas."

MRS. ROBERT (MARY LOU) PARROTT
Upper Marlboro, Maryland

Almond Pie

3 or 4 eggs, beaten
⅓ cup sugar
1 cup syrup
dash of salt
½-¾ cup nuts (walnuts can be used)

Beat the eggs well. Add sugar, syrup, and salt, and mix. Add vanilla and nuts. Pour into prepared pie shell and bake until the filling is set. Test as you would test custard. Bake in 350° F. oven.

"Hint: after making the pie shell, pour melted butter (1 teaspoon) over the bottom of the shell and spread evenly. This keeps the crust from becoming soggy."

MRS. GARTH (NORMA) HYDE
Missoula, Montana

Peanut Butter Pie

1 3-ounce package cream cheese
1 cup powdered sugar
¾ cup crunchy peanut butter (room temperature)
1 9-ounce container of Cool Whip
2 baked 9-inch pie shells

Mix together cream cheese, powdered sugar, and peanut butter; then mix in the Cool Whip. Pour in pie shells and refrigerate.

MRS. RALPH W. (RUBYE) MARLOWE
Albertville, Alabama

Fluffy Peanut Butter Pie

½ cup peanut butter, smooth or crunchy
8 ounces cream cheese, softened
1 cup powdered sugar
½ cup milk
1 9-ounce package nondairy whipped topping
1 9-inch graham cracker crumb crust or 9-inch baked
    pastry shell
¼ cup finely chopped peanuts (optional)

Whip cream cheese until soft and fluffy. Beat in peanut butter and sugar. Slowly add milk, blending thoroughly into mixture. Fold topping into mixture. Pour into prepared crust. Sprinkle with chopped peanuts, if desired. Freeze until firm and serve. For storage longer than 4 to 6 hours, wrap the pie well for freezing to prevent dehydration.

DON CORNWELL
Mission, Kansas

Editor's note: when Don Cornwell brought us one of these delicious pies, there was a scripture verse stamped in the aluminum pie plate: *"Let your moderation be known unto all men" (Philippians 4:5).*

He hath shewed thee, O man, what is good: and what doth the Lord require of thee, but to do justly, and to love mercy, and to walk humbly with thy God? (Mic. 6:8).

For every one that exalteth himself shall be abased; and he that humbleth himself shall be exalted (Luke 18:14).

Peanut Butter Pie

Crust
¾ cup crushed pretzels
3 tablespoons sugar
6 tablespoons melted butter

Combine and press into pie pan.

Filling
1 envelope unflavored gelatin
¼ cup sugar
¼ teaspoon salt
1 cup milk
½ cup creamy peanut butter
2 eggs separated
¼ cup sugar
2 cups Cool Whip

Mix sugar, gelatin, and salt in saucepan; add milk and egg yolks. Cook over medium heat, stirring until it boils; add peanut butter and stir until blended; chill. Beat egg whites until foamy; add sugar gradually, and beat until stiff. Fold peanut butter mixture into egg whites, fold in Cool Whip, and spoon mixture into crust and chill. Sprinkle a little of the crust mixture on top if desired.

MRS. RAY (DOROTHY) MARLIN
Indianapolis, Indiana

He has an oar in every man's boat, and a finger in every pie (Cervantes).

Lemonade Pie

1 can Eagle Brand milk
1 can frozen lemonade
1 small container of Cool Whip
1 graham cracker pie crust

Mix in large bowl: Eagle Brand milk, can of lemonade (thawed and mixed thoroughly). Stir in thawed Cool Whip. Pour into pie shell and refrigerate until serving.

"A delicious pie—quick to make—requires short chilling. These ingredients can be kept on hand ready for emergencies."

MRS. DUDLEY (LOIS) ANDERSON
Gallup, New Mexico

Creamed Cheese Pie

¾ cup all-purpose flour
1 teaspoon baking powder
½ teaspoon salt
1 egg
1 3½-ounce package vanilla pudding mix (not instant)
3 tablespoons butter
½ cup milk
1 can peaches or blueberry pie mix
1 8-ounce package cream cheese
½ cup sugar
3 tablespoons peach juice
1 teaspoon sugar
½ teaspoon cinnamon

I saw a new heaven and a new earth: for the first heaven and the first earth were passed away; and there was no more sea (Rev. 21:1).

Mix the first 7 ingredients at medium speed for 2 minutes; place in deep greased pie pan. Place can of peaches or blueberry pie filling over mixture. Mix cream cheese, ½ cup sugar, peach juice, spread over peaches to 1 inch of pie. Sprinkle 1 teaspoon sugar and cinnamon over top of pie. Bake 30-35 minutes at 350° F. Serve hot.

MRS. ALECK (ETHELYN) ULMET
Louisville, Kentucky

Honey Cheese Pie

Crust and Topping

⅓ cup butter or margarine
¼ cup honey
3 tablespoons brown sugar
3 cups granola, coarsely crushed

Filling

1 envelope plus 2 teaspoons unflavored gelatin (about 5 teaspoons)
¼ cup water
2 tablespoons lemon juice
1 8-ounce package cream cheese, softened
½ cup honey
⅛ teaspoon salt
1 8-ounce carton plain yogurt
2 cups heavy cream, whipped

For crust and topping
Combine butter, honey, and brown sugar in medium-sized sauce-pan; cook over low heat, stirring occasionally, until butter is melted and sugar dissolves. Stir in cereal; (reserve ¼ cup cereal mixture for topping) mix well. Press remaining cereal mixture onto bottom and sides of lightly oiled 10-inch pie pan; chill.

For filling
Soften gelatin in combined water and lemon juice; stir over low heat until dissolved. Beat together cream cheese, honey, and salt until well blended. Gradually add yogurt and dissolved gelatin mixture, mixing until well blended. Chill until slightly thickened (about 5 minutes). Fold in whipped cream; spoon onto crust. Sprinkle ¼ cup reserved cereal mixture over top. Chill until firm.

MRS. JAMES A. (DONNA) SCARTH, JR.
Portland, Oregon

Molasses Coconut Pie

2 cups sugar
4 tablespoons flour
3 eggs, beaten
3 cups milk
1 cup molasses
2 cups coconut
5 tablespoons butter, browned

Mix sugar, flour, and eggs together. Add milk, molasses, and co-conut. Add browned butter and pour into two unbaked pie shells. Bake at 375° F. until nicely browned.

MRS. WILLIAM (MAE) MOWEN
Ephrata, Pennsylvania

Banana Split Pie

1 prebaked 9- or 10-inch pie crust
1 quart or more chocolate, vanilla, and strawberry ice
    cream
1 banana
1 tablespoon lemon juice
1 small container Cool Whip
nuts, cherries

Line bottom of pie shell with sliced bananas. Sprinkle with lemon juice. Press into shell slightly softened ice cream. Firm in freezer, before covering with Cool Whip. Nuts and cherries for garnish. Freeze. Take out of freezer a few minutes before serving. Serve with homemade fudge sauce.

MRS. DICK (JODY) GROSS
Wenham, Massachusetts

Better shun the bait than struggle in the snare (John Dryden).

Praline Pumpkin Pie

Pie filling
  3 eggs, whipped
  3 tablespoons lightly browned butter
  ⅓ cup granulated sugar
  ½ cup firmly packed brown sugar
  ½ teaspoon salt (scant)
  1 tablespoon flour
1¾ cups cooked pumpkin
  1 level teaspoon cinnamon
  ¼ teaspoon nutmeg
  ¼ teaspoon allspice
  ¾ cup canned milk

Praline Topping
  3 tablespoons granulated sugar
  ½ cup finely chopped pecans
dash of cinnamon
  1 9-inch pie crust, unbaked, brushed with melted butter

Place ingredients for filling in order given into blender jar and blend thoroughly until smooth. Pour into pie shell. Bake in 425° F. oven for 15 minutes; reduce heat to 350° F. and bake 25 minutes. At end of baking period, sprinkle praline topping and bake until pie is firm and almost rising in center.

"This pie may be served with or without a whipped cream garnish, which may be passed in a chilled glass bowl."

MRS. CHUCK (JEANNE) MILLHUFF
Olathe, Kansas

Raspberry Chiffon Pie

Red Layer
  1 package raspberry gelatin
1¼ cups water
  2 10-ounce packages frozen raspberries
  1 teaspoon lemon juice

White layer
  1 cup whipping cream (or small package Dream Whip)
  1 6-ounce package cream cheese
¾ cup powdered sugar

Baked 10-inch pie shell

Dissolve raspberry gelatin in boiling water. Add frozen raspberries and lemon juice. Refrigerate until slightly thickened.
Mix cream cheese with powdered sugar and add to whipped
cream. Into baked pie shell, put ½ of white layer then ½ of red
layer. On top add rest of white layer and cover with red. Refrigerate.

MRS. LEON (DORIS) DOANE
Olathe, Kansas

Oreo Pie

  3 egg whites
¾ cup sugar
½ teaspoon vanilla
¼ teaspoon salt
½ cup chopped pecans
10 crushed Oreo cookies
  1 9-ounce container Cool Whip, thawed

Beat egg whites until stiff, gradually adding sugar. After egg
whites are stiff, fold in other ingredients, except Cool Whip.
Spread in lightly buttered 9-inch pie pan. Bake at 325° F., 35
minutes. When cooled spread Cool Whip over the top. Chill until
serving.

MRS. ROBERT (BEVERLY) ALLEN
Louisville, Kentucky

Chart House Mud Pie

½ package Nabisco chocolate wafers
½ cube butter, melted
  1 quart coffee ice cream
1½ cups fudge sauce

Crush wafers and add butter, mix well. Press into 9-inch pie plate. Cover with soft coffee ice cream. Put into freezer until ice cream is firm. Top with cold fudge sauce (it helps to place in freezer for a time to make spreading easier). Store in freezer approximately 10 hours. Slice mud pie into eight portions and serve on a chilled dessert plate with a chilled fork. Top with whipped cream and slivered almonds.

MRS. CHARLES (BUNNY) ONEY
Westerville, Ohio

Cherry Nut Cream Pie

1 small box vanilla wafers, crushed
1 cup Angel Flake coconut, toasted in oven
½ cube melted butter or margarine
1 can sweetened condensed milk
¼ cup lemon juice
½ pint whipping cream, whipped (or lo-cal substitute)
1 can red sour (tart) pitted cherries
1 cup chopped nuts

Make crust out of first three ingredients. Mix condensed milk and lemon juice (will thicken). Fold in whipped cream, cherries, and nuts. Fill crust and chill 3-4 hours or overnight. Garnish with nuts, crumbs, or whatever.

MRS. PAUL (PEARLE) BENEFIEL
Glendora, California

You may wander far, but God's love has a very long arm (Selected).

Black Bottom Pie

16 regular size marshmallows
1 regular size package (6 ounce) chocolate chips
2 ½-pints whipping cream
1 teaspoon vanilla
½ cup milk
1 Hershey chocolate bar (25c size)
1 baked 9- or 10-inch pie shell
¼ cup chopped nuts

Melt chocolate chips, marshmallows, and milk in top of double boiler or use your microwave oven. Stir until well mixed. Chill 15-20 minutes. Whip whipping cream and sweeten to taste. Fold ½ of this whipped cream, chopped nuts, and vanilla into chilled chocolate mixture. Pour into baked pie shell. Chill in refrigerator several hours. Cover top of pie with remainder of whipped cream. Grate Hershey bar (using potato peeler); let chocolate curls fall on top of pie. Chill until served.

MRS. DAVID (GENEVA) BARTON
Riverside, California

Plott Pie

3 egg whites
1 teaspoon vanilla
¾ cup sugar
1 teaspoon baking powder
1 package German chocolate, grated
1 cup Ritz cracker crumbs
½ cup chopped pecans

Beat egg whites with vanilla to soft peaks. Combine sugar and baking powder. Gradually add to egg whites, beating to stiff peaks. Set aside 2 tablespoons German chocolate, fold in the rest of the chocolate along with cracker crumbs and pecans. Spread into 9-inch pie pan. Bake at 350° F. for 25 minutes. Topping: whip ½ pint whipping cream with 2 tablespoons sugar. Spread cream on cooled pie. Sprinkle with reserved chocolate.

MRS. DENNIS (ELSIE) KINLAW
Wilmore, Kentucky

Preacher Pie

(for the Circuit Rider)

1 egg, well beaten
4 rounded tablespoons sugar
1 rounded tablespoon flour
4 rounded tablespoons molasses (or white Karo)
1 tablespoon butter
½ teaspoon vanilla
nuts (if available)

Blend well and pour in unbaked pie shell. Bake at 350° F. It is thin but rich.

MRS. I. L. (RUTH) STIVERS
Lonsdale, Arkansas

Impossible Pie

4 eggs
½ cube butter (at room temperature)
1 cup sugar
½ cup flour
¼ teaspoon salt
2 cups milk
½ teaspoon vanilla

1 cup coconut
½ teaspoon baking powder

Pour all ingredients, except coconut, in a bowl or blender. Stir in coconut. Pour mixture into a 10-inch pie pan that has been sprayed with non-caloric pure vegetable spray for cookware. Bake at 350° F. for 45 minutes or until done. When done crust will be on the bottom, custard in the middle and toasty coconut on top. Serve while still warm, otherwise it will flatten.

Mrs. Gordon A. (Rhoda) Olsen
Eugene, Oregon

Japanese Fruit Pie

2 8- or 9-inch unbaked pie shells
1 cup raisins (White ones are especially good)
1 cup chopped pecans
1 small can (1 cup) Angel Flake coconut
2 cups sugar
2 sticks melted margarine or butter
5 eggs
2 tablespoons vinegar

Mix butter, eggs and sugar, and then all remaining ingredients; pour evenly into unbaked pie shells. Bake in oven 350° F. for 35-40 minutes, until set. Remove from oven. Serve warm or cold.

Mrs. J. R. (Thetis) Hucks
Chester, South Carolina

If we confess our sins, he is faithful and just to forgive us our sins, and to cleanse us from all unrighteousness (1 John 1:9).

Lemon Chiffon Pie Filling

3 eggs
1 cup sugar
½ cup fresh lemon juice
3 tablespoons boiling water
¼ teaspoon salt

Beat 3 egg yolks and add ¾ cup of sugar and salt, lemon juice, grated lemon rind, and hot water. Cook over slow flame until it boils and let it boil about 1 minute. Add ¼ cup of sugar to egg whites after they are beaten stiff. Add by spoonfuls to mixture. Pour into baked crust and brown in oven (under broiler). Watch very carefully or it burns.

Mrs. Doris McDowell
Walnut Creek, California

One cannot go sincerely to his brother to point out a fault without recognizing and admitting faults of his own. Thus in communication between brother and brother is the promotion of unity of the Spirit (Carl McClain).

You just can't do wrong and get by. Today let's do right and get blessed (John Hancock).

Samuel said, Hath the Lord as great delight in burnt offerings and sacrifices, as in obeying the voice of the Lord? Behold, to obey is better than sacrifice, and to hearken than the fat of rams (1 Sam. 15:22).

Frozen Coconut Chocolate Freezer Pie

Crust
1 ⅓ cups flaked coconut
  2 tablespoons melted butter
  ¼ cup crushed graham crackers
  2 tablespoons sugar

Filling
  1 6-ounce package semisweet chocolate morsels
  1 3-ounce package cream cheese, softened
  ⅓ cup granulated sugar
  2 tablespoons milk
  dash of salt
  1 2-ounce envelope dessert topping mix

Crust: mix ingredients together, press into 8-inch pie pan. (Save about ⅛ of mixture and bake in separate pan to sprinkle on top of pie.) Bake 10 to 12 minutes at 375° F.
Filling: melt chocolate morsels over hot water. In small mixer bowl blend cream cheese, sugar, milk, and salt with the melted chocolate. Prepare topping mix and fold into chocolate mixture. Pour into cooled crust, sprinkle crumbs on top. Freeze.

MRS. PAUL K. (EMILY) MOORE
Mount Pleasant, Michigan

Rhubarb Custard Pie

1 cup cooked rhubarb, drained
1 cup sugar
3 beaten egg yolks
2 rounded tablespoons of flour
2 teaspoons minute tapioca
pinch of salt

Mix together and add 2 cups milk. Put in an unbaked pie shell. Bake 425° F. for 45 minutes. Then add meringue.

Meringue
  3 egg whites
  3 tablespoons cold water
  1 teaspoon baking powder
  6 tablespoons granulated sugar
  pinch of salt

Put all ingredients, except sugar, in mixing bowl. Beat until stiff. Add sugar gradually. Pile on pie, bake at 425° F. for a few minutes (until lightly browned). Watch carefully.

MRS. FLETCHER (ARLENE) WRIGHT
Cape Elizabeth, Maine

Heavenly Chocolate Pie

Meringue
  2 egg whites
  ½ teaspoon vinegar
  ¼ teaspoon cinnamon
  ½ cup sugar

Filling
  1 6-ounce package chocolate chips
  2 egg yolks
  ¼ cup water
  1 cup whipping cream
  ¼ cup sugar
  ¼ teaspoon cinnamon

Have ready one baked pie shell. Make a stiff meringue with above ingredients, with which line pie shell, heaping up the sides. Bake at 325° F. for 15 to 18 minutes. Melt package of chocolate chips over hot water. Meanwhile beat egg yolks, and water and add to melted chocolate. Spread ½ of chocolate mixture over cooled meringue in shell. Whip cream, adding sugar and spice. Then blend in the rest of the chocolate mixture. Pile into pie. Chill thoroughly. Garnish with shaved chocolate. Makes 8 servings.

MRS. FRANK (MABEL) LAY
Portland, Oregon

I desired mercy, and not sacrifice; and the knowledge of God more than burnt offerings (Hos. 6:6).

Old-fashioned Southern Chess Pie
(Alabama Recipe)

  3 eggs
  1½ cups sugar (may be reduced to 1 cup if pie is too rich for individual taste)
  ½ stick melted margarine
  ⅓ cup buttermilk
  2½ tablespoons yellow cornmeal (white may be used)
  1 teaspoon pure vanilla or butternut-vanilla flavoring

Mix together and pour into unbaked pie shell. Bake at 350° F. for 40 minutes. Add coconut sprinkled on top, or pecans if desired.

"Delicious old southern recipe and the easiest pie I have ever made. It is an enriched egg custard type of pie. Does not last very long around our house."

MRS. CHARLES (LAVERNE) OLIVER
Helena, Alabama

Custard Rhubarb Pie

3 cups sliced rhubarb
2 egg yolks
1 cup sugar
2 tablespoons flour
1 tablespoon butter
1 unbaked 9-inch pie shell
favorite meringue recipe

Pour boiling water over rhubarb. Let stand for five minutes. Drain off water, retaining about three tablespoons on rhubarb. Beat egg yolks well and add the sugar, flour, and butter. Pour this mixture into the rhubarb. Fill unbaked pie shell and bake at 350° F. for about 45 minutes, until custard is set and knife inserted in center comes out clean. Put meringue on top and brown.

Mrs. Charles (Marge) Higgins
Nampa, Idaho

Coconut Custard Pie

4 eggs
¼ cup butter
1 teaspoon vanilla
2 cups milk
¾ cup coconut
½ cup Bisquick
½ cup sugar

Put all ingredients in blender at "blend" setting for 2 minutes. Pour in ungreased 9-inch pie pan. Bake at 350° F. for 40-50 minutes. Done when brown on top and firm. *Do not* open oven while baking.

Mrs. Larry (Pat) Neff
Owosso, Michigan

You cannot lose when you ask, for you will receive God's help. As you seek, you will find His way; and as you knock, the door will be opened for you to live daily in His will (Jim Monck).

Rhubarb Pie

4 cups rhubarb
3 tablespoons flour
1½ cups sugar
1 egg
1 teaspoon vanilla

Mix flour and sugar with rhubarb. Add beaten egg and vanilla. Put in unbaked pie shell. Add top crust and bake 45 minutes to 1 hour.

"Serve this to people that do not like rhubarb. They will think this is delicious!"

Mrs. O. E. (Neola) Beeson
Council Bluffs, Iowa

Rhubarb Pie

   3 cups (fresh or frozen) rhubarb chopped
   2 tablespoons flour
   1 egg
   1 ½ cups sugar

Mix flour with chopped rhubarb. Beat egg well, add sugar gradually, continue to beat until light. Mix both mixtures together and pour into your pie shell. Cover with top crust. Brush crust with milk. Bake 20 minutes at 400° F., then 20 minutes at 350° F.

"Delicious served warm!"

Mrs. David (Linda) Aaserud
Bangor, Maine

Crisp Never-Fail Pie Crust

For single pie crust
   1 cup flour
   ½ teaspoon salt
   ⅓ cup corn oil
   3 tablespoons cold water

For 2 two-crust pies
   4 cups flour
   2 teaspoons salt
   1 ⅓ cups corn oil
   ¾ cup cold water

Combine flour and salt in bowl. Mix water and oil together. Pour over flour and stir lightly with fork, only until mixed. Roll out between waxed paper, peel off one piece of paper, place pie plate upside down on crust and slip hand underneath and pop into pan. Trim crust and crinkle edges. Prick bottom, if one shell, and bake. Bake at 450° F. for 8-10 minutes.

Mrs. James (Donna) Scarth
Portland, Oregon

Snowball Cake

2 envelopes unflavored gelatin
¼ cup cold water
1 cup boiling water
1 cup crushed pineapple
1 cup pineapple juice
1 cup sugar
½ teaspoon salt
juice of one lemon
1 carton whipped topping
coconut
1 angel food cake

Dissolve gelatin in cold water. Add boiling water and crushed pineapple with juice, sugar and lemon juice. Put in refrigerator to partially jell. Then add ⅔ carton of whipped topping and fold in mixture. Tear angel food cake into bite-size pieces, fold into mixture, and pour into 9 x 13" dish. Chill overnight. Frost with the remaining whipped topping and sprinkle coconut over the top. Alternate method: Use a medium-sized can of crushed pineapple and add all at once, including the juice. Also, all of the whipped topping can be folded in at once, if so desired, and coconut may be included in mixture.

MRS. BRUCE (RUTH) TAYLOR
Marion, Indiana

Carrot Cake

2 cups flour
2 teaspoons baking powder
1½ teaspoons salt
2 teaspoons cinnamon
1½ cups cooking oil
2 cups sugar
4 eggs
2 cups grated carrots
1 8-ounce can crushed pineapple, drained
¾ cup chopped pecans

Sift dry ingredients together. Mix oil, sugar, and eggs, beating after each addition. Add dry ingredients and mix well. Add carrots, pineapple, pecans. Grease and flour 9 x 13" pan, bake 40-50 minutes at 350° F.

Icing: cream together, 1 8-ounce package cream cheese, 1 stick margarine, 1 box powdered sugar, 2 teaspoons vanilla.

MRS. MARVIN (ARLENE) SNOWBARGER
Emporia, Kansas

Carol's Carrot Cake

2 cups flour
1½ cups sugar
1 teaspoon cinnamon
2 teaspoons baking soda
¾ cup buttermilk
1 8½-ounce can crushed pineapple
½ cup oil
3 eggs
1 teaspoon mace (optional)
½ teaspoon salt
2 teaspoons vanilla
1 cup coconut
1 cup chopped walnuts
2 cups grated carrots

Combine dry ingredients; blend in oil, eggs, and buttermilk. Add remaining ingredients. Bake at 350° F. for 45 minutes.

Frosting
½ cube margarine
½ 8-ounce cream cheese
½ box powdered sugar

Beat until creamy.

"This is the best carrot cake ever! The buttermilk, pineapple, and coconut make it super moist."

MRS. RICHARD (CAROL) PARROTT
Corvallis, Oregon

Be ye kind one to another, tenderhearted, forgiving one another, even as God for Christ's sake hath forgiven you (Eph. 4:32).

God . . . hath visited and redeemed his people (Luke 1:68).

Lemon Pudding Cake

1 package lemon flavored instant pudding
1 box cake mix (white or yellow)
4 eggs
1 cup water
½ cup oil

Blend all ingredients and beat 2 minutes. Bake in bundt or tube pan at 350° F. for 55 to 60 minutes, or until cake springs back when lightly pressed. Cool in pan for 15 minutes and remove. Glaze: Gradually add 1 tablespoon hot milk and a few drops yellow food coloring to 1 cup sifted powdered sugar in a bowl and blend well.

MRS. CHARLES (BETTY) PATTON
Knoxville, Tennessee

Mandarin Sno-ball Cake

2 envelopes unflavored gelatin
4 tablespoons cold water
1 cup boiling water mix well
1 cup sugar
1 tablespoon lemon juice
1 No. 2 can crushed pineapple with juice
1 11-ounce can mandarin oranges, drained
3 envelopes Dream Whip
1 angel food cake (homemade or bought)
1 7 ounce package flake coconut
1 box Dream Whip

Chill first 7 ingredients until softly thickened. Prepare the 3 envelopes of Dream Whip and fold into gelatin mixture. Break up an angel food cake into small bits and layer cake onto bottom of 9 x 13" dish. Pour gelatin mix over layer of cake. Use the other half of angel food cake bits and place over gelatin mixture. Pour the other half of gelatin mix on second half of cake. Top with 1 box (2 envelopes) of Dream Whip (mixed as directed on box). Sprinkle 1 package flake coconut on top. Chill till ready to serve.

MRS. LAUREN (JUNE) COUSINS
Monroeville, Pennsylvania

Lemon Gelatin Cake

1 package lemon cake mix
1 3-ounce package dry lemon gelatin
¾ cup water
¾ cup salad oil
4 eggs

Mix above ingredients. Beat for 4 minutes on medium speed. Pour into 9 x 13" cake pan. Bake 35-40 minutes, in 350° F. oven. Remove from oven and let stand 20 minutes. Poke holes in top of cake with an ice pick and dribble the following mixture over the top: Mix 2 cups powdered sugar and ½ cup lemon juice.

"Other flavors may be used, such as orange cake mix and orange gelatin. This cake keeps well. It also may be made ahead and frozen."

MRS. GEORGE (KAY) SCUTT
Valparaiso, Indiana

Pound Cake

2 sticks soft margarine
3 cups sugar
6 eggs
3 cups plain flour
1 cup whipping cream
1 teaspoon vanilla
½ teaspoon walnuts or 1 teaspoon lemon

Mix well soft margarine and sugar, add eggs one at a time. Alternately add flour and cream. Add flavoring, pour in greased tube pan. Bake (in preheated oven) 325° F. for 1½ hours or until golden brown on top.

"This makes up a good basic pound cake, can be glazed. Goes well with fruits and ice cream."

Mrs. Clarence (Evangeline) Coleman
Lexington, South Carolina

Lemon Pound Cake

1 package yellow cake mix
1 package instant lemon pudding
¾ cup water
½ cup salad oil
4 eggs

Glaze:
1 cup powdered sugar
¼ cup lemon juice

My little children, let us not love in word, neither in tongue; but in deed and in truth (1 John 3:18).

Beat eggs until thick and lemon colored, add cake mix and pudding mix (dry), water and salad oil. Beat at medium speed for 10 minutes. Pour into 2 foil-lined loaf pans. Bake in 350° F. oven about 50 minutes.

Glaze:
Cook juice and sugar to boiling point. Punch holes in warm cake and drizzle over top.

Mrs. Wil (Polly) Spaite
Porterville, California

For I have given you an example, that ye should do as I have done to you (John 13:15).

Cream Cheese Pound Cake

2 sticks margarine
1 stick butter
1 8-ounce package cream cheese
3 cups sugar
6 eggs
3 cups cake flour
2 teaspoons vanilla flavoring
1 teaspoon lemon extract (optional)
pinch of salt

Cream margarine, butter, and cream cheese together, then add sugar. Cream again. Add eggs, one at a time, and beat alternately with flour. Add flavoring. Preheat oven to 325° F. and bake for 1½ hours. When cake has baked for 1 hour; cover with piece of aluminum foil and bake for 30 minutes longer. Bake in tube pan.

MRS. J. D. (THELMA) BAREFOOT
Chesapeake, Virginia

Sterling Pound Cake

3 cups sugar
2 sticks margarine, softened
1 cup cooking oil
6 eggs
1 cup milk
3 cups flour
1 teaspoon coconut extract
1 teaspoon almond extract
1 cup flaked coconut
½ teaspoon salt

Mix sugar, margarine, and oil. Add eggs, one at a time. Mix well. Add milk, flour, extracts, coconut, and salt. Be sure batter is well blended. Pour into greased tube pan. Bake at 350° F. for 1½ to 2 hours.

MRS. H. C. (GERRY) HATTON
Sterling, Illinois

Coconut Pound Cake

2½ sticks margarine
3 cups sugar
6 eggs (room temperature)
3 cups flour
¼ teaspoon salt
¼ teaspoon baking soda
1 small (8-ounce) carton sour cream
1 teaspoon vanilla
6 ounces coconut

Cream margarine and sugar together. Add the eggs one at a time. Beat well. Sift flour, salt, and baking soda together. Add alternately (to creamed mixture) with sour cream. Add vanilla and beat well. Fold in the coconut. Pour in a well-greased and -floured tube pan (bundt pan is great). Bake in a preheated oven, 300° F., for 1½ hours or until done.

"Very delicious! Needs no frosting. A great favorite for many people."

MRS. GORDON (ALICE JEAN) WETMORE
Kansas City, Missouri

They called them, and commanded them not to speak at all nor teach in the name of Jesus. But Peter and John answered . . . we cannot but speak the things which we have seen and heard (Acts 4:18-20).

Barbara's Pound Cake

2 sticks margarine, at room temperature
½ cup shortening, at room temperature
3 cups sugar
5 eggs
3 cups flour
½ teaspoon baking powder
¼ teaspoon salt
1 cup milk
1 teaspoon lemon flavoring
1 teaspoon vanilla flavoring

Do not substitute. Mix margarine and shortening together well. Add sugar, mixing well. Gradually add eggs, one at a time. Then add flour sifted with baking powder and salt, alternately with milk, lemon flavoring, and vanilla flavoring. Bake at 325° F. for 1 hour and 20 minutes.

"My children (all grown) like this for birthday cake! This is a very tasty, moist pound cake. Batter should be very smooth and creamy and easy to pour. If too thick, add more milk. Use electric mixer on medium speed."

MRS. REEFORD L. (BARBARA) CHANEY
Richmond, Virginia

Jam Cake

    5 eggs, beaten
    2 cups sugar
    3 cups flour
    1 cup butter
    1 cup buttermilk
    1 teaspoon soda
    ¼ teaspoon salt
    ½ teaspoon cinnamon
    1½ teaspoons cloves
    1½ teaspoons allspice
    1 cup raisins
    1 cup black walnuts, chopped
    1 cup jam, strawberry or blackberry

Thy word is a lamp unto my feet, and a light unto my path (Ps. 119:105).

Cream butter and gradually add the sugar. Cream together until light and fluffy. Add well-beaten eggs. Sift flour, spices and salt together. Dissolve soda in buttermilk and add it and the flour mixture alternately to the egg, sugar, butter mixture, and beat after each addition. Lightly dredge the fruit and nuts with extra flour and add to the mixture. Next add the jam. Stir to get good distribution. Grease and paper-line bottom of a 10-inch tube pan. Pour in batter and bake 1 hour and 15 minutes at 325° F. or until done. Ice with caramel icing.

MRS. WESLEY (PAULINE) POOLE
Fairfield, Ohio

Easy Jam Cake

    1 cup butter
    1 cup sugar
    4 eggs
    3 cups plain flour
    1 teaspoon soda
    1 teaspoon cinnamon
    1 cup buttermilk
    1 cup blackberry jam with seeds
    1 cup pecans (optional)

Cream butter and sugar, add eggs, then flour, soda, and cinnamon alternately with milk, then jam. One cup broken pecans may be added if desired. Bake in 2 greased and floured round 8-inch pans in a 350° F. oven, for approximately 35 minutes. Frost with your favorite caramel or white frosting.

MRS. WILLIAM (BETTY) SLONECKER
Nashville, Tennessee

Prune Cake

2 cups flour
pinch salt
1 teaspoon soda
1 teaspoon cinnamon
1 teaspoon allspice
1 teaspoon nutmeg
1½ cups sugar
1 cup cooking oil
1 cup buttermilk
3 eggs
1 teaspoon vanilla
1 cup nuts, chopped
1 cup prunes, chopped

Glaze:
1 cup sugar
½ cup buttermilk
½ teaspoon vanilla
1 tablespoon white syrup
1 stick butter

It behoved Christ to suffer, and to rise from the dead the third day: and that repentance and remission of sins should be preached in his name among all nations, beginning at Jerusalem (Luke 24:46-47).

Sift together: flour, salt, soda, cinnamon, allspice, and nutmeg. Mix in bowl: sugar, oil, buttermilk, eggs, and vanilla. Mix all together. Fold in nuts and prunes. Grease a stem pan (line with paper and grease paper). Bake 1 hour, 15 minutes at 350° F. Cool 15 minutes and remove from pan. Mix glaze and cook over medium flame, stirring constantly, until it turns caramel color. Pour over cake.

"Cake keeps well, if you hide it! It is a good change from fruit-cake, at Christmas, but delicious anytime."

Mrs. Donald (Lillian) Irwin
Quincy, Massachusetts

When we come to the end of our own manipulations and in our desperation acknowledge Jesus as Lord, He is there (Mary Lou Steigleder).

Swedish Prune Fruit Cake

2 cups brown sugar
1 cup butter
1 cup prunes, cooked and chopped
1 cup prune juice
3 egg yolks (save egg whites)
3 cups flour
nuts and dates (amount optional)
1 teaspoon cinnamon
1 teaspoon cloves
1 teaspoon allspice
1 teaspoon soda
½ teaspoon nutmeg
1 pound mixed dried fruit
½ pound raisins

Mix all ingredients (except egg whites). Fold in the 3 beaten egg whites. Bake 1¾ hours at 250° F. in 9 x 5" greased loaf pans or 1 bundt cake pan. Glaze.

"A delicious moist cake that we have always enjoyed. Credit for this recipe goes to Kelly Johnston, Newport, Oregon."

MRS. CARL (DORIS) CLENDENEN
Salem, Oregon

Mississippi Mud Cake

Cream together

2 sticks margarine
2 cups sugar
2 tablespoons cocoa

Then add

4 eggs
1½ cups flour
1⅓ cups coconut
1 teaspoon vanilla
1½ cups nuts
dash salt

Mix well. Bake in 9 x 13" pan. While still hot, spread jar of marshmallow creme over cake. Frosting: ½ cup margarine, ⅓ cup milk, 3½ tablespoons cocoa; bring to a boil. Remove from heat and add: 1 pound powdered sugar, 1 cup nuts. Spread on cake. (You can reheat if it gets too thick.)

MRS. HAROLD (MERRY) LITTLE
Modesto, California

Apple Cake

2 eggs
2 cups sugar
1¼ cups salad oil
1 teaspoon vanilla
1 teaspoon cinnamon
1 teaspoon salt
3 cups flour
3 cups chopped apples
½ cup chopped nuts
1 teaspoon soda

Combine sugar, eggs, oil, and vanilla. Beat well. Sift flour, salt, cinnamon, and soda together. Roll apples and nuts in part of flour mixture and add to sugar and egg mixture. Finally add the remaining flour mixture. Pour into 9 x 13 x 2" pan. Bake until done (approximately 1 hour), at 325° F.

MRS. MARK L. (VIRGINIA) FRAME
New Castle, Indiana

Fresh Apple Cake

2 cups flour
2 teaspoons soda
¾ or 1 teaspoon cinnamon
1 teaspoon salt
½ cup cooking oil
2 cups sugar
2 eggs
4 cups chopped apples
2 cups black walnuts

Glaze
1 cup sugar
¼ teaspoon soda
¾ tablespoon butter
1 tablespoon white Karo
½ cup buttermilk

Sift first four ingredients and sugar. Put in oil and eggs and beat until fluffy. Add chopped apples and nuts. Bake 45 minutes in 350° F. oven. Cool just enough to take out of pan. Prepare Glaze while cake is cooling.

Glaze: boil all ingredients for 5 to 8 minutes. Glaze the top of the cake.

MRS. GERALD L. (KAY) MORGAN
Marietta, Ohio

The more we learn of Christ, the more we become like Him. The more we become like Christ, the more truth He can share with us (Wanda Milner).

This I say then, Walk in the Spirit, and ye shall not fulfill the lust of the flesh (Gal. 5: 16).

German Apple Cake

3 eggs
1 cup salad oil
2 cups sugar
1 teaspoon vanilla
1 teaspoon baking soda
2 cups flour
2 teaspoons cinnamon
½ teaspoon salt
1 cup chopped nuts
1 can apple pie filling

Beat eggs and oil together. Mix all other ingredients and then add egg mixture and 1 cup chopped nuts and 1 can of apple pie filling. Bake in 9 by 12 baking pan at 350° F. for 45-60 minutes.

Frosting:
2 small packages cream cheese
3 tablespoons butter
1 teaspoon vanilla
1¼ cups powdered sugar

Blend cream cheese and vanilla and butter--then add sugar.

"This cake is delicious and rich and keeps very well."

MRS. ED (ELLEN) ANDERSON
Long Beach, California

Apple Ugly Cake

Section 1
1 cup sugar
1½ cups flour
1 teaspoon baking soda
1 teaspoon salt
1 teaspoon cinnamon

Section 2
½ + 1/6 cup salad oil
1 egg
1 teaspoon vanilla

Section 3
2 cups apples, peeled and chopped
¼ cup raisins

Mix together ingredients in section 1. Stir in section 2. Mix well. Add section 3. Bake one hour at 325° F.

MRS. AUSTIN (MARGARET) WRIGHT
Warren, Ohio

Raw Apple Cake

2 cups sugar
1½ cups oil
3 eggs
3 cups flour
1 teaspoon soda
1 teaspoon salt
1 teaspoon vanilla
3 cups uncooked apples, finely chopped
1 cup pecan pieces

Glaze:
1 cup brown sugar
1 stick margarine
¼ cup milk

Bring to slow boil. Cook two minutes, pour over cake.

Blend together oil, sugar, and eggs. Add sifted dry ingredients, mixing thoroughly. Fold in apples and nuts, add vanilla. Bake one hour at 350° F. in either rectangular pan or well-floured tube pan. Top with glaze.

MRS. COLEMAN C. (MILDRED) MOORE
Kannapolis, North Carolina

Through him we both have access by one Spirit unto the Father (Eph. 2:18).

High Altitude Johnny Appleseed Cake

Sift together
2 cups flour
1 cup sugar
1 teaspoon salt
1 teaspoon cinnamon
½ teaspoon nutmeg
¼ teaspoon cloves

Add
1 cup raisins
1 cup chopped walnuts
½ cup melted butter

Combine
1½ cups thick, hot applesauce
2 teaspoons soda

Add to dry ingredients. Beat until well blended. Pour into greased loaf pan. Bake at 350° F. for 1 hour.

"This recipe is for high altitude preparation (our altitude is 4,300 feet.)"

MRS. ARTHUR F. (DORIS) TALLMAN
Sparks, Nevada

Cheese Cake

First layer
25 Ritz crackers
½ cup powdered sugar
1 stick margarine

Second layer
1 package Dream Whip (mix according to package)
1 package cream cheese
1 cup powdered sugar
1 can fruit pie filling, cherry or your favorite

First layer: Roll Ritz crackers, mix sugar, and melted margarine. Pat in bottom of baking dish.
Second layer: Beat or mix cream cheese and sugar till smooth. Fold in Dream Whip. Spread over first layer. Then cover with pie filling. Leave in refrigerator overnight.

"I usually use 10 or 15 more crackers, we like a thicker crust."

MRS. JAMES (FAITH) EMMERT
Yukon, Oklahoma

Cheese Cake

2 pounds cream cheese, room temperature
1 cup whipping cream
4 to 5 eggs
1 cup milk
2 cups sugar
3 tablespoons flour
1 teaspoon cornstarch
pinch of salt
2 teaspoons vanilla
2 tablespoons melted butter
any good graham cracker pie crust recipe

Mix together with hand mixer the softened cheese with all of the dry ingredients which have first been mixed together. Add eggs, one at a time, blending after each one. Add all other ingredients except the cream and butter. Fold these last two into the mixture with spoon. Pour into springform pan which has been lined with graham cracker crust. Bake in very hot oven (500° F.) for five minutes or until edge of crust is golden brown. Reduce heat to 250° to 275° F. and bake 1 hour and 15 minutes (may take a little longer depending on your oven). Cool for several hours before removal from pan.

MRS. THOMAS M. (KAY) HERMON
Little Rock, Arkansas

Cheese Cake

Crust
  3 tablespoons melted butter
  1 tablespoon sugar
  ½ cup chopped pecans
  1 cup graham cracker crumbs

Filling
  3 8-ounce packages cream cheese
  1 cup sugar
  3 eggs
  ½ teaspoon vanilla

Topping
  1 pint sour cream
  3 tablespoons sugar
  ½ teaspoon vanilla
  coarsely chopped nuts

When ye pray, use not vain repetitions, as the heathen do; for they think that they shall be heard for their much speaking (Matt. 6:7).

Combine crust ingredients and press firmly around 9" cheese cake pan. Soften cream cheese at room temperature then cream with the sugar. Add eggs one at a time, then the vanilla. Spoon mixture into the crumb-lined pan and bake 20 minutes at 375° F. Take immediately from oven.
Mix first three topping ingredients and spread on top of cheese layer. Bake 5 minutes at 500° F. Remove from oven and sprinkle a few coarsely chopped nuts over the top. Refrigerate a few hours until thoroughly chilled.

Mrs. Donald (Linda) Cain
McCory, Arkansas

Gingerbread Fruit Upside-down Cake

⅛ stick margarine
½ cup brown sugar
½ cup raisins
½ cup chopped nuts
3-4 sliced apples
gingerbread cake mix

I would rather walk in the dark with God than go alone by sight (Selected).

Put first 4 ingredients in bottom of 9 x 13" Pyrex baking pan; cover with a layer of apple slices. Mix gingerbread mix according to package directions; cover fruit mixture and bake according to package directions. (350° F. for 40 minutes.) Serve warm with whipped topping or ice cream.

Mrs. Paul (Juanita) Forgrave
Columbus, Ohio

Best Gingerbread

½ cup sugar
1 egg
¼ cup light molasses (Brer Rabbit)
1 cup flour (don't you dare add more!)
1 teaspoon soda
¼ teaspoon each cinnamon, ginger, nutmeg, salt
½ cup melted butter (you must use butter)
½ cup hot water

Mix sugar, egg, and molasses. Sift flour, soda, and spices, add to sugar mixture. Add hot water to melted butter (¼ only), add to the flour mixture. Bake in square pan 8 x 8" greased and floured, about 20 minutes at 350° F. When done, while still in pan, pour the remaining ¼ cup melted butter over gingerbread. (I use a pastry brush.) Serve warm, it doesn't need whipped cream.

Mrs. Hugh C. (Audrey) Benner
Leawood, Kansas

How big is God? How great is He? Is it true that there is nothing that He cannot do? And all that God is, Christ is. All that God can do, Christ is able to do, for in our wonderful Savior dwells ALL the fullness of God (Leslie Miller).

Super Chocolate Cheesecake

18 chocolate wafers (enough for 1 cup)
¼ cup melted butter
¼ teaspoon cinnamon
1 8-ounce package semisweet chocolate chips or bar
1½ pounds (24 ounce or 3 8-ounce packages) cream cheese, room temperature
1 cup sugar
3 eggs
1 teaspoon cocoa (not instant)
1 teaspoon vanilla
2 cups sour cream

Crush chocolate wafers with rolling pin to make 1 cup. Mix crumbs into melted butter, add cinnamon. Press crumb mixture into bottom of an 8-inch springform pan; buckle sides on, chill. Melt chocolate chips in top of double boiler. In large bowl, beat cream cheese until fluffy and smooth. Beat in sugar and add eggs, one at a time, beating after each addition. Beat in melted chocolate along with cocoa and vanilla. Blend thoroughly. Beat in sour cream. Pour into prepared springform pan. Bake 1 hour and 10 minutes. The cake will still be runny, but becomes firm as it chills. Cool at room temperature, then chill in refrigerator for at least 5 hours before serving.

"Garnish with whipped cream and chocolate curls or sprinkles. Leftovers freeze well."

Mrs. L. Wesley (Naomi) Johnson
Nampa, Idaho

White Chocolate Cake

4 ounces white chocolate or almond bark
½ cup hot water
2 cubes of butter
1¾ cups sugar
4 egg yolks
1 teaspoon vanilla
2½ cups flour
1 teaspoon soda
pinch of salt
1 cup of buttermilk
1 cup of chopped pecans
1 cup coconut
4 egg whites (do not beat stiff)

Dissolve chocolate in hot water and set aside to cool. Combine the butter and sugar, and mix until creamy. Add the chocolate mixture. Mix egg yolks one at a time, then the vanilla. Add sifted flour, soda, salt, buttermilk, pecans, coconut, and the egg whites. Bake in greased oblong cake pan (not layer pan). Start cake in slow oven and in 30 minutes you can turn oven to 350° F. Cake is done when brown on top or a toothpick comes out clean and dry.

Icing
1 cube butter
1 8-ounce cream cheese

Mix well and add 1 box powdered sugar. Add ½ cup ground pecans, ½ cup coconut, and 2 teaspoons vanilla.

MRS. FOREST (AZALIA) FREEMAN
Capitan, New Mexico

Banana Split Cake

Graham cracker crust
2 cups graham cracker crumbs
½ cup margarine, melted

Layers
1 cup margarine, melted
2 eggs, beaten well
1 box powdered sugar
5 bananas, sliced
1 large can crushed pineapple, drained
1 large container Cool Whip
slivered almonds

Prepare crust. Mix ingredients for layer one (resembles pudding). Spread on crust. Add layer two: 5 sliced bananas. To this add layer 3, crushed pineapple. Top with Cool Whip and slivered almonds. Chill until ready to serve.

MRS. DAN (MARTHA) WRIGHT
Waco, Texas

Not as the offence, so also is the free gift. For if through the offence of one many be dead, much more the grace of God, and the gift by grace, which is by one man, Jesus Christ, hath abounded unto many (Rom. 5:15).

He only is my rock and my salvation: he is my defence; I shall not be moved (Ps. 62:6).

Another Banana Split Cake

2 packed cups vanilla wafer crumbs
2 sticks margarine
2 cups powdered sugar
2 egg whites
3 bananas, sliced length-wise
1 No. 2 can crushed pineapple, drained thoroughly
Dream Whip
chopped nuts and cherries

Use oblong cake pan. First layer: vanilla wafer crumbs mixed with 1 stick margarine. Second layer: powdered sugar, egg whites, and 1 stick margarine; beat for 10 minutes. Third layer: sliced bananas. Fourth layer: crushed pineapple. Fifth layer: Dream Whip. Sixth layer: chopped nuts and cherries.

MRS. HERB (MIRIAM) HALL
Olathe, Kansas

Flower Garden Cake

6 egg yolks, beaten
¾ cup sugar
1½ teaspoon lemon rind, grated
¾ cup lemon juice
1 large angel food cake
1½ envelopes unflavored gelatin
¼ cup cold water
6 egg whites
¾ cup sugar
1 cup chunk pineapple
½ cup cherries, cut into small pieces
½ cup chopped pecans
whipped cream topping

Make a custard out of the first four ingredients. Cook in top of a double boiler until it coats a spoon. Remove from heat and add gelatin dissolved in cold water.

To egg whites (beaten very stiff), add sugar, and fold into other mixture. Break angel food cake into bite-size pieces in a large mixing bowl. Fold custard mixture over cake. Add chunk pineapple, cherries, and pecans. Pour into buttered tube pan. Cover with wax paper and put into refrigerator overnight. Remove from pan when ready to serve and ice with whipped cream.

MRS. CHARLES (MARGE) HIGGINS
Nampa, Idaho

Raspberry Cake

1 can or package of frozen raspberries, thawed
¾ cup raspberry juice (add water if needed)
1 package white cake mix (Duncan Hines Deluxe II)
4 eggs
½ cup oil
1 package raspberry gelatin

Combine cake mix, gelatin, eggs, and beat 2 minutes at medium speed; add oil and liquid, beat additional 2 minutes. Fold raspberries into mix; pour into bundt or angel pan. Bake at 350° F. for 35 minutes or until done. Makes 10-12 servings.

Icing:

1 8-ounce cream cheese
¾ package powdered sugar
½ cube butter

Blend and spread on cake. I add a drop of red coloring for a pale pink frosting.

"This is a good Sunday cake because made on Saturday, the flavors blend and it keeps particularly well."

MRS. MARLYN (MARY) ANDERSON
Tigard, Oregon

Gumdrop Cake

1 pound white raisins
1-2 pounds gumdrops, cut
1 cup walnuts
4 cups flour
1 teaspoon salt
1 cup butter
2 cups sugar
2 eggs
1½ cups applesauce, unsweetened
1 teaspoon soda in 1 tablespoon hot water
1 teaspoon vanilla
¼ teaspoon each cloves, nutmeg
1 teaspoon cinnamon

They said, We will drink no wine: for Jonadab the son of Rechab our father commanded us, saying, Ye shall drink no wine, neither ye, nor your sons for ever (Jer. 35:6).

Beat eggs until foamy, add sugar and butter. Cream well. Slowly add flour, continuously beating, add salt and spices and applesauce, vanilla and soda. Fold in raisins, walnuts, and gumdrops. Bake in well-greased 9 x 13" pan at 275° to 300° F. for 1½ to 2 hours or until toothpick comes out relatively clean.

MRS. GEORGE (WANDA) ALMGREN
Bakersfield, California

Mocha Angel Cake

1 pint whipping cream
1 tablespoon instant coffee
Chill together 2 hours.
3 tablespoons cocoa
1 package slivered almonds

Add 1 cup sifted powdered sugar. Beat. Add ½ package slivered almonds which have been toasted in oven. Slice angel cake horizontally so there are three equal layers. Spread whipped cream mixture on layers and top. Top with balance of toasted almonds.

Mrs. Robert (Jewel) Ferris
Redlands, California

Nella's Poppyseed Cake

Cake
1 cup buttermilk
1 cup shortening
3 cups sugar
3 cups flour
6 whole eggs
¼ teaspoon soda
½ teaspoon salt
1 teaspoon vanilla
1 teaspoon almond extract
1 teaspoon butter flavoring
1 tablespoon poppyseeds

Glaze
⅓ cup orange juice
1⅔ cups powdered sugar
1 teaspoon vanilla
1 teaspoon almond extract
1 teaspoon butter flavoring

Cake:
Soak the poppyseed in buttermilk overnight. Cream together well, shortening and sugar, and add eggs one at a time. Sift flour, soda, and salt, and add to the creamed mixture. Add buttermilk with vanilla, almond extract, and butter flavoring. Bake in a greased and floured bundt pan 325° F. for 1 to 1½ hours. Cool 10 minutes, then remove from pan; add the glaze.

Glaze:
Bring to a boil and pour over the cake while it is still warm.

"The poppyseed will make the cake look 'musty,' but when you have tasted it, you will say, 'I "must" have some more.'"

Mrs. Harold (Nella) Harcourt
Kilgore, Texas

Frozen Cake

½ gallon vanilla ice cream or ice milk
1 large angel food cake, torn into small pieces
2 packages frozen strawberries
1 large size Cool Whip
1 cup chopped nuts

Mix well with potato masher or similar tool. Spoon into container. Freeze. Serve frozen. Makes 10 to 15 servings.

"This is a good make-ahead dessert. A good way to use angel food cakes when they are on sale!"

Mrs. Ford (Barbara) Boone
Baton Rouge, Louisiana

But thou, when thou prayest, enter into thy closet, and when thou hast shut thy door, pray to thy Father which is in secret; and thy Father which seeth in secret shall reward thee openly (Matt. 6:6).

Coca-Cola Cake

Cake
2 cups unsifted flour
2 cups sugar
2 sticks margarine
3 tablespoons cocoa
1 cup Coca-Cola
½ cup buttermilk
2 beaten eggs
1 teaspoon soda
1 teaspoon vanilla
1½ cups miniature marshmallows

Icing
1 stick oleo
3 tablespoons cocoa
6 tablespoons Coca-Cola
1 box powdered sugar
1 cup pecans, chopped

Combine flour and sugar in large bowl. Heat oleo, cocoa, and Coca-Cola to boiling. Pour over flour and sugar, stir well. Add buttermilk, eggs, soda, vanilla, and miniature marshmallows. Pour into greased and floured long cake pan. Bake at 350° F. for 30 or 35 minutes.

Icing:
Combine oleo, cocoa, and Coca-Cola, heat to boiling. Pour over powdered sugar and beat well. Add chopped pecans, spread on cake.

Mrs. James W. (Jean) Daniel
Henryetta, Oklahoma

O come, let us sing unto the Lord: let us make a joyful noise to the rock of our salvation (Ps. 95:1).

Hummingbird Cake

(with cream cheese frosting)

Cake
- 3 cups all-purpose flour
- 2 cups sugar
- 1 teaspoon salt
- 1 teaspoon soda
- 1 teaspoon ground cinnamon
- 3 eggs, beaten
- 1½ cups salad oil
- 1½ teaspoons vanilla extract
- 1 8-ounce can crushed pineapple, undrained
- 2 cups chopped pecans or walnuts divided
- 2 cups chopped bananas

Frosting
- 2 8-ounce packages cream cheese, softened
- 1 cup butter or margarine, softened
- 2 16-ounce packages powdered sugar
- 2 teaspoons vanilla extract

For to me to live is Christ, and to die is gain (Phil. 1:21).

Cake:

Combine dry ingredients in a large mixing bowl; add eggs and salad oil, stirring until dry ingredients are moistened. Do not beat. Stir in vanilla, pineapple, 1 cup chopped pecans, and bananas. Spoon batter into 3 well-greased and -floured 9-inch cake pans. Bake at 350° F. for 25 to 30 minutes or until cake tests done. Cool in pans 10 minutes; remove from pans and cool completely.

Frosting:

Combine cream cheese and butter; cream until smooth. Add powdered sugar, beating until light and fluffy. Stir in vanilla. Spread frosting between layers and on top and sides of cake. Sprinkle with 1 cup chopped pecans. Makes one 9-inch, 3-layer cake; 15-18 slices.

"This cake is super moist and super delicious!"

MRS. JERALD R. (THELMA) LOCKE
Bethany, Oklahoma

Never-Fail Cupcakes

- 1½ cups flour
- 1 cup sugar (I use ½ brown and ½ white)
- ½ cup cocoa
- 1 teaspoon soda
- ½ cup shortening or margarine
- 1 egg
- ½ cup buttermilk or sour milk

½ cup hot water
1 teaspoon vanilla

Sift dry ingredients together into large mixing bowl. Add all other ingredients in order given. After the last item is added beat until the batter is smooth. Fill cups ½ full of batter for 18 cupcakes. Bake at 350° F. Also makes a large sheet cake. I bake this in 3 pie pans and shape the warm cake as a pie shell. Cool. Drizzle with chocolate syrup and nuts. Cover with foil and freeze. I call this Chocolate Sundae Pie.

"This recipe was given to me by a German farm lady in Colorado in about 1930, the start of my childhood recipe collection.

MRS. K. S. (BETTY) RICE
Kansas City, Missouri

Lazy Daisy Oatmeal Cake

1¼ cups boiling water
1 cup oatmeal, uncooked
½ cup butter or margarine
1 cup granulated sugar
1 cup firmly packed brown sugar
1 teaspoon vanilla
2 eggs
1½ cups sifted flour
1 teaspoon soda
½ teaspoon salt
¾ teaspoon cinnamon
¼ teaspoon nutmeg

Pour boiling water over oats; cover and let stand 20 minutes. Beat butter until creamy; gradually add sugars and beat until fluffy. Blend in vanilla and eggs. Add oats mixture; mix well. Sift together flour, soda, salt, cinnamon, and nutmeg. Add to creamed mixture. Mix well. Pour batter into well-greased and -floured 9-inch square pan. Bake 50-55 minutes at 350° F. Do not remove cake from pan.

Frosting
¼ cup butter or margarine, melted
½ cup firmly packed brown sugar
3 tablespoons cream (canned or half-and-half)
⅓ cup chopped nuts
¾ cup shredded or flaked coconut

Combine all ingredients. Spread evenly over cake. Broil until frosting becomes bubbly. Delicious served warm or cold.

MRS. BOB (MARY LEE) HUFF
Alexandria, Indiana

Whipped Cream Cake

½ pound butter
3 cups sugar
3 cups cake flour
6 eggs
½ pint whipping cream, not whipped

Add extracts, if desired:
½ teaspoon vanilla
½ teaspoon lemon or
½ teaspoon almond

Blend all ingredients. Then mix, on medium speed, for 3 minutes. Put into well-greased and -floured tube pan. Bake at 350° F. for 1 hour and 15 minutes.

Mrs. Coleman C. (Mildred) Moore
Kannapolis, North Carolina

There is no higher or finer freedom than the ability to refrain from something we would like to do because of its possible injury to others (Richard S. Taylor).

Chocolate Sheet Cake

Cake
2 cups sugar
2 cups flour
½ cup buttermilk
1 teaspoon soda
2 eggs
½ teaspoon salt
1 teaspoon vanilla
2 sticks margarine
4 tablespoons cocoa
1 cup hot water

Frosting or Topping
1 stick margarine
4 tablespoons cocoa
6 tablespoons buttermilk
1 pound box powdered sugar
1 teaspoon vanilla
1 cup nuts

Cake:
Melt margarine, add cocoa and hot water. Bring to a rapid boil. Pour over dry ingredients. Add buttermilk, eggs, and vanilla. Bake in large cookie sheet (greased) for 15-20 minutes at 350° F.

Frosting:
Melt margarine, add cocoa and buttermilk. Bring to a boil, add powdered sugar, vanilla, and 1 cup nuts. Mix thoroughly and place on cake while warm. When cool, cut in bars.

Mrs. R. J. (Maudie) Clack
Madison, Wisconsin

Bear ye one another's burdens, and so fulfill the law of Christ (Gal. 6:2).

Trust in the Lord with all thine heart; and lean not unto thine own understanding (Prov. 3:5).

Italian Cream Cake

1 stick margarine
½ cup vegetable shortening
2 cups sugar
5 eggs
2 cups sifted flour
1 teaspoon soda
1 cup buttermilk
1 teaspoon vanilla
½ cup pecans
1 small can coconut

Cream margarine, shortening, sugar, and eggs. Add remaining ingredients and mix. Bake in 3 lined 9-inch layer pans. Bake in 350° F. oven for 30 to 35 minutes.

Frosting
1 8-ounce package cream cheese
1 teaspoon vanilla
½ stick margarine
1 box confectioners' sugar

Cream all together with mixer. Add nuts on top of frosting.

MRS. GENE (LINDA) MONEYMAKER
Indianapolis, Indiana

Editor's Note: This was one of the winners of the cake-baking contest at the Indianapolis District laymen's retreat.

Daniel purposed in his heart that he would not defile himself (Dan. 1:8).

Brownstone Front Cake

¾ cup shortening
2 cups brown sugar
3 eggs, separated
2½ cups flour
1 cup sour milk
1 teaspoon vinegar and 1 teaspoon soda
1 teaspoon vanilla
1 teaspoon cinnamon
1 teaspoon nutmeg
1 cup walnuts, chopped

Cream shortening and sugar. Add egg yolks, flour, sour milk, vinegar, and soda. Then add flavoring and spices. Fold in egg whites and nuts. Bake at 325° F. for 1 hour. If you use layer pans, bake the cake 35 minutes, testing with a toothpick. Frost with any favorite caramel icing.

MRS. RUSSELL J. (PATRICIA) LONG
Barberton, Ohio

In the Lord put I my trust: how say ye to my soul . . .? (Ps. 11:1).

French Chocolate Cake and Glaze

½ cup softened butter
1 cup almonds, ground fine
¾ cup chocolate chips or three 1-ounce squares
⅔ cup sugar
3 eggs
¼ cup fine bread crumbs
grated rind of 1 large orange

Chocolate glaze
1 1-ounce unsweetened chocolate square
¼ cup chocolate chips or one 1-ounce semisweet chocolate square
2 tablespoons honey
¼ cup soft butter
toasted almonds
candied cherries

Cake:
Preheat oven to 375° F. Butter bottom and sides of 8-inch round cake pan. Line with wax paper. Melt chocolate over hot or boiled water. Work butter (may use beater) until light and soft. Gradually add sugar, beating constantly. Add eggs one at a time, beating after each. Stir in melted chocolate, grated orange rind, nuts, and bread crumbs. Mix well with spatula. Bake 25-45 minutes (test). Cool on rack 30 minutes. Turn out and completely cool. Glaze and trim with almonds and cherries.

Glaze:
Combine chocolate, butter, and honey, melt over hot water. Take off heat and beat hard by hand until pourable, then glaze and trim.

"This is a French recipe given to my daughter when in Europe. It is delightful."

MRS. M. R. (EVELYN) HANSCHE
Racine, Wisconsin

Butter Cake

2 sticks butter (½ pound)
1¾ cups sugar
5 eggs
2 cups sifted cake flour
½ teaspoon vanilla (optional)

Mix softened butter and sugar at medium speed until blended. Add one egg at a time, beating between additions. Add flour and beat until well blended (add vanilla, if desired). Pour into greased and floured tube or bundt pan. Preheat oven to 350° F.;

bake for 50 minutes or until toothpick comes out clean. Allow 15 or 20 minutes to cool. Loosen around edges and remove.

"This is a smaller version of the pound cake."

MRS. PHIL (MILDRED) SMITH
Falls Church, Virginia

Gooey Butter Cake

1 egg
1 box Duncan Hines Buttercake mix
1 stick margarine, melted
1 cup chopped nuts

Topping
1 box powdered sugar
1 8-ounce package cream cheese (room temperature)
2 eggs

Mix cake ingredients with hands until crumbly. Pat lightly into greased and floured 9 x 13" pan. Mix topping ingredients with electric mixer and pour over cake. Bake at 325° F. for 35 to 40 minutes.

MRS. CLAYTON (WANDA) KING
Nashville, Tennessee

Orange Slice Cake

1 cup butter
1 teaspoon soda
2 cups sugar
4 eggs
3½ cups flour
½ cup buttermilk
1 pound candy orange slices, cut in small pieces
½ pound dates, cut in pieces
1 4-ounce can coconut
2 cups chopped pecans or walnuts
1 tablespoon orange rind, grated

O Lord, how manifold are thy works! in wisdom hast thou made them all: the earth is full of thy riches (Ps. 104:24).

Combine butter, sugar, stir in eggs. Add soda to buttermilk and add alternately with flour. Add orange slices, coconut, dates, pecans and orange rind. Turn into a 10-inch greased tube pan. Bake 2 hours in 300° F. oven. Allow to cool in pan overnight, setting on a cooling rack. This 5-pound cake should be mixed by hand as beaters will make it light and fruit will go to the bottom.

Finding acceptance with joy, whatever the circumstances of life—whether they are petty annoyances or fiery trials—this is a living faith that grows (Mary Lou Steigleder).

MRS. GEORGE (EILEEN) TEAGUE
Ellicott City, Maryland

Chocolate Wacky Cake

1½ cups sugar
2¼ cups flour, sifted
6 tablespoons cocoa, sifted
1½ teaspoons soda
pinch of salt
1½ teaspoons vanilla
1½ tablespoons vinegar
9 tablespoons melted shortening or oil (½ cup + 1 table-spoon)
1½ cups cold water

Put all ingredients in large mixing bowl and beat till well mixed. Bake in oblong pan at 350° F. for 25-30 minutes.

Fudge Frosting
1 cup brown sugar
3 tablespoons cocoa, sifted
4 level tablespoons shortening
¼ cup milk
1 teaspoon vanilla
1 to 1½ cups confectioners' sugar, sifted

Combine brown sugar, cocoa, shortening and milk in saucepan. Boil slowly 3 minutes. Cool. Add vanilla and confectioners' sugar. Note: I add ⅔ cup chopped nuts to this fudge frosting. Because the frosting is more difficult to spread after the nuts have been added, I put a thin layer of frosting on the cake before adding the nuts to the remaining frosting.

Pour out your heart before him (Ps. 62:8).

MRS. PAUL (JERRI) MANGUM
West Chester, Pennsylvania

Pumpkin Cake

2 cups white sugar
4 eggs
1½ cups corn oil
1 teaspoon salt
3 teaspoons cinnamon
2 teaspoons soda
2 teaspoons baking powder
2 cups canned pumpkin
1 cup chopped nuts
3 cups flour

Glaze:
3 ounces cream cheese
dash of salt
1 tablespoon milk
½ teaspoon vanilla
½ pound icing sugar

I am sure that in our devotions God judges not only our Bible reading and prayers but also our use of bicycles and feet, and cars and hands and lips (B. Maurice Hall).

Cream together sugar, eggs and corn oil; sift together flour, salt, cinnamon, soda, and baking powder, and add to creamed mixture alternately with pumpkin; add nuts. Pour into greased cake pan (best in angel food or bundt cake pan), and bake at 350° F. for 50-60 minutes. Glaze while cake is still warm.

MRS. BLAIN (CAROL) MACLEOD
Sherwood, P.E.I., Canada

Magic Christmas Cake

1 pound flake coconut
1 pound nuts, chopped
1 pound dates, cut small
2 cans Eagle Brand milk
½ cup red and green cherries, cut very small (optional)

Mix well, all above, using a wooden spoon. Pour into greased angel food pan. Bake 1 hour (30 minutes at 350° F. and 30 minutes at 400° F.).

"I find this an excellent cake to replace the regular fruit cake. It may be served alone or with whipped cream or ice cream. It is rich."

MRS. FRED (ZENORA) ERDMANN
Great Falls, Montana

Yum Yum Cake

1 package white cake mix
2 tablespoons salad oil
1 8-ounce package cream cheese
1 package vanilla instant pudding
1 cup milk
crushed walnuts
1 pint whipping cream or Cool Whip
1 large can crushed pineapple

Bake cake on cookie sheet according to directions. Drain pineapple. Mix cream cheese and slowly add milk. When well mixed, add pudding and continue mixing until thick. Spread pudding mixture over cold cake. Spread on pineapple. Whip cream and spread over pineapple. Sprinkle with nuts. Makes 10-12 servings.

"This cake can be made 24 hours ahead. It is rich!"

MRS. EARL (HAZEL) LEE
Pasadena, California

Cookies and Other Desserts

Jerome Cookies

graham crackers
1½ sticks butter
1 cup sugar
1 egg
½ cup evaporated milk
1 cup chopped nuts
1 4-ounce can coconut

Icing
2 cups powdered sugar
½ stick melted margarine
3 tablespoons evaporated milk
1 teaspoon vanilla

Line a 9 x 13" pan with whole graham crackers. Melt butter. Add sugar. Beat egg in evaporated milk then add to butter/sugar mixture. Bring to a boil, stirring constantly. This will thicken. Add nuts, coconut, and 1 cup crushed graham crackers. Spread over crackers in pan and then put another layer of crackers on top.

For icing: mix all the ingredients together and stir till smooth. Spread over second layer of graham crackers. Chill several hours.

"Can store cookies in a container in cabinet after they have been refrigerated."

MRS. RONALD (DONNA) PEACH
Kingsport, Tennessee

Sugarless Cookies

1¼ cups water
⅓ cup salad oil
2 cups seedless raisins
2 teaspoons cinnamon
½ teaspoon nutmeg

Combine above and boil for 3 minutes. Let cool.

2 eggs beaten (or egg substitute)
2 teaspoons liquid sweetener
2 tablespoons water
1 teaspoon baking soda
½ teaspoon salt
2 cups flour
⅓ cup chopped walnuts
1 teaspoon baking powder

Dissolve salt, soda, and sweetener in 2 tablespoons water, add to beaten eggs, then stir into cooled mixture. Sift flour and baking powder together and mix all together, drop by teaspoons on greased cookie sheet. Bake in 375° F. oven until lightly browned, about 10 or 12 minutes.

"These need to be stored in refrigerator because no sugar is used."

MRS. I. F. (LUCILLE) YOUNGER
Nampa, Idaho

Delectable Sugar Cookies

1 cup butter
1 cup shortening
1 cup powdered sugar
1 cup granulated sugar
2 eggs, beaten
4 cups flour
1 teaspoon cream of tartar
1 teaspoon soda
1 teaspoon vanilla
½ teaspoon lemon

Cream shortening and sugar. Add beaten eggs. Add sifted dry ingredients and flavoring. Chill dough. Make small round balls. Flatten with glass dipped in sugar. Place half of nut or maraschino cherry in center if desired. Bake at 350° F. for 8-10 minutes or until a delicate brown. The dough can be kept in the refrigerator and the cookies baked fresh as needed.

MRS. G. B. (AUDREY) WILLIAMSON
Colorado Springs, Colorado

Mother's Brown Sugar Cookies

1 egg
½ teaspoon almond flavoring
1 cup brown sugar
½ cup sifted flour
½ teaspoon salt
¼ teaspoon soda
1 cup nuts
1 cup coconut

Beat egg. Add flavoring and sugar. Combine flour, salt, soda;
add to sugar mixture. Add nuts and coconut. Spread in greased
and floured 9 x 9" pan. Bake 20-25 minutes at 350° F.

"These cookies are soft when removed from oven. Let Cool in
pan.

MRS. DONALD (LILLIAN) IRWIN
Quincy, Massachusetts

Chinese Chews

2 sticks margarine, melted
1 box light brown sugar
2 beaten eggs
2 cups plain flour
1½ cups nuts
1 teaspoon vanilla

Heat first 2 ingredients to low boil. Let cool slightly. Add other
ingredients and mix. Preheat oven to 300° F., bake 30 minutes.

"Especially good at Christmas, Thanksgiving, and other festive
occasions."

MRS. HAROLD (MARTHA) LINER, SR.
Camden, South Carolina

Seven Layer Cookie

¼ pound margarine
1 cup coconut
1 small package chocolate chips
1 small package butterscotch chips
1 cup graham cracker crumbs
1 cup pecan nuts
1 can Eagle Brand milk

Melt margarine in pan. Grease sides of pan. Sprinkle crumbs evenly in pan. Cover with coconut, chocolate and butterscotch chips. Then pour milk evenly over all. Sprinkle nuts on top. Bake 30 minutes in 350° F. oven.

"Serve with ice cream topping."

MRS. FRED (GRACE) BERTOLET
Lake Worth, Florida

Tea Cookies

½ pound margarine
1½ cups sifted confectioners' sugar
1 egg
1 teaspoon vanilla
2½ cups sifted flour
1 teaspoon baking soda
1 teaspoon cream of tartar
¼ teaspoon salt

Beat egg and add to soft margarine. Add sugar and rest of ingredients and mix. Drop by spoonfuls on cookie sheet and bake at 350° F. for 10-12 minutes. When you remove from oven (and cookies are hot) put a half cherry in center of each cookie.

"A red or green cherry makes a very nice Christmas Holiday cookie."

Blessed are they that keep his testimonies, and that seek him with the whole heart (Ps. 119:2).

MRS. MORRIS E. (ESTHER) WILSON
Rochester, New York

Southern Pecan Drops

1 egg white, beaten stiff
1 cup sugar (¼ of the cup white sugar and the rest brown sugar)
1 pinch salt
1 teaspoon vanilla
2 cups pecan halves

Beat egg white until stiff. Whip sugar into egg white. Fold rest of ingredients into egg and sugar mixture. Drop on greased cookie sheet. Bake 30 minutes at 300° F.

"This cookie is nice to serve at a ladies' tea."

Labour not for the meat which perisheth, but . . . believe on him whom he hath sent (John 6:27-29).

MRS. FORREST (MARGARET) WHITLATCH
Des Moines, Iowa

Coconut Honey Balls

1 cup butter
½ cup sugar
1 teaspoon vanilla
1 teaspoon almond extract
2 cups sifted flour
1 cup pecans
1 cup coconut

Glaze
½ cup honey
⅓ cup pineapple juice
2 teaspoons vinegar
2 tablespoons butter

Cream butter. Add sugar, vanilla, and almond extract, creaming well. Add sifted flour, pecans, and coconut. Mix well. Shape dough into balls, using a teaspoonful for each. Place on ungreased baking sheets. Bake at 350° F. for 15-18 minutes. Dip in glaze.

Glaze:
In saucepan combine honey, pineapple juice, vinegar, and butter. Simmer 5 minutes. Cool to lukewarm.

MRS. HERB (MIRIAM) HALL
Olathe, Kansas

Christmas Cookies

1 pound chopped dates
½ box raisins
½ pound candied cherries (part red, part green)
½ pound chopped nuts
2½ cups sifted flour
1 teaspoon soda
1 teaspoon salt
2 teaspoons cinnamon
1 cup butter or margarine
1½ cups sugar
2 eggs

Chop dates and cut cherries in quarters, using a bit of flour to prevent stickiness. Sift flour, soda, salt, and cinnamon together. Preheat oven to 350° F. Cream butter until soft, then add sugar gradually, working until smooth. Beat in eggs thoroughly. Stir in sifted flour mixture. Add fruits and nuts. Dough will be very stiff. Drop batter from teaspoon onto an ungreased cookie sheet. Bake 10 minutes. Cool slightly then remove from cookie sheet. Makes 150-170 small cookies.

MRS. T. C. (EDRELL) SANDERS, JR.
Columbus, Ohio

Pineapple Nut Cookies

½ pound butter or margarine
1 cup white sugar
1 cup brown sugar
2 eggs
1 cup drained crushed pineapple
1 teaspoon vanilla
1 cup nuts
1 teaspoon soda
4 cups flour

Cream the butter and sugars until light and fluffy. Add eggs and mix well. Add the pineapple and vanilla and mix well. Mix soda and flour together and gradually add to the above mixture. Add nuts. Drop on greased cookie sheet. Bake about 12 minutes in 350° F. oven.

"These are better if stored in a tight container for at least a day."

DON CORNWELL
Mission, Kansas

Date Crystal Cookies

Combine and let stand
    1 cup date crystals
    ½ cup boiling water

Cream
    2 cups brown sugar
    1 cup shortening

Add
    2 beaten eggs
    3 cups sifted flour
    1 teaspoon soda
    1 teaspoon baking powder
    ½ teaspoon salt

Add date crystals

Fold in
    1 cup nuts
    1 teaspoon vanilla

Most men have within themselves the secret longing to be head of a dynasty. Few men achieve it—to be a good father is sufficient challenge for most of us (Edward S. Mann).

I am among you as he that serveth (Luke 22:27).

Refrigerate overnight. Bake in 375° F. oven for 8-10 minutes. Makes 50 cookies.

"I order my date crystals from: Hi-Jolly, Mesa, Arizona. A 3-pound bag costs about $2.50."

MRS. WINSTON (MERRETA) KETCHUM
Vancouver, Washington

Cathedral Window Cookies

½ stick butter or margarine
1 12-ounce package Hershey chocolate chips
2 eggs
1 10-ounce package miniature marshmallows
2 cups chopped pecans

In double boiler, or low heat, melt butter or margarine. Add chocolate chips, melt. Add eggs slightly beaten. Cool. Add marshmallows and nuts. Form in 2 or 3 rolls on wax paper with powdered sugar, cool and cut when needed.

"This is a good and pretty party cookie. Can be stored for a long time."

MRS. A. MILTON (GRACE LEE) SMITH
Sapulpa, Oklahoma

Chinese Almond Cookies

1 cup shortening
1 cup sugar
3 cups flour
1 teaspoon baking soda
½ teaspoon salt
1 egg
2 teaspoons almond extract

Mix dry ingredients together and cut in shortening. Add egg and extract, then knead well till dough is mealy, and no longer sticks to hands, or side of bowl. Make walnut sized balls, flatten slightly on ungreased pan. Dip small dowel (or similar rod) in red food coloring and decorate center of the cookie with a dot. Bake at 350° F. for 10-15 minutes.

"Cookie should have melting quality when eaten, otherwise it lacks kneading."

MRS. MIYOJI (NATSUKO S.) FURUSHO
Hanapepe, Kauai, Hawaii

Peanut Butter Rice Krispies Treat

Melt
1 stick butter (or margarine)
1 large package miniature marshmallows
¾ cup peanut butter

Add
½ box (13 ounces) Rice Krispies

Mix ingredients and put into 9 x 13" pan, smooth. Top with thin layer of chocolate frosting, or sprinkle with chocolate chips. Place in warm oven for 5 minutes and smooth as frosting. Refrigerate 30 minutes.

MRS. GEORGE (MARTHA) GARVIN, JR.
River Forest, Illinois

Fruit Cake Cookies

2 sticks margarine, melted
1½ cups sugar
2 eggs
2½ cups flour
1 teaspoon soda
1 teaspoon cinnamon
¼ teaspoon salt
4 ounces candied cherries
4 ounces candied pineapple
1 package chopped dates
2 cups pecans or walnuts

Mix well—drop on cookie sheet. Bake until golden brown in a 350° F. oven.

MRS. FOREST (AZALIA) FREEMAN
Capitan, New Mexico

My soul longeth, yea, even fainteth for the courts of the Lord: my heart and my flesh crieth out for the living God (Ps. 84:2).

Oatmeal Carmelitas

1 cup flour
1 cup quick rolled oats
¾ cup firm-packed brown sugar
½ teaspoon soda
¼ teaspoon salt
¾ cup margarine, melted
1 cup (6 ounces) semisweet chocolate
½ cup chopped pecans or walnuts
¾ cup caramel ice cream topping
3 tablespoons flour

Combine flour, oats, brown sugar, soda, salt, and melted margarine. Blend at low speed to form crumbs. Press half crumbs into bottom of 11 x 7" pan. Bake at 350° F. for 10 minutes. Remove from oven. Sprinkle with chocolate pieces and nuts. Blend caramel topping with 3 tablespoons flour. Lace this over chocolate and nuts to cover. Sprinkle with remaining crumb mixture. Bake 15-20 minutes more till brown. Chill 1 to 2 hours before cutting. Makes 24 cookies.

Oh that men would praise the Lord for his goodness, and for his wonderful works to the children of men! (Ps. 107:8).

MRS. RAY (CAROLYN) SANDERS
Woodland, California

Mother's Old-fashioned Cookies

Sift together
  4 cups flour
  1 teaspoon baking powder
  1 teaspoon soda
  ½ teaspoon salt
  1½ teaspoons cinnamon
  ¼ teaspoon nutmeg
  ¼ teaspoon cloves

Add
1 cup water to 2 cups of raisins and cook until water is reduced to ½ cup of liquid. Cool. (You may grind the raisins and add ⅔ cup of boiling water.)

Cream together
  1 cup shortening
  2 cups sugar
  3 eggs, beaten
  1 teaspoon vanilla
  1 cup chopped nuts

Mix with sifted dry ingredients. Drop by teaspoonsful onto a greased cookie sheet and bake at 375° F. for 15 minutes.

"This makes a large amount. Some of the batter may be kept in the refrigerator for a while to be used later. During the holidays, add candied fruits, dates, figs, etc., as you desire. If your family does not care for the raisins, grind them up and no one will know that these little goodies are there!"

MRS. ROSS E. (IRENE) PRICE
Colorado Springs, Colorado

Lemon Cookies

  2 cups granulated sugar
  1 cup butter or margarine
  1 cup buttermilk
  1 teaspoon soda
  2 eggs
  3½ cups flour
  1 teaspoon baking powder
  1 orange (juice and rind grated)

Make stiff batter, drop on buttered cookie sheets. Bake at 375° F. for 8-10 minutes.

Icing: beat 1 cup powdered sugar into juice and grated rind of one lemon, spread on hot cookies.

MRS. RAY (IRENE) HORTON
Sciotoville, Ohio

Coconut Bars

½ cup butter
½ cup light brown sugar
1 cup flour (regular)
2 eggs, beaten
1 cup light brown sugar
1 cup pecans, chopped
1 teaspoon vanilla
1½ cups flake coconut
¼ teaspoon salt
3 tablespoons flour

Cream butter, add the ½ cup light brown sugar, and blend thoroughly. Add flour. Mix and spread in 8 x 10" pan. Bake at 375° F. for 10 minutes. Beat eggs lightly and add to all remaining ingredients. Mix thoroughly. Pour this mixture over mixture which has been baked. Bake 20 minutes longer. Cool and cut into small squares or bars.

"This is a delicious, chewy coconut bar."

MRS. RAY (DOROTHY) SHADOWENS
Clarksville, Tennessee

Chocolate Cherry Bars

1 package fudge cake mix
1 21-ounce can cherry fruit filling
1 teaspoon almond extract
2 eggs, beaten

Frosting
1 cup sugar
5 tablespoons butter or margarine
⅓ cup milk
1 6-ounce package chocolate chips

O satisfy us early with thy mercy; that we may rejoice and be glad all our days (Ps. 90:14).

Using solid shortening, grease and flour a 9 x 13 pan. In large bowl, combine first four ingredients. By hand, stir until well mixed. Pour into prepared pan. Bake for 30 minutes, or until done. While bars cool, prepare frosting. In small saucepan, combine sugar, butter, and milk. Boil, stirring constantly 1 minute. Remove from heat, stir in chocolate chips until smooth. Pour over partially cooled bars.

I will say of the Lord, He is my refuge and my fortress; my God, in him will I trust (Ps. 91:2).

"For variation you may use: spice cake mix, apple pie filling, and butterscotch chips. Very good!"

MRS. R. C. (MARGARET ANN) RAYCROFT
Monroe, Michigan

Chocolate Peanut Squares

1 cup white sugar
1 cup dark brown Karo syrup
6 cups Special K cereal (large package)
1 16-ounce jar crunchy peanut butter
1 16-ounce package chocolate chips, semisweet
1 16-ounce package butterscotch chips

Mix and melt sugar and syrup over hot water. Put cereal and peanut butter in large bowl but do not mix until you have poured the hot mixture over it, then stir. Press into well buttered (bottom and sides) 9 x 13" cake pan. Melt the chocolate and butterscotch chips over hot water. Stir well. Spread over other mixture. Cut into squares.

MRS. J. FRED (NEVA) PARKER
Prairie Village, Kansas

God that made the world and all things therein . . . giveth to all life, and breath, and all things (Acts 17:24-25).

Baked Fudge Bars

1 stick margarine
3 squares chocolate (or ½ cup cocoa plus 3 tablespoons margarine)
2 cups sugar
3 eggs, beaten
½ cup nuts, broken
1½ cups all-purpose flour

In pan, melt margarine and chocolate. Add sugar, stir. Add beaten eggs and stir. Blend flour and add nuts last. Add vanilla if desired. Bake in slow oven, 325° F. for 35-40 minutes in 9 x 11" Pyrex or heavy pan.

MRS. GENE (EVELYN) FULLER
Lubbock, Texas

Old-fashioned Brownies

4 squares (4 ounces) chocolate
¾ cup shortening (margarine)
2 cups sugar
1 teaspoon vanilla
4 eggs, unbeaten
1½ cups flour
1 teaspoon baking powder
1 teaspoon salt
1 cup chopped walnuts

Melt chocolate and shortening over low heat. Add sugar, eggs, vanilla, and beat well. Add flour, baking powder, and salt, stir until smooth. Add chopped walnuts and mix well. Pour into a greased 9 x 13" oblong pan. Bake at 350° F. for 25 to 30 minutes. Cool in pan and top with a chocolate icing. Makes about 24 servings.

CORDIE LEE DAVIS
Southington, Ohio

Saucepan Brownies

1 stick margarine
3 heaping tablespoons cocoa
2 cups sugar
pinch of salt
1 teaspoon vanilla
3 eggs
1½ cups flour
1 cup chopped nuts

Melt margarine in saucepan. Remove from heat. Add cocoa, sugar, salt, and vanilla and mix. Add eggs and mix well. Add flour and nuts and mix. Pour batter into greased and floured 9 x 12" pan. Bake at 375° F. for 17 to 20 minutes. Cool and cut in squares. May frost if preferred.

MRS. CARL (BARBARA) SUMMER
Bethany, Oklahoma

Charlie Brown Brownies

3 squares unsweetened chocolate
½ cup butter (1 cube margarine)
1¼ cups brown sugar
1 cup white sugar
3 eggs
¼ teaspoon salt
1 cup flour
1 cup walnuts
2 teaspoons vanilla

Melt chocolate and butter. Add other ingredients one at a time; hand stir. Pour into 7½ x 12" pan. Bake 275° F. for 50 minutes. Cool and cut into small rectangles.

MRS. ROBERT H. (EVELYN) SUTTON
Eugene, Oregon

Canadian Fudge Squares

Boil
½ cup margarine
1 cup white sugar
½ teaspoon salt
1 egg
2 tablespoons cocoa

In bowl break up:
12 double graham wafers
½ cup chopped walnuts

Over low heat, boil first five ingredients. Bring to full rolling boil, while stirring. Pour over wafers and nuts. Stir quickly and press into 9 x 9" pan. Cool. Cover with your favorite icing.

MRS. RUTH JONES
Chilliwack, B.C., Canada

Scottish Currant Squares

1 pie crust dough normally used for a 9-inch pie
1 package currants
2½ slices white bread
½ cup sugar
1 teaspoon ginger
1 teaspoon cinnamon

Cover currants and bread with water and soak for 1 hour. Roll out half the pastry dough until it will cover the bottom and 1 inch up the sides of a 9 x 13" pan. Drain the water off the currants and bread and mix well. Add sugar, ginger, and cinnamon, and mix again. Spread the filling mixture over the crust. Roll out remaining dough until it will just cover the filling. Seal by folding the dough from the bottom crust over the top crust. Make fork punctures on crust and bake at 400° F. until light brown.

"This is a recipe my parents brought from Scotland. The squares are always a favorite at church fellowship times, and with my family as well."

MRS. ANDERSON (ANN CUBIE) REARICK
East Rockaway, New York

Quick Crescent Pecan-Pie Bars

1 8-ounce can refrigerated quick crescent dinner rolls
1 egg, beaten
½ cup chopped pecans
½ cup sugar
½ cup corn syrup
1 tablespoon butter or margarine, melted
½ teaspoon vanilla

Preheat oven to 375° F. Lightly grease 9 x 13" pan. Separate crescent dough into 2 large rectangles. Press rectangles over bottom and ½ inch up sides of prepared pan to form crust; seal perforations. Bake crust at 375° F. for 5 minutes. In medium bowl, combine remaining ingredients. Pour over partially baked crust. Bake at 375° F. for 18 to 22 minutes until golden brown and filling is set. Cool, cut into bars. Makes 2 dozen bars.

"This recipe was submitted in a Pillsbury Bake-off contest by a Christian lady. She won $25,000 for it. Unfortunately, I was not the lady."

MRS. FRANCIS L. (EILEEN) SMEE
Visalia, California

The Word is mine to take, personalize, and use this day. I'll insert my name in every promise and walk firmly ahead (Mary Lou Steigleder).

Cherry Coconut Bars

Pastry
¾ cup sifted flour
½ cup butter
3 tablespoons confectioners' sugar

Filling:
2 eggs, slightly beaten
¾ cup sugar
¼ cup flour
½ teaspoon baking powder
¼ teaspoon salt
½ teaspoon vanilla or almond flavoring
¾ cup chopped nuts
½ cup coconut
½ cup cherries

Faith cometh by hearing, and hearing by the word of God (Rom. 10:17).

Heat oven to 350° F. Mix pastry. Spread in 8-inch greased pan. Bake 20 minutes. Stir filling together. Spread over top of baked pastry. No need to cool. Bake 25 minutes. Cool and cut into bars.

MRS. RAY (JANET) JACKSON
Pleasant Hill, California

Chocolate Chip Bars

½ cup butter or margarine
⅓ cup granulated sugar
⅓ cup packed brown sugar
1 egg
1 cup flour
1 teaspoon vanilla
½ teaspoon soda
½ teaspoon salt
½ cup semisweet chocolate chips
½ cup chopped nuts (optional)

Cream butter and sugars. Add remaining ingredients; blend well. Spread in greased 9 x 13" pan (cookie sheet, if recipe is doubled); bake at 375° F. for 15-20 minutes or until light, golden brown.

MRS. AARON (MARY) KNAPP
Omaha, Nebraska

Paul's Pumpkin Bars

4 eggs
2 cups sugar
1 cup cooking oil
1 16-ounce can (2 cups) pumpkin
2 cups flour
2 teaspoons baking powder
1 teaspoon baking soda
2 teaspoons cinnamon powder
1 teaspoon salt
1 teaspoon vanilla

Icing
1 3-ounce package cream cheese, softened
½ cup butter, softened
1 teaspoon vanilla
2 cups sifted powdered sugar

In mixer bowl, beat together eggs, sugar, pumpkin, oil, and vanilla, till light and fluffy. Stir together flour, baking powder, cinnamon, salt, and soda. Add to pumpkin mixture and mix well. Spread mixture in ungreased 15 x 20 x 1-inch baking pan. Bake for 35 to 40 minutes at 350° F. Cool. Frost and cut in 1-inch bars.

To make icing: cream together cream cheese and butter. Stir in vanilla, add powdered sugar, a little at a time, beating well till mixture is smooth. Spread icing on cooled pumpkin bars, then sprinkle walnut chips over icing. Put in refrigerator until icing is set, then cut into bars. Makes 24 bars.

MRS. PAUL (VERNELL) PRICE
Eureka, California

Carrot Bars

4 eggs
2 teaspoons soda
1 teaspoon salt
2½ cups flour
2 cups sugar
2 teaspoons cinnamon
1½ cups cooking oil
½ cup walnuts, large pieces
3 small jars strained carrots (baby food)

Frosting
3 cups (scant) powdered sugar
6 ounces warm cream cheese
½ teaspoon vanilla
½ cube softened butter or margarine

Combine ingredients in order given, taking no pains to mix individually. Bake 30 minutes at 325° F. on greased 11 x 16 x ½" jelly roll pan or cookie sheet. Can use 12 x 18 x ½ also. Frost when cool.

"A simple carrot cake. Keeps and freezes well."

MRS. BOB (DODIE) SMEE
Visalia, California

Lemon Bars

1 stick margarine or ½ cup butter
¼ cup powdered sugar
1 cup flour

Mix all thoroughly and press in an 8 x 9" or 9 x 9" pan and bake for 15-20 minutes at 350° F.

While crust is baking, beat together:
2 eggs
2 tablespoons lemon juice
1 cup sugar
2 tablespoons flour
½ teaspoon baking powder

Pour mixture over baked crust and bake 25 minutes at 350° F. or until light brown. Should be soft inside. Cut into bars and sprinkle with powdered sugar.

"A family favorite. Can be served alone or as an excellent accompaniment for fruit or sherbet."

MRS. P. L. (JUNE) LIDDELL
Howell, Michigan

Lemon Bars a la Thaxton

1 cup all-purpose flour
½ cup butter or margarine
¼ teaspoon salt
¼ cup confectioners' sugar
2 eggs
1 cup sugar
3 tablespoons lemon juice
½ teaspoon baking powder

Mix together flour, butter, salt and confectioners' sugar. Pour into greased 8 x 8 x 2" pan. Bake 20 minutes at 350° F. Combine eggs, sugar, lemon juice, and baking powder; pour over baked pastry. Return to oven; bake at 350° F. for 25 minutes. Cut into bars while still warm. May be made a day in advance.

MRS. D. W. (MUZETTE) THAXTON
Spring, Texas

Easy Graham Bars

3½ cups graham cracker crumbs
1 cup Milnot or evaporated milk
1 cup white sugar
¼ cup oil
1 package chocolate chips
½ cup broken nutmeats

Mix all ingredients, pour into greased 9 x 13" pan. Bake 20-30 minutes, in a 350° F. oven. Cut in squares. Sprinkle with powdered sugar.

MRS. SAM (VELDA) ROBERTS
Alexandria, Indiana

Let us be held steady by His Word, so that in time of need we may rejoice, "My God is real, for I can feel Him in my soul!" (Oleta Spray).

Sea Foam Nut Squares

2 cups sifted flour
1 teaspoon baking powder
½ teaspoon salt
⅛ teaspoon soda
½ cup shortening
¼ cup white sugar
2 cups firmly packed brown sugar
2 eggs
2 tablespoons cold water
½ teaspoon vanilla
¼ cup milk
1 cup chopped nuts

Sift together the flour, baking powder, salt, and soda. Set aside. Cream the shortening and gradually add the white sugar, and ½ cup firmly packed brown sugar. Cream together until light and fluffy. Add 2 egg yolks and 2 tablespoons cold water and mix well; add vanilla. Add milk alternately with dry ingredients to creamed mixture and blend well. Spread in greased and floured 10 x 15" pan or in two 9 x 9 x 2" pans.

Beat two egg whites until stiff but not dry. Add 1½ cups firmly packed brown sugar a little at a time, beating well after each addition. Spread over cooky dough and sprinkle with 1 cup chopped nuts. Bake in slow oven—325° F. for 25 to 30 minutes. Cut into bars or squares while still warm.

"These nut squares have a delicious chewiness and a rich brown-sugar candy flavor. They are different and great for a party."

MRS. WILLIAM C. (ESTHER) DAMON
Haslett, Michigan

Marshmallow Squares

¾ cup butter or margarine
⅓ cup brown sugar
1½ cups flour
  2 tablespoons gelatin
½ cup cold water
  2 cups sugar
½ cup hot water
½ cup maraschino cherries
½ cup almonds or walnuts
¼ teaspoon almond flavoring
food coloring

Cream butter or margarine, add brown sugar, add flour until ball of dough forms. Press into 9 x 13" pan, prick surface. Bake at 325° F. for 30 minutes. Sprinkle gelatin over cold water and soften. Bring sugar and hot water to boil for two minutes. Remove from heat and add softened gelatin. Stir until dissolved and then beat until stiff—requires several minutes. Fold in cherries, nuts, coloring, and flavoring. Spoon mixture over baked shortbread in pan and cool for several hours. Sprinkle top with coconut, if desired, and cut in squares or bars.

"A recipe I received while living in Nova Scotia."

MRS. BRUCE (RUTH) TAYLOR
Marion, Indiana

Crunchy Date Bars

1 stick butter
1 cup light brown sugar
1 cup chopped dates
½ cup chopped nuts
2½ cups Rice Krispies
1 teaspoon vanilla
powdered sugar

Grease a 9 x 13" pan and dust with powdered sugar. Boil butter, brown sugar and dates together for 5 minutes. (Use medium heat.) After date mixture cools slightly, add vanilla and mix with Rice Krispies and nuts. Spread in pan with a large greased spoon and dust top with powdered sugar.

"These are easy; no oven required; and are delicious!"

MRS. DAN (ELEANOR) ROAT
Havana, Illinois

Corn Flake Candy

6 cups corn flakes
1 cup sugar
1 cup white syrup
1 cup peanut butter

Butter a large mixing bowl. Mix sugar and syrup in pan. Bring to a rolling boil. Measure corn flakes into buttered bowl. Remove syrup from stove and add peanut butter. Mix until smooth and pour over corn flakes. Mix until all are coated. Drop by spoonfuls on wax paper.

"Quick and easy to make. Good for the sweet tooth."

MRS. HARVEY (MAXINE) HENDERSHOT
Nashville, Tennessee

Cherry Divinity

3 cups sugar
¾ cup white syrup
¾ cup water
3 egg whites
2 cups chopped nuts
1 3-ounce package cherry gelatin (or any flavor depending on color desired)

Mix sugar, syrup, and water in saucepan, stirring until syrup begins to boil. Boil until syrup spins a thread or makes hard ball by dropping a few drops into a cup of water. Meanwhile, in mixer beat egg whites until they begin to stiffen. Add the dry gelatin and beat until peaks form. Slowly pour syrup into whites as you continue the beating. Beat until candy loses it gloss; fold in the nuts. Drop by teaspoonsful on waxed paper. Mix the nuts in by hand.

MRS. CHARLES (LAVERNE) OLIVER
Helena, Alabama

Date Candy

3 cups sugar
1½ cups cream
1½ tablespoons butter
1 package dates, cut up
1 teaspoon vanilla

Cook sugar, cream, and butter to soft ball. Add dates and cook about 1 minute. Remove from fire, add vanilla. Beat until hard enough to pour in your pan or cookie sheet.

MRS. JAMES (FAITH) EMMERT
Yukon, Oklahoma

Order my steps in thy word: and let not any iniquity have dominion over me (Ps. 119: 133).

Vienna Slices

2 cups all-purpose flour
¼ teaspoon salt
1 teaspoon baking powder
1 cup sugar
⅔ cup sweet butter
4 eggs, separated
2 tablespoons milk
1 teaspoon lemon extract
½ cup apricot jam
1 cup chopped pecans

That the generation to come might know them, even the children which should be born; who should arise and declare them to their children (Ps. 78:6).

Preheat oven to 350° F. Sift flour, baking powder, ½ cup sugar. Cut in the butter as if for pie crust. Combine slightly beaten yolks, milk, and lemon extract. Add to dry ingredients and mix well. Put the dough in a 9 x 12 x 2" pan and press it onto bottom and sides to about ½" thickness. Spread jam on top. Gradually beat remaining sugar into beaten egg whites, until stiff. Spread over jam and sprinkle nuts on top. Bake for 30 minutes. When cool, cut into 2-inch slices.

MRS. WALLY (GINGER) LAXSON
Athens, Alabama

Coconut Pecan Balls

1 pound coconut
1 pound pecans, chopped
1 pound powdered sugar
1 cup melted butter
2 tablespoons vanilla
1 12-ounce package chocolate chips
¼ of ¼-pound stick paraffin

Mix coconut, pecans, powdered sugar, melted butter and vanilla. Roll into balls. Place on wax paper and chill. Melt chocolate chips and paraffin over hot water. Roll balls in this mixture. Store in tight container to keep moist.

"This is a special Christmas candy at our house."

Mrs. J. V. (Pat) Morsch
Orlando, Florida

Caramel Corn

2 sticks margarine
2 cups brown sugar
1 teaspoon salt
½ teaspoon soda
1 teaspoon vanilla
6 quarts popped corn

Combine ingredients and stir, bringing to a boil. Cook five minutes without stirring. Take from heat, add ½ teaspoon of soda and 1 teaspoon of vanilla. Pour over 6 quarts of popped corn. Mix well. Pour into 2 long cake pans. Put in oven 1 hour at 250° F. Stir every 15 minutes. Take out and cool. Separate corn. Put in plastic containers so it is airtight.

Mrs. Alton (Eulela) Goerlitz
Lyndon Station, Wisconsin

Never-Fail Meringue

1 tablespoon cornstarch
6 tablespoons white sugar
½ cup water
3 egg whites
few grains of salt

Mix cornstarch, sugar, water, and salt and cook till thick and clear. Cool slightly. Beat egg whites until frothy. Continue beating while slowly pouring cooked mixture into egg whites. Beat five more minutes. Cover cooled filling in pie, sealing edges to crust. Bake at 450° F. for 5-7 minutes until golden.

MRS. FRANK (MABEL) LAY
Portland, Oregon

Karmel Korn

2 cups brown sugar
½ cup white syrup
1¼ sticks margarine
⅛ teaspoon cream of tartar
6 quarts popped corn (can use more)

Boil ingredients 5 minutes slowly. Remove from stove. Add 1 heaping teaspoon soda. Stir until mixed well. Pour over popped corn. Put in 200° F. oven for 1 hour, stirring every 10-15 minutes.

"Always a hit at parties. Crisp and crunchy like that you buy."

MRS. PHILLIP (SHIRLEY) RILEY
Jamestown, North Dakota

Problems? Pray. Can't get through? Call on God's people for help. Confess your need. You'll find great lift in the concern and compassion of the clean Christian people who pray (Louis A. Bouck).

Fudge

4½ cups sugar
1 can condensed milk
Pam
3 6-ounce packages semisweet chocolate chips
2 cups nuts

Spray pan with Pam. Cook sugar and condensed milk over medium heat. Bring to boil and boil 7 minutes, stirring constantly. Have ready in large bowl, semisweet chocolate chips, nuts, ½ pound butter—chopped in pieces. Pour boiling mixture over this. Stir until dissolves and begins to stiffen. Add 1 tablespoon vanilla. Pour in 9 x 13" Tupperware dish. Refrigerate until sets.

MRS. IRA L. (CAROLYN) EAST
Wilmington, Ohio

The law of the Spirit of life in Christ Jesus hath made me free from the law of sin and death (Rom. 8:2).

❧ Beverages ❧

Holiday Punch

1 3-ounce package cherry gelatin
1 cup boiling water
1 6-ounce can lemonade
3 cups cold water
1 quart cranberry juice
1 bottle (1 pint, 12 ounce) ginger ale

Dissolve gelatin in boiling water. Add lemonade, cold water, and cranberry juice. Put ice in bowl, add punch mixture and then ginger ale.

"This punch is ideal for a Christmas supper party but it is also very refreshing on a hot, summer day."

MRS. WILLIAM (DORIS) RESTRICK
Wallingford, Connecticut

Oh, for a faith that will not shrink,
Tho' pressed by ev'ry foe.

Party Punch

1 large box of gelatin
3 cups sugar
4 cups water
1 small bottle almond extract
2 bottles ginger ale
1 46-ounce pineapple juice
1 46-ounce orange juice
1 bottle Realemon

Boil water and sugar one minute. Mix gelatin according to instructions on box. This can be stored in the ice box until ready to use. When ready to use add the gingerale, pineapple, and orange juice, Realemon (small bottle), and almond extract. Makes 40-50 servings.

MRS. A. MILTON (GRACE LEE) SMITH
Sapulpa, Oklahoma

Orange-Mint Punch

1½ cups sugar
1½ cups hot water
1 cup fresh mint leaves
1 small can frozen orange juice
2 small cans frozen lemonade
2½ quarts water
1 large bottle ginger ale

Stir sugar and water in a saucepan and simmer for 5 minutes. Pour over mint leaves to steep. Strain after 2 hours. Combine this minted syrup with all except ginger ale. Refrigerate. When ready to serve, add cold ginger ale and ice.

"This recipe was given to me by Oklahoma City First Nazarene Church friends in about 1950. A favorite with family and friends in the summer."

Mrs. K. S. (Betty) Rice
Kansas City, Missouri

White Grape Punch

1 quart white grape juice
1 quart soda water
1 quart ginger ale
1 large can frozen lemonade (concentrate)
2-3 frozen limes whole

Freeze limes overnight. Mix all above ingredients together (follow lemonade directions). Limes serve as garnishes—do not squeeze.

"An unusual thirst quenching summer punch!"

Mrs. Samuel (Joyce) Henck
Pittsford, New York

Party or Shower Punch

3 bottles lemon-lime drink such as Bubble-up
1½ cups pineapple juice, (or to your taste)
vanilla ice cream

Combine all ingredients.

"This punch can be made any color—even blue! The secret is to add your coloring to the liquid before adding the ice cream."

Mrs. H. C. (Gerry) Hatton
Sterling, Illinois

Save me, O God, by thy
name, and judge me by thy
strength (Ps. 54:1).

Pink Fruit Punch

6 cups sugar
6 cups water
2 packages strawberry Kool-Aid
1 12-ounce can frozen lemon juice
1 12-ounce can frozen orange juice
1 46-ounce can pineapple juice

Combine sugar and water. Boil for 5 minutes. Cool. Add remaining ingredients. When ready to serve the punch, add 2 quarts of ginger ale plus enough water to make three gallons.

"Instead of adding the water, I add enough ice to make three gallons."

MRS. VIRGIL (VIRGINIA) APPLEGATE
Cincinnati, Ohio

Mmmmm Punch

1 quart pineapple sherbet
1 quart vanilla ice cream
24 ounces pineapple juice
3 12-ounce cans ginger ale

Soften sherbet and ice cream slightly. Mix in pineapple juice. Pour into punch bowl. Add ginger ale. Makes 1 medium bowl. Perfect to "keep coming" for large groups. Serves 25-30 punch cups.

"Makes delicate white punch. May substitute other sherbet and ice cream flavors to vary color and taste. always complimented."

MRS. ROBERT (CAROLYN) SCOTT
Orange, California

Fruit Punch

1 3-ounce package wild strawberry gelatin
1 46-ounce can pineapple juice
1 cup sugar
juice of 4 lemons (½ cup Realemon)
1 teaspoon vanilla flavoring
1 teaspoon almond flavoring
water to make 1 gallon

Mix all ingredients and add water to make 1 gallon. (1 gallon plastic milk containers are good to use.) Chill 6 to 8 hours before serving. Can be kept for several days in the refrigerator.

Mrs. Alex (Greeta) Cubie
South Windsor, Connecticut

Punch

Punch
½ cup sugar
1½ cups water
1 2-inch stick cinnamon
1 tablespoon whole cloves
2 No. 2 size cans pineapple juice
2 cups orange juice
2 12-ounce bottles sparkling water

Fruited ice ring
fresh strawberries
orange slices
lemon slices
maraschino cherries
mint leaves

What things were gain to me, those I counted loss for Christ. . . . if by any means I might attain unto the resurrection of the dead (Phil. 3:7-11).

Combine sugar, water, cinnamon, and cloves. Boil 5 minutes. Strain and cool. Add fruit juices and chill. Add sparkling water just before serving. Fruit ring: Arrange layer of berries, fruit slices, and mint leaves in ring mold. Just barely cover with water and freeze. Repeat layers till ring is filled. Unmold and float in punch. As ice ring melts, fruit floats in punch.

Mrs. Roy (Carolyn) Sanders
Woodland, California

Jamaican Punch

1 cup pineapple juice
1 banana
1 12-ounce can frozen Hawaiian Punch
2½ 12-ounce cans water

Abhor that which is evil; cleave to that which is good. . . . Be not overcome of evil, but overcome evil with good (Rom. 12:9, 21).

Mix above ingredients in your blender. Add 2 or 3 ice cubes and blend again. Makes it cold and "icy." Serve immediately.

Mrs. Roy (Ruth) Green
Eugene, Oregon

Orange Julius

½ 6-ounce can frozen orange juice concentrate
½ cup milk
½ cup water
¼ cup sugar
½ teaspoon vanilla
5 or 6 ice cubes

Mix in blender until smooth.

MRS. LELAND (IRENE) WURST
Albuquerque, New Mexico

Hot Mulled Cider

½ cup brown sugar
¼ teaspoon salt
2 quarts cider
1 teaspoon whole allspice
1 teaspoon whole cloves
3 inch stick cinnamon
dash nutmeg

Combine brown sugar, salt, and cider. Tie spices in small piece of cheesecloth and add to cider. Slowly bring to a boil; cover and simmer 20 minutes. Remove spices. Serve hot with orange-slice floaters. Use cinnamon sticks as muddlers. Makes 10 servings.

MRS. DEAN (ROXIE) WESSELS
Olathe, Kansas

Now the God of peace, that brought again from the dead our Lord Jesus . . . through the blood of the everlasting covenant, make you perfect in every good work to do his will (Heb. 13:20-21).

Slush

6 tart lemons or Realemon juice
6 oranges or 1 small can frozen juice
6 large ripe bananas, mashed or crushed in blender
1 large can pineapple juice
6 cups water
5 cups sugar
2 large bottles of 7-Up

Mix first four ingredients together. Heat water and sugar together until sugar dissolves, then cool. Mix with juices and pour into shallow containers and freeze. Remove from freezer about 30 minutes before serving and after thawing a bit, crush in blender and mix with the 7-Up.

MRS. OVID (LAURA) YOUNG
Bourbonnais, Illinois

Index